Our Man in Paris

Our Man in Paris

A Foreign Correspondent,
France and the French

JOHN LICHFIELD

WITHDRAWN
FROM
STOCK

Signal Books
OXFORD

For Margaret, my best source

THE
INDEPENDENT

The publishers gratefully acknowledge *The Independent's* kind permission
to reproduce and republish the articles in this book

First published in 2010 by
Signal Books Limited
36 Minster Road
Oxford
OX4 1LY
www.signalbooks.co.uk

A catalogue record for this book is available from the British Library

ISBN 978-1-904955-73-3 Paper

Design: Bryony Clark
Cover illustration: Russ Cook
Cartoons: Russ Cook
Printed by Bell & Bain, Glasgow

CONTENTS

Introduction (1)

PART ONE: Paris   7

An Urban Minefield, *March 1997* (8); Paris in the Rain, *July 1997* (10); Urban Theatre, *July 1998* (12); A Gardienne Angel, *July 1998* (15); The Parisian Paradox, *June 1999* (16); A Visit to Oscar, *October 2000* (18); Trouble in Store, *April 2001* (21); Tourist Guide, *May 2002* (22); A Cockfight, *June 2002* (23); Fun-du-Siècle, *September 2002* (25), The Parisian Paradox 2, *September 2002* (27); The Hidden Gallery, *November 2002* (28); Christmas in Paris, *December 2002* (30); Guitar Solo, *January 2003* (32); French Verbals – Regular and Irregular, *January 2003* (34); Death of a Good Samaritaine, *May 2003* (36); In Search of Seurat – and Air, *May 2003* (38); A Pigeon Fancier, *June 2003* (40); An Urban Rabbit Tail, *November 2003* (40); Manhattan-sur-Seine, *November 2003* (42); Café Society, *January 2004* (44); Death of the Garret Room, *February 2004* (46); A Trou Story, *April 2004* (48); A Brush with the Police, *April 2004* (50); Neighbour Wars, *May 2004* (51); Ruder than the French, *May 2004* (53); A Star is Reborn, *July 2004* (53); An Unscheduled Stop, *August 2004* (55); A Hot Flush, *October 2004* (56); Metro Rage, *November 2004* (58); Café Society 2, *April 2005* (58); One of the Greatest, *May 2006* (61); Making Paris Bigger, *September 2006* (62); How Paris Really Works, *June 2007* (64); Paris on Strike, *November 2007* (66); A Meeting with George W, *January 2009* (68); Eating Out, *March 2009* (69); How I Became a Snob, *June 2009* (70); Picasso Comes Home, *March 2010* (72)

PART TWO: Normandy   75

Cold Comfort Ferme, *December 1998* (76); Cold Comfort Ferme 2, *January 1999* (78); Geronimo, *May 1999* (80); Jour de Fête, *July 1999* (82); Cold Comfort Ferme 3, *October 1999* (84); Cold Comfort Ferme 4,

November 1999 (86); Geronimo 2, *March 2000* (88); Cold Comfort Ferme 5, *July 2000* (90); A Mushroom Hunt, *November 2000* (92); An Historic Moment, *April 2001* (95); An English Country Garden, *August 2001* (97); Rural History Lesson, *May 2002* (101); Pas Dans Mon Backyard, *February 2003* (103); April is the Prettiest Month, *April 2003* (105); The Saint in the Hedge, *May 2003* (107); Killers in the Forest, *January 2005* (109); Pas Dans Mon Backyard 2, *January 2005* (111); Rural History Lesson 2, *May 2005* (113); Travels with Donkeys, *August 2005* (114); A Country Home, *August 2006* (117); Feel Good Facteur, *July 2007* (118); My French Son, *August 2007* (120); A Wife-Swap Shop, *August 2008* (122); Lament for a Lost Landscape, *April 2010* (124)

PART THREE: The Education System   127

A Kiss from Teacher, *January 1997* (128); A Rabbit for the Weekend, *March 1997* (130); Toto the Snail Has Hay-Fever, *September 1997* (132); My Son, the Author, *April 2000* (135); A Police Call, *January 2003* (138); Another Police Call, *April 2003* (139); Saturday School, *September 2003* (139); Sic Transit..., *June 2004* (141); September – the Cruellest Month, *September 2004* (143); Dictating the Future, *December 2004* (145); Egalité, Fraternité, Hypocrisie, *June 2006* (147); Do it Yourself, *June 2007* (150); What a Kiss Can Do, *July 2008* (151)

PART FOUR: Food and Wine   153

Cuisine – Haute or Haughty, *March 1997* (154); Fast Wine, *October 2002* (156); Repas – Ready to Eat, *March 2003* (159); Slow Burn Fast Food, *May 2003* (161); School Meals, French Style, *November 2003* (163); Mancunian Haute Cuisine, *March 2005* (165); Beaune of Contention, *August 2006* (167)

PART FIVE: Politics   171

On the Front Line, *March 1997* (172); A Pont Too Far, *May 1997* (174); Paranoia Politics, *April 2002* (177); Letter from America, *February 2003*

(179); Stop, a Movement Has Started, *July 2003* (181); Streets of Name, *July 2003* (183); Death of a Cat, *August 2003* (185); Chirac, the American, *November 2003* (188); The Sarko Show, *December 2007* (188); The Dreaded Banlieues, *June 2008* (191); The 99th Département, *October 2008* (192); Carla, the Cartoon, *November 2008* (195); Bring Back Jacques, *April 2009* (198); Jamais on a Sunday, *July 2009* (201)

PART SIX: Living with *Les Français* and Others 207

The Town I Loved So Well, *March 1997* (208); Les Vacances de Monsieur L, *September 1997* (210); The French – At Play and Work, *October 1999* (212); My Wife's Affair, *June 2001* (215); The Grand Tour, *July 2001* (217); Enfants Terrible, *September 2001* (220); Hero of the Nation, *October 2001* (221); French Friends, *May 2002* (223); In the Swim, *June 2002* (225); Ah, les Anglais, *June 2002* (226); De-Constructing the Maison Secondaire, *October 2002* (226); Vous, Not Tu, You Brute, *November 2002* (229); Rude? Nous?, *July 2003* (229); Tu or Vous 2, *December 2003* (231); The French Way of Christmas, *December 2003* (233); French Letters, *September 2004* (235); Driving Legally, Without a Licence, *November 2004* (237); Tree Hugging, *December 2004* (239); Conga Dancing for European Unity, *March 2005* (240); Three Men on a Walk, *April 2005* (242); Right Track? Or Left?, *May 2005* (244); Armani Man, *May 2005* (245); Armani Man 2, *June 2005* (246); Crossing Borders, *April 2006* (248); Painful Memories, *May 2006* (250); A Miracle Play, *July 2006* (252); French Letters 2, *February 2007* (254); Rotten Weather, *July 2007* (256); Far From Elementary, *January 2008* (258); The Melting of the Frozen North, *February 2008* (260); Secret Society, *March 2008* (262); Painful Memories 2, *April 2008* (264); Sarko Invades Normandy, *June 2008* (266); A Country Wedding, *August 2008* (268); Celebrating the 2CV, *September 2008* (269); Train Spotting in France, *October 2008* (273); Fame, With Strings Attached, *March 2009* (274); The End of *Le Monde?* Never, *May 2009* (276); Bottom Gear, *October 2009* (277)

INTRODUCTION

Journalists are seekers of sensation, lovers of the extraordinary. The ordinary is the business of social historians, statisticians, novelists and other bores. Who wants to know about what happened yesterday if it is the same thing that happened last week and last month and last year?

Actually, we all do. Especially if it is the ordinary/extraordinary: not what happens in our own lives, or to our own families, but in the lives of the people next door. Or the country next door.

We British are very nosy about our nearest neighbours; much nosier, it has to be admitted, than they are about us. We especially like to hear of the petty, or not so petty, failures or problems of our cross-Channel cousins.

We have an inferiority-superiority complex about the French. They are unreliable, devious, selfish, rude and oversexed. Their food is over-rated. Château Supercilious is rubbish compared to Koala Creek. They are always on strike / blocking the Channel Tunnel / directing busloads of Afghans to Calais / making incomprehensible movies / giving billions of euros in UK-funded subsidies to greedy, hopeless French farmers.

At the same time, we have an unpleasant suspicion that the French are better looking than we are / have better and more sex / eat better / have better weather / better footballers / a better health service / more open space / higher mountains / more beaches / better schools / better motorways / better railways / better lives.

The French spend less time staring over the Channel than we do. They have other, equally irritating/fascinating neighbours to the north, east and south. They are, in any case, chiefly fascinated by themselves or, *à la limite*, the Americans. All the same, our schizophrenic suspicions are mirrored by persistent French prejudices, and anxieties, about the British.

We are, seen from across the Channel, emotionally retarded / badly dressed / under America's thumb / uninterested in food / awkward about sex. We are either frigidly conventional or wildly eccentric or callously violent. We are also, the French fear, more enterprising than they, more innovative and less hung-up by tradition.

The typical British man, according to French stereotypes, either: a) wears a bowler hat; b) has purple hair; c) has a shaven skull and knuckle-dusters. The typical British woman either: a) wears a dull, sensible skirt; b) has purple hair; c) gets drunk before breakfast.

We think of the French as a race of vague, over-emotional, unreliable poets. The French see themselves as a race of rational mathematicians and engineers. We think of ourselves as a race of polite, pragmatic, creative introverts. The French see us as a race of devious, drunken, emotionally-challenged egotists.

My son Charles is an accidental and often unwilling hero of many of the articles in this book. He went through the French education system from six to eighteen. He then went to university in Britain assuming, with a sigh of relief, that he was leaving his parents and going home at the same time. The British students, although friendly, insisted that Charles was irredeemably French. The young Britons appeared equally odd to his French-educated eyes: they are, he says, a generation of "vegetarian alcoholics".

Our two countries, so close and so historically entwined, live largely back-to-back lives. The Channel is still one of the world's great cultural fault lines, like a European Rio Grande. And yet we are more interconnected than at any time since the Hundred Years War. Over 300,000, mostly young, French people now live in Britain. Over 250,000, mostly middle-aged or older, British people now live full-time in France.

For thirteen years, I have been one of them, as the Paris correspondent of *The Independent* and *The Independent on Sunday*. The articles reprinted here are only a small fraction of the thousands of stories that I have written in that time. In theory, these were the ephemeral articles; the throwaway columns; the soft diaries about my family's life in France, the chance encounters with odd, or ordinary, French people, both in Paris and in my beloved adopted village in Normandy.

There is little here about high-politics or diplomacy or elections or plane crashes or riots or floods or murders. There is nothing—or very little—on the serial soap operas which have dominated news from France in the last thirteen years: the unfortunate accident of Diana Princess of Wales; the Anglo-French beef war; the insoluble conundrum of the illegal immigrants piling up in Calais; the problems of the multi-racial suburbs; the French stand against the Iraq war; the French "non" to a European constitution; the final years of *Chiraquie* and the rise of Nicolas Sarkozy.

I wrote many articles about such things. They all seemed hugely important the time. And yet I noticed something strange. The letters or emails that I received from readers were rarely about my (hem hem) hard-hitting, ground-breaking news articles or deeply-considered, carefully-crafted opinion articles. Readers responded far more often to a diary column about how my kids were dealing with the French school system; or the casual iniquities of my struggling, hippy-farmer neighbour in Normandy; or my wife's discovery of a forgotten gallery in the Musée d'Orsay.

In writing about such things, I was often breaking the first rule of news journalism. I was trying to describe the ordinary, rather than the extraordinary. And yet the ordinary and the everyday—if it is someone else's ordinary—sometimes touch people more than the dramatic and the would-be important. Hence, one assumes, the triumph of the blogosphere. Who cares now about Jacques Chirac's campaign speeches in 2002? Or the reasons for the French ban on British beef in 1999?

At times I was given a fixed space in the newspaper each week in which to write about whatever amused or interested me. At other times, the columns and diaries had to compete for space with floods, or fires, or wars, or the diaries of other foreign correspondents who were also trying to describe the ordinary-extraordinary in their own countries. Sometimes, I was burning to get something off my chest. More often the blank space and deadline loomed like an appointment with the hangman (or guillotine operator). There are articles here that were written in desperation to fill a space. Others describe events which touched me deeply, like the death in his own small plane of my friend, Bernard, the flying dairy farmer.

Sometimes, I allowed the incidents and characters to speak for themselves. At other times—too often maybe—I felt compelled to generalise and link the events to broader themes or changes in French life. Often, I see, I contradicted myself.

But so what? If these articles are worth rescuing, from the database or the recycling bin, it is because they are snapshots of changing moods and changing times. They do not represent an attempt to "explain France" or to "rubbish France". They may occasionally stray towards the usual traps of Froglit (a thriving genre in the UK), comic exaggeration or comic romanticisation. But they are not, overall, an attempt to define "the French", because there is no such people.

There is Parisian France and Provincial France and Southern France and Northern France and Elite France and Grass-roots France and Rural France and Suburban France. There is Old France and there is Young France. All of them appear here, some more than others.

There are running themes such as France's difficulties with modernity and globalisation; the hypocrisy of Official France towards the slow death of Rural France; the tendency of Political France and Media France to debate, and to attempt to reform, French myths rather than realities. There is much on Parisian rudeness and the many exceptions to it that one finds. There is the contradiction between France's official devotion to Egalité and Fraternité and the selfish arrogance that is inculcated in the country's Official Elite (now, I hope, declining).

There is also, I hope, much Savoir-faire and Joie de Vivre.

———

The book is dedicated to my wonderful wife, Margaret, who is the true source of many of the ideas and observations and incidents. Apart from the experiences of my son Charles, it also draws—often to their fury—on the lives of my daughters Clare and Grace, whose exposure to French schools, French teachers and French children taught me more about France than daily reading of the often excellent French press.

I would also like to thank James Ferguson of Signal Books for resurrecting these long-forgotten columns, which, like Norman mayflies or Parisian plumbing, were only meant to live for a day. And I should declare my debt to successive editors and foreign desk colleagues at *The Independent* and *The Independent on Sunday*, who encouraged, commissioned, and then printed, all this stuff in the first place.

PART ONE

Paris

When I first visited Paris, at the age of fourteen with my Belgian godmother, I couldn't see what all the fuss was about. The buildings were black, just like at home in the north of England. The people were rude. The buses looked like they had been brought out of a museum.

The next time I visited the City of Light, fourteen years later in 1978, I was a poor immigrant who had a job working overnight at the French news agency. The buildings were no longer black; the people were just as rude. I used to go on long urban rambles through what was still, in parts, a gritty town, recognisably the home of Edith Piaf and a dozen black and white French gangster movies.

On the Rue St Denis, the prostitutes were so thick on the ground that they could have linked arms like a giant chorus line. One night, on the Grands Boulevards, I saw the *patron* pull a revolver from behind the bar and invite a drunken customer to leave. That never happened in Bolton.

When I returned to Paris as a foreign correspondent in December 1996, much had changed. As mayor from 1977, Jacques Chirac had pushed immigrants and poor whites out of large parts of the city. Paris was cleaner (apart from the dog-stricken pavements). It was safer. It was prettier. It was duller.

That process has continued over the last thirteen years. Great icons of Parisian eccentricity and authenticity, like the Samaritaine department store, have vanished. President Sarkozy has driven the ladies from the Rue St Denis into the two Bois or into cheap hotels (where they are more than ever at the mercy of their pimps).

Paris remains a great city for tourists or the well-off or the middle-aged. It is the most beautiful city in the world. Young Parisians find it a teeny bit dull.

■ An Urban Minefield

MARCH 1997

Our friend Sandra, an Irish woman married to a Frenchman, says that the *vrai parisien* pedestrian can always be distinguished from the visitor or newcomer. The unwary outsider stares up at the startlingly elegant buildings on every side. The Parisian always looks down. He or she is, from bitter experience, scanning the pavement ahead for dog poo.

Paris has a serious dog problem, more serious, it is said, than any other city in the world. Partly this is because it has more dogs—300,000—than any other city. But that is not all. Other cities, including other French cities, have taken aggressive steps to curb this urban scourge. Paris has adopted a policy of, as it were, *laissez-faire*.

On my walk to work the other day I decided, in the name of investigative journalism, to measure the extent of the affliction. I counted eighteen deposits in the first thirty yards. Walking to school with the children is a one mile slalom course to avoid what Charles calls, from grisly memory, the "squelchy ones".

Continuing my fearless inquiries, I uncovered several disturbing facts. Dogs leave twenty tons of faeces on the streets of Paris daily (who has weighed them you ask? We will come to that later). An average of 650 people a year are hurt so badly after slipping on dog shit in Paris that they have to be taken to hospital. This works out at nearly two victims a day; broken collar bones are the most frequent injury.

The City of Paris pays £5 million a year to a company which operates more than 100 machines, resembling golf carts, called *caninettes*. Their job is to scour dog poo from the most affected pavements once or twice a day. (The normal street cleaning is supposed to take care of the gutters.) The caninettes make their most intensive rounds just after the morning rush-hour and just after the late film on television. Experience has shown that this is when owners and dogs most frequently resort to the public canine toilets, known to everyone else as the streets.

I contacted the technical director of the operation, Dominique Bellanger, who admitted it was not feasible to get around all the 1,500 miles of Parisian streets daily. His team, he said, concentrates on the "most polluted areas". (It is his company which has measured the harvest from Parisian dogs.) The caninettes do a good job but, as M. Bellanger concedes, the expectation that they will pass by encourages lazy dog-owners to use the pavements, not the gutters.

We are used to thinking of Britain as a nation of doting dog-owners, but we have nothing on the French. In the Bois de Boulogne on a fine Sunday, Parisians parade in their hundreds around the ornamental lakes, with every conceivable species of mutt, turning the Bois into some vast, open-air Crufts. The sentimentality which the French rarely bestow on one another is available sometimes for children and always for dogs.

Paris, like California, has dog psychiatrists; even dog and cat astrologers. There are 80,000 dogs with private health insurance in France. Close to my office is a dog shop. In the window are dog mittens, fashionable dog coats, haute-cuisine dog biscuits, dog toys—including stuffed animals (pets for dogs?)—and packets of the "finest-quality straw from the Pays d'Auge" (*appellation contrôlée* produce for pets?)

There is not a pooper-scooper in sight. I inquired within. The shop did not sell them: no demand apparently, despite the 300,000 dogs living in Paris. Over the years, committees have been formed by the town hall to study the issue, scientific studies have been commissioned, and information campaigns have been aimed at dog-owners (encouraging more *fraternité* and less *liberté*).

Other French cities have, so to speak, stamped on the problem. Grenoble led the way in the 1980s with instant fines, prosecutions for persistent offenders, even the seizure of pets. At the same time, the city built 120 "sanitary dog spaces" and conducted a permanent civic-awareness campaign. Similar policies, as well as a tax on dog-owners, were proposed to the city of Paris as long as eight years ago. They were rejected by the then mayor, who said such "repression" would not work and would penalise the old and the poor.

The mayor was, of course, Jacques Chirac, who is notoriously soft-hearted about animals. At one point the future president lectured dog food manufacturers on the need to make their offerings conducive to drier and more compact dog poo. He was, it is said, reluctant to do anything which might offend so many thousands of dog-owning voters.

Nothing much is likely to change soon. Complaints about dog dirt are the third most frequent reason for letter-writing to the Paris town hall (ahead of fear of crime). But this has been true for many years now. The Agriculture Minister, Philippe Vasseur, will shortly present a law to parliament on the control of pets. It is aimed mostly at controlling savage dogs such as pit bulls and at the better regulation of cat and dog sales. It also proposes a free, if limited, veterinary service for poorer pet owners. There is no suggestion of a licence or tax to control dog numbers, as some had urged.

Non-dog-owning Parisians should console themselves with the wisdom of the 19th-century poet Gérard de Nerval, who provoked the dog lovers of his day by promenading with a lobster at the end of a pink ribbon. When questioned on his motives, he replied that lobsters "know the secrets of the sea, they don't bark..." He might have mentioned at least one other reason, in a crowded city, to prefer a crustacean to a dog.

■ Paris in the Rain
JULY 1997

Stubborn, unyielding rain is unpleasant in any city, but there is something especially maddening about rain in Paris. Despite the excellence of its public transport, and the pedestriacidal tendencies of its traffic, the French capital is a walking city. If you cannot stroll comfortably from place to place, much of the pleasure of living in Paris is spoilt.

When it rains, unless your destination is close to a Metro station, or you brave the demolition derby in the streets, you have to walk. In Paris, as in most other cities, the buses and taxis dissolve in water.

In other places I have lived (Bolton, Brussels, London), rain was tediously predictable. In Paris, the rain is malevolent. It rushes out of pipes placed at head-height by the city's archaic plumbing system. It gathers in great globules on the beautiful, wrought iron balconies and falls with astonishing accuracy down the back of your neck.

If you have an umbrella, the aggravated raindrops cannon off the pavement and soak your trousers, or, if you are a woman, so I am told, bounce impossible distances up your tights. Parisian street gutters tend to resemble mountain streams in the driest weather (part of the municipal cleansing system). In heavy rain, the gutters become raging Amazons.

What on earth, I was once asked, is the purpose of those rolled up pieces of sacking, or blanket, or carpet, tied in string, which litter the gutters of Paris? Are they the bed-rolls of foreign students, who fell long ago into the sewers? Are they provided, thoughtfully but untidily, by the Town Hall to allow prams to ascend the high curbs?

I believe I know the unpoetic answer to this existential mystery. Long ago, I worked a night shift in Paris and would walk home at 6am. I would see the African foot soldiers in the city's great army of street cleaners manipulating the unappealing bundles with their sweeping brushes. They are designed to block and direct the flow of water which cleans the gutters of dog poo and other detritus.

Who said the French are not a resourceful people?

Back to the rain. It was on the wettest day of the week that I had to look after the children. Initially it was just Charles, who is seven. Clare, aged three, had been packed off to her best school-friend, Charlotte. After a couple of hours the girls decided to re-stage the Holyfield-Tyson fight and I was summoned to remove Clare before they reached the ear-severing stage.

What can you do with children in Paris in the rain? There are dozens of places the children have come to enjoy: the marvellous Jardin d'Acclimatation in the Bois de Boulogne, which is a permanent fairground set in beautiful gardens; the donkeys in the Jardins du Ranelagh; the toy yachts in the Jardin du Luxembourg (actually they don't like that one, but I do).

The problem is that, apart from being costly, all these activities are impossible in the rain. Only one option was left: the puppets.

There are fifteen puppet shows listed in the Paris entertainment guide. My favourites are the Marionettes du Ranelagh in the 16th *arrondissement*. But they have a suspect corrugated iron roof. The last time we went there in the rain, it was like having a cold shower with your clothes on. The Marionettes in the Champs Elysées are in the open-air and, anyway, disappointing. It was agreed that we would try the marionettes in the Luxembourg gardens, which have their own miniature opera house.

Puppet shows are a revelation of national character: an admission of the nation's true self, or an assertion of what the nation secretly believes itself to be. In Britain, we have to put up with the tedious Mr Punch: boorish, violent and self-opinionated. In Paris, the puppet shows are much funnier and more varied, with wonderfully elaborate costumes and scenery.

They almost all chronicle the adventures of Monsieur Guignol, a French everyman: cheerful, playful, feckless, resourceful, loyal, polite but finally not too respectful of authority. He is usually dressed as an 18th-century butler, with a strange waxy three-cornered hat and a long pigtail.

It is Monsieur Guignol's task to resolve, with a mixture of silly puns and slapstick, the bizarre complications which arise in a classic children's story (for instance *Little Red Riding Hood* with a cuddly wolf who only eats pasta). The one we saw this week was a cock-eyed mixture of *Sleeping Beauty* and *Cinderella*. We emerged after 45 happy minutes into... bright sunshine.

■ Urban Theatre
JULY 1998

The last time I lived in Paris, twenty years ago, I worked nights. I would wake in the early afternoon, too dazed to accomplish much, and wander over to the then recently opened Pompidou Centre.

Among the street performers on the esplanade before the building, my favourite, my great hero, was a man in his late thirties who looked vaguely like the French film director François Truffaut. He played a carpenter's saw with a violin bow. Or rather he didn't play it. His act was one long digression in which he would never play more than a screeching note or two before breaking off to harangue and insult and amuse the crowd.

When a large enough audience had assembled, he would seize on a handful of children and adults. Before they quite knew what was happening, they would be performing a dottily hilarious version of a fairytale, colliding with events from that day's news: *Little Red Riding Hood*, say, with Valéry Giscard d'Estaing as The Wolf.

Sometimes the plays never really took off. On other occasions they would last for an hour or more and become wonderful, rambling, surreal satires. By the end, performers and audience—children and adults—would be weak with laughter.

Twenty years later, the esplanade in front of the Pompidou Centre, partly closed for renovations until the year 2000, is a faint echo of the vibrant place that it once was. But my hero, I was delighted to find, is still there. He does not use the saw and bow any more. These days, his only props are a stick, a whistle, a toy mobile telephone and a bowler hat, from which he never quite gets around to producing a rabbit.

His name is John Guez (he is part-Spanish, part-French, born in Tunisia but his father was in the US Army). He is now 56 and white-haired but still youthful, almost childlike. M. Guez has performed outside the Pompidou Centre every day—rain permitting—for the last 22 years, since the building opened. He is a former door-to-door baby wear salesman, married to a teacher of French. "I am here not really to make my living but to observe life. My wife is an understanding woman. She knows that I like to go out and play with the people on the street and she doesn't mind." He describes himself as "part of the Maquis. Part of the Resistance against modern life, against the Star System, against the world of fast food and the TV zapper."

M. Guez would hate to admit it, but he has become a Parisian institution.

Sometimes, to his annoyance, the habitués in his audience start the required sound effects, the wind in the trees, a dog barking in the night, before he has instructed them to do so. An institution—and a marriage agency.

On one occasion, a couple with two children came up to him

after his show. They said: "You won't remember us but..." They explained they had first met when he pulled them out of the crowd ten years earlier to play parts in one of his plays. Similar meetings have occurred on several occasions since.

Yesterday the theme was (roughly speaking) *Sleeping Beauty* or *Rapunzel* mixed up with the World Cup. A shy girl from New York was selected to be the princess. Two young Frenchmen were the rival princes. Three children, brothers and sisters, were a kind of Greek chorus, or panel of TV experts, repeating M. Guez's comments on the hopelessness of the other performers, Ronaldo, the French soccer team and the iniquities of sports sponsorship.

"Regardez ses godasses," they recited in horrified tones. "Ils ne sont pas des Adidas" (Look at his shoes, they are not Adidas.)

There was, suddenly, a vacancy for a witch.

"That shouldn't be difficult to find," Guez said. "There is a pile of witches in the audience today."

By the time the play ended, there were 200 people watching and nine actors. The two young Frenchmen were bullied into performing a shadow sword fight, with the princess as a prize for the loser. "Le vainqueur aura son coeur. Le vaincu aura son..." (he broke off).

This is the theme of the day; the loser is also the victor.

Afterwards, M. Guez said that he had been disgusted by the "unthinking elation" of the French at their World Cup victory, a reaction that spared no time for the feelings of the Brazilians. "In life, there are the obvious victories but there are also the internal victories. The victories that no-one else sees."

Is this why he makes the street his stage? "Yes, every day I start with nothing. Every day, I force myself to perform better, to achieve something out of nothing. Every day is a victory over myself. I make a little money (he gives change to those people that he thinks are paying too much). But my reward is to see the joy of others, and especially the joy of the children."

But what happened to the saw and bow. "Ah the saw and bow, yes. I decided eventually, after many years, that I was not a polished enough performer with the saw to appear in public. Now I only perform at home, for my own pleasure. And to annoy the neighbours."

■ A Gardienne Angel
JULY 1998

The concierge came to the door of our flat, looking even more bedraggled than usual and a little wet. Had we, she wanted to know, being throwing water out of the window into the courtyard five floors below? Er, no, we replied, at first indignant and then amused.

Concierges are not supposed to be called concierges any more. The word is regarded as pejorative, carrying connotations of amateur espionage and moral judgements passed behind twitching lace curtains. They are now to be called *gardiennes*, which also means "female goalkeepers".

Our female goalkeeper is a gentle, hard-working, competent woman but a little strange. Her job is to deliver the mail, put out the rubbish, clean the hall and stairs and keep out undesirables. She is given to talking (and laughing) to herself loudly, cooking cabbage stews which perfume the entire building, and having noisy parties with her friends on Friday nights.

Madame is a Bosnian Serb and a Jehovah's Witness. This combination seems to have made her a sweet-natured paranoid. Her mood swings from friendly to chillingly distant, which means the mail arrives up to three days after even the French postal service intended. Conversations with our gardienne are best kept to domestic subjects. Any deviation from that rule is likely to produce a) a lecture on the iniquities of the Bosnian Moslems, who are "trying to conquer Europe", or b) an inquiry as to whether you wish to learn about "the love of Christ" in the French version of the *Watchtower*.

Despite these oddities, the consensus in the building is that we are lucky to have Madame. The gardienne is a dying breed. There were 60,000 in Paris in 1950; there are now fewer than 25,000. They have been flushed out of their tiny ground-floor apartments by the coming of electronic coded devices for opening doors.

It is regarded as a great cachet to have a gardienne. If you walk down any Parisian street early in the morning, you can tell which buildings have them and which do not. The gardiennes are there, in close formation, washing the front steps and pavements outside their buildings; the electronic devices are not.

All of which is by way of saying that we would not dream of pouring water on Madame from a height of five floors. A couple of moments after she left, shaking her head, we looked out of the window to see her in the courtyard with two of our least friendly neighbours. All three were looking down at a great puddle of water in the courtyard and then looking up at our window and pointing. We could hear the words "les anglais" and possibly even "hooligans", a word recently imported into the French language. We grew indignant all over again, especially my wife, who is not English but Irish.

Then we remembered. Charles, aged eight, had been taking a shower at the time of the incident. Upon questioning, he freely admitted to pointing the shower attachment out of the bathroom window for no particular reason. He asked for at least 37 previous offences to be taken into consideration. (This was why Madame was in the courtyard looking up at our flat in the first place.)

The next day I presented myself at her door with a large pot plant to apologise. She roared with laughter and then, sheepishly, handed over several days' mail.

■ The Parisian Paradox
JUNE 1999

Here is a story of a child's shoe, a piano and the Parisian paradox. The paradox is that Parisians can be the most tolerant people on earth. And, at the same time, by common consent, the rudest.

The shoe in question belongs to Beatrice, my daughter's best friend, aged five. Every other Friday, Beatrice, who is half-Irish and half-Swedish, comes to lunch and to play at our home. School lunchtimes are so lengthy in Paris (two hours), and the weekends so crowded with family activities, that the social life of Parisian children occurs largely in the middle of the school day.

Every second Friday afternoon, the two girls are taken back to school by our Filipina occasional baby-sitter, Rowena. Like most of the foot soldiers in the large army of Filipinas in Paris, Rowena hardly speaks a word of French.

Last Friday, the trio were getting off the Metro when Beatrice's shoe detached itself from her foot and fell between the train and the platform. Beatrice was distraught. The two little girls approached the woman in the ticket office and told her the sad story. The ticket office woman was, by all accounts, charming. She made a telephone call and an engineer arrived. He ordered the current of Line Six cut off for twenty minutes.

Trains stopped; passengers spilt out; others joined them. Nothing and no-one could move until the shoe was recovered. The Metro is not the London Tube, where waiting twenty minutes for a train is normal. Parisians are used to catching a train within two minutes. But when the station staff pointed out the problem no-one complained. It was accepted, with good humour, that this was an entirely proper reason to shut down Line Six.

Three weeks earlier, the whole of the underground and bus system had been closed for two days after a Metro security officer collapsed and died on the job from natural causes. The employees of the Parisian transport company went on strike insisting—against all the evidence—that the man had been assaulted by two illegal jewellery vendors.

Parisians, for the most part, tolerated this absurd strike with resignation and good humour. In neither incident—the shoe or the strike—could such forbearance be expected in London.

The piano in question belongs to my wife, Margaret. Several months ago, she started to play again after a twenty-year interval. Last week she got into the lift with an elegant, hatchet-faced, sixty-something woman who lives above us. She has never shown any interest in talking to us. Abruptly, she asked: "Is it you who plays the piano?" My wife admitted that it was. The woman looked her in the eye and said: "You're not making any progress, you know."

Such first-degree, premeditated rudeness could only happen in Paris. Foreign visitors often assume it is aimed at them. It is not. Parisians are equally rude to one another.

French friends say it goes back to the Second World War, or even the Revolution, when neighbours often betrayed one another to the authorities. A lawyer friend reports that neighbour-versus-neighbour court cases are one of the great boom areas of the French legal system. One recent case concerned an excessively loud coffee-grinder.

So there is the paradox. Parisians can be tolerant, almost to a fault. In their attitudes to strikes, dog dirt, little girl's shoes fallen onto the Metro tracks, they display an almost Buddhist resignation. And yet in their personal relations, they have a breath-taking capacity for waspish and often arrogant defence of their personal space.

When the shoe was finally restored to Beatrice, the two girls were more than half an hour late for afternoon school. The big door was shut. The school's security officer came out and screamed at them to go away. The school rules stated, she said, that once the door was closed no-one could be allowed in. Clare put her hands on her hips and screamed back. It was not her fault—it was not even Beatrice's fault. She didn't want to go home; she wanted to go to school.

The two girls were admitted. One sharp tongue had recognised, and bowed to, another. After two years, little Clare has become, for good or ill, a *Parisienne*.

■ A Visit to Oscar
OCTOBER 2000

"Yet each man kills the thing he loves,
  By each let this be heard,
  Some do it with a bitter look,
  Some with a flattering word.
  The coward does it with a kiss,
  The brave man with a sword!"

  – Oscar Wilde, "The Ballad of Reading Gaol"

At Oscar Wilde's tomb, many a tourist desecrates the thing he loves. Some do it with a scribbled signature, some with a flattering word in Italian. The real obsessives do it with a kiss, or, in this case, scores and scores of pale mauve paint kisses, carefully imprinted by someone called Régine.

Graffiti in the Père Lachaise cemetery in Paris has a long and ignoble history. The most recent and egregious victim is the tomb of Wilde, who died a hundred years ago next month. His grave is now the most decorated and desecrated place in what claims to be the most visited cemetery in the world.

Almost all of the scribbling is perpetrated by people who claim to be fans of the author, a large number of whom seem to be Italians. "You taught me what is love," writes Luca from Pescara. "What's the craic?" asks Aisling from Dublin. One, unsigned and fading, inscription, reads "Traitor", without further explanation.

The worst single, recent outbreak of idolatry is a rash of painted kisses covering the whole of the front, and part of the sides, of what would otherwise be a startlingly beautiful tomb—a naked angel, sculpted by Sir Jacob Epstein, paid for by an anonymous "lady".

The angel guarding Oscar Wilde was originally a well endowed male, but his manhood was chiselled off years ago. One version of events says that the head keeper of the cemetery thought this detail offensive (it did not stop him keeping the stolen part, or parts, as a paperweight).

The graffiti in Père Lachaise is a more recent outbreak of philistinism. It began when Jim Morrison, lead singer with the American rock group The Doors, was buried here in 1971. For many years, Morrison's grave was a multicoloured disgrace. Worse, seemingly every fourth tomb on the route to Morrison's grave was callously daubed with large arrows or scrawled with inscriptions such as "This way to Jim".

A couple of days ago the French press reported that families with relatives buried in the cemetery had started a campaign to oust Morrison's body. They were fed up, it was said, with the commotion and untidiness surrounding his grave. A petition was reported to be circulating.

The story was entirely untrue. There is no campaign and no petition, according to officials at the cemetery. In any case, the commotion and untidiness are no more. Morrison's grave has been scrubbed clean. All the arrows and scribbled signs have been gone for years.

There are one or two modest new graffiti on the Morrison tombstone. Fans sometimes thoughtfully leave hand-rolled joints for Jim. Otherwise, the grave of James Douglas Morrison is now as sombre and anonymous as the sepulchres of the respectable and wealthy 19th-century Parisians, which stand all around.

Père Lachaise is an odd place for Morrison to end up. It is an odd place for Wilde to end up, even if it includes other artist-rebels such as Marcel Proust, Edith Piaf and Honoré de Balzac. The cemetery has quiet, leafy lanes and individual houses for whole dynasties of the bourgeois dead. It is a kind of necro-suburb, the antithesis of the dense, noisy city for the living outside the high cemetery wall.

Odd or not, both Morrison and Wilde lie there "in perpetuity". Jim Morrison is here because he died of a heart attack while on tour in Paris, aged 28. Oscar Wilde is here because he died in poverty in the Hôtel d'Alsace, 13 Rue des Beaux Arts, in Paris in November 1900, aged 46. He fled to the French capital after he was disgraced and jailed for his homosexual love affair with Lord Alfred Douglas (a name that also appears among the scribbled signatures on his grave).

Wilde's tomb was last fully restored in 1992. Officials at the cemetery, who seemed unaware of the Wilde centenary next month, said yesterday that every effort was made to prevent vandalism and to clean off inscriptions on all tombs. But they said that some graffiti had proved very hard to erase.

Morrison's grave now has a full-time guard. Wilde's, the cemetery officials admitted, does not. Many hundreds of Wilde lovers will visit the tomb for the centenary of his death next month. They will discover that other Wilde aficionados have stupidly killed the dignity and beauty of the thing they love.

■ Trouble in Store
APRIL 2001

A mournful, end-of-empire atmosphere descended on the Boulevard Haussmann in central Paris yesterday. At 3.30 p.m., Marks & Spencer closed its doors forever. Not since Dunkirk has there been such a distressing British retreat from France. One almost expected a helicopter to land on the roof and fly away to Baker Street with the last pair of Extra Large thermal underpants and the last jar of English pickles.

The atmosphere in the final days was, however, more Moscow circa 1989 than Hong Kong circa 1998. More Marx than Marks. In the speciality food department, there were several million unsold boxes of Kenyan tea and shelves full of Plum and Sesame stir-fry sauce but little that people wanted to buy.

Where were the crumpets, the mince-pies, the chicken tikka massala? All gone. There had, it is true, been an emergency last minute infusion of ready made sandwiches (very popular with Parisians) and lettuce. But many shoppers were wandering around disconsolately with nothing in their baskets.

Upstairs, the womenswear department was still well stocked, despite a forty per cent off sale (which, in itself, tells the story of the M&S continental demise). But the menswear department was roped off. "Nothing left up there," said a jolly security guard, "nothing left but the walls and even they have been sold."

All of this suggests that, with more careful targeting, M&S could have kept a foothold on the continent. The flagship store on the Boulevard Haussmann was profitable to the end (other shops in France much less so). There was a huge Parisian and expatriate clientele for M&S sausages, cheese, bacon, ready made Indian meals and men's underwear. If Marks had retained a smaller shop somewhere in Paris, concentrating on the lines which sold well, it would have been a great success.

Even now, there is a great business opportunity for Tesco or Sainsburys to move in and keep the British sausage alive in Paris. All that remains, south of Calais, for British food addicts are a gaggle of speciality shops selling Branston Pickle at £5 a jar.

In its heyday, the Boulevard Haussmann store was one of the most fashionable spots in the French capital. Princess Grace of Monaco used to shop there (and not everyone believed her story that she was only buying stuff to give away to her charities).

The last manager of the store, Guy Bodescot, recalls the confusion caused in the early days in the mid 1970s when M&S refused to supply French translations of its labels. The London headquarters gave way only when it was discovered that Parisian shoppers were buying packets of dried flowers and using them (unsuccessfully) as herbal teas.

The first translations, supplied from London, were equally unsettling. M&S brand marmalade was guaranteed to be "sans préservatifs", which means literally "without condoms".

■ Tourist Guide
MAY 2002

Journalists of the old school arriving in a country unfortunate enough to be in the news would question taxi drivers and quote them as "sources close to the government" or "diplomatic officials". No journalist would ever do that today, of course.

The other night I was being driven through Paris by a source close to the government, who was extremely pessimistic about the French economy, especially the tourist economy. "You can't make a living anymore" he said. "There are no Americans coming to Paris these days. They're all scared to go abroad again. There used to be the Japanese but they've got no money for taxis anymore. They all stay out in cheap hotels in the suburbs and travel around in buses."

"What about the British?" I ventured.

"Ha, the British. They were always too mean to take taxis but now, in any case, they come over on the train for a day, have a ham sandwich and go back again."

Er, the French? "Ha, the French. They're never here. Not the wealthy ones anyway. With this 35 hour week, they're always on holiday. I tell you this country is going straight into the wall," he said, accelerating his car almost into the boot of the one in front to emphasise his point.

I checked his assertion that there are fewer tourists than normal in Paris this year, with the city's tourist board and with our friend, Michel, who owns a small hotel in the heart of the Left Bank (rates on request). Yes, they said, it is true, that the Japanese have deserted the city centre hotels. Yes, it was true that there were many fewer Americans post 11 September.

However, they said, the Americans have been flooding to Paris in great numbers again since mid-May. Why the change? It must be the example set by President George W. Bush, who visited four European countries in just over a week (a modest total by the traditional standards of American tourists).

Not only has he saved the world from terrorism, W. is making the world safe for tourism. Europe has much to be grateful for.

■ A Cock-fight
JUNE 2002

Paris is full of surprises, of hidden worlds. The worlds usually ignore one another. Occasionally, they clash.

Amid the shabby clamour of Pigalle, with its peep shows, sex shops, fast food joints and rip-off hostess bars, there is a short, genteel avenue which might have been plucked from Kensington or Holland Park. It could be a movie set of Edwardian London for a remake of *Mary Poppins*. There are cobbles and trees and early 19th-century houses, set in their own small grounds.

Victor Hugo and Gustave Flaubert spent some time there. The great French gypsy jazz musician Django Reinhardt lived there for many years. To get past the high iron gate into the avenue, you have to know the entrance code. Once the gate clangs behind you, the other Paris—the Paris of car horn concertos, Polish tour buses and motorbikes slaloming through crowded pavements—vanishes. You enter a parallel world of rural charm, in the heart of the most densely packed city in Europe.

Too rural for some. You might think that the residents of this island of peace would complain about disturbances from the fretful, Parisian world outside. No. It is the Parisians who live in apartments overlooking the avenue who are complaining. They say that they are being driven crazy by inappropriate, farmyard noises from the bucolic universe next door.

Five weeks ago, Henri de Bodinat, who lives in one of the houses on the avenue, gave a cockerel to his wife Clémence for her birthday. The de Bodinats have kept hens in their garden for two years. In that time, they have eaten 1,300 Parisian free range eggs. They are not the only hen fanciers in the neighbourhood. The fashion designer, Jean-Paul Gaultier, who lives two doors away, used to keep hens (designer hens?) which once invaded the de Bodinats' garden.

Anyway, Henri de Bodinat, fifty, a music publisher, thought that his hens might like some male company. The cockerel—named "Coucou" or cuckoo, after his speckled grey and white colouring, and his race, the Coucou de Bretagne—took his farmyard duties seriously. He saw no reason to abandon his habits in the big city. He began crowing at six a.m.

The neighbours complained. The de Bodinats locked Coucou in the hen-house at night to encourage him to adopt slothful, urban habits and to sleep later. The cockerel continued, however, to crow during the day, frequently and very loudly.

One day, M. de Bodinat was abused by a man from a balcony of one of the typically Parisian, seven storey buildings overlooking the avenue. "Shut up that cock, or I'll shut it up for you" was, more or less, the angry man's message. Two days later, the police came around. Is there a law against cocks crowing during the daytime in Paris? M. de Bodinat asked them. They had to admit that there probably was not.

A few days later, the police came back. "There are near-brothels just around the corner, terrible screams at night from the streets all around. You'd think the police would have had other things to do in Pigalle," M. de Bodinat said. "They told me that the commissariat (local police headquarters) had had fifty complaints. They were fed up with answering the phone. They said the cock had to go or we would be taken to court."

The de Bodinats' immediate neighbours in the avenue learned of the threat to silence "Coucou" and were appalled. "We had many messages of support. People were talking about getting up a petition to save the cock. They thought that he added considerably to the countryside atmosphere of the avenue," said M. de Bodinat.

Nonetheless, the de Bodinats declared a truce. A few days ago, they sent Coucou to live in the country for the summer.

The near neighbours miss him. The de Bodinats' four children miss him. Presumably, the hens miss him. It seems that even Jean-Paul Gaultier misses him. The great couturier is restoring his house. His latest addition is a splendid, gold-coloured weather-vane, in the shape of a cockerel.

Emboldened by all this support, the de Bodinat family has decided to have a cock-fight after all. A lawyer friend has promised to conduct any legal action for free. In September, Coucou, the cockerel, will return from exile and the feathers will fly.

■ Fun-du-Siècle
SEPTEMBER 2002

After a five year rearguard action of heroically mean minded stubbornness, I have been defeated at last. I took the children to Disneyland, Paris.

By sticking close to my five-year-old daughter, I managed to avoid all the scary rides. Grace and I spent the day on the attractions "not recommended for people under the age of one".

This was not quite my first exposure to Disneydom. I went to the original Disneyland in California twelve years ago and visited the new (crushingly dull) Walt Disney Studios, Paris, movie theme park when it opened in March this year.

Given the sweet vulgarity of the Disney Corporation's parallel universe, my first impression on each occasion was one of pleasant surprise. Everything was more tasteful than I expected; or rather, given the opportunities for bad taste which a Disney theme park offers, everything is more restrained than you have a right to expect.

After a while—seeing the submissive seventy minute queues for glorified roundabouts and ghost trains and rollercoasters—I was reminded of the Christmas that I spent in a Center Parcs holiday resort in France a couple of years ago. I wanted to make contact with the escape committee and tunnel under the wire.

If the people running the Soviet bloc had been more ruthless and imaginative, they could have made a lasting success of the Communist system by making it more like Disneyland. An enclosed universe in which one simplified world-view is relentlessly imposed; in which all national cultures and folk-stories are rewritten to fit a preconceived pattern; in which people are deprived, or relieved, of all initiative and choice; in which pleasure is rationed by endless queuing; in which the food is disgusting: such a world, it seems, need not be a failure.

Disneyland Paris attracts twelve million people a year, making it by far the most successful tourist attraction in France, with twice as many visitors as the next most successful places, the Louvre and the Eiffel Tower.

Disney has invented commercial totalitarianism. There are few benches in Eurodisney and none of the pleasant areas of lawns and flowers which exist in most other theme parks. Once inside the magic kingdom, you are expected to rush from one queue, or one shop, or one overpriced fast food stall to the next, spending money and Having Fun.

Children apart, no-one looks very happy but plenty of adults come on their own, over and over again. Disneyland has one of the best recidivism rates of any park of its kind.

Disneyland reminded me of that wonderful cult TV series from the 1960s, Patrick McGoohan's *The Prisoner*, in which lobotomised holiday makers disport themselves in a proto-Club Med on the North Wales coast.

But, strangely, the spiritual dangers of theme parks were also pointed out by Saint Walt himself.

One of the Disneyland rides that I took several times with Grace (only a forty minute queue for a five minute trip) was the Pinocchio ghost train. In a scary part of the ride, Pinocchio and the other children are sent to the sinister "Fun Island", just as they are in the Disney film version of the story. The children spend their time disporting themselves on roundabouts and rollercoasters (no queues) until they turn into donkeys.

The French sociologist, Gérard Mermet, in a new edition of his marvellous book *Francoscopie* published this month, divides 21st-century humanity into three categories: the mutants, the *mutins* (mutineers) and the *moutons* (sheep). "Mutants" are those people—mostly young, mostly male—who thrive in a globalised world which is constantly changing and where taste is simultaneously personal and international. "Mutineers" are those who wish to hold onto the more familiar rungs of traditional and national culture. "Moutons" (the majority) avidly consume global culture but have, at the same time, a vague sense of bewilderment and loss, which can easily be exploited by demagogues, in politics, and the media.

I expect that I'm a mutineer; but one so awkward that I also detest most of my fellow mutineers.

P.S. I admit it. My children adored Disneyland.

■ The Parisian Paradox 2
SEPTEMBER 2002

Parisians are the rudest and kindest of people. Everything depends on whether they know you or not.

In French schools, children are encouraged to bring in a cake on their birthday. My wife and I stayed up late one night last week trying to fashion a cake, or finally two cakes, from odds and ends of cake mixes and flour. The result looked, and tasted, like a couple of mouse mats, but we decorated them with several tons of Smarties, and Grace, whose fifth birthday it was, appeared satisfied.

The only problem was getting the cakes to school. My car was parked miles away. I decided to take the Metro, with two cakes and two small children, in the morning rush hour. The last time I tried anything so daring, the other passengers were charming. On this occasion, they gave no quarter. I was shoved and elbowed in and out of two crowded trains, finally holding the cakes on a tray high over the heads of a carriage-full of frozen faces.

The cakes survived. The teachers in the school claimed later to have enjoyed eating them. "Did you also make the Smarties yourself?" one teacher said. "They were especially good." This is the French idea of a joke.

Just as I was contemplating emigration, the bossy woman in my regular sandwich shop—a woman who harries unknown, foreign customers mercilessly and who has met Grace once—insisted on giving me a pretty porcelain box and candle-holder for her birthday.

■ The Hidden Gallery
NOVEMBER 2002

One of the most popular museums in the world has a room stuffed with great paintings which visitors seldom see. It is a secret gallery, except for those who have stumbled on the secret. The small room is poorly signposted and hidden in an awkward corner of the Musée d'Orsay in Paris. It contains twenty impressionist, post-impressionist and *fauviste* paintings by artists ranging from Van Gogh to Monet, from Cézanne to Seurat, from Pissarro to Derain.

In any other city, in any other gallery, the room would be swarming with visitors. Not here. Paris has a surfeit of publicly-owned art (vast sections of the Louvre and Beaubourg collections are never shown). The Musée d'Orsay has the world's most extraordinary collection of impressionist paintings on its celebrated and permanently besieged top floor.

Our room—we have come to think of it as our room—is on the floor below. It goes unnoticed and unloved.

The hidden gallery was discovered accidentally by my wife a few months ago. She wandered down the back stairs at the museum, along a narrow corridor, around two corners and found herself all alone with a Monet, two Bonnards, two Cézannes, two Renoirs, a Gauguin, two Vlamincks, a Seurat, a Van Gogh etc., etc.

I spent over an hour in there with two of my children the other day. (What else can you do in Paris with children on a rainy day?) In

that time, only four other people came into the room. The expression
on their faces said either: "oh no, not more impressionists" or "this
is not the loo" and they walked out again.

Clare, aged eight, likes to "copy" paintings with felt-tip pens.
A Van Gogh took her two minutes; Monet a little longer. ("They
did it better," she admitted.) Grace, aged five, lay flat on the floor
for thirty minutes, with her coloured pens spread around her,
doing a freelance version of a beautiful Renoir painting of a vase
of gladioli.

The custodian did not bother either of them. Why should he?
They weren't in anyone's way.

The room is on the middle floor of the building, in the south-
west corner; follow the confusing signs, if you can. It is called the
"Collection Max et Rosy Kaganovitch". Officials at the Musée
d'Orsay admit that the collection is obscurely placed, easy to miss
and poorly displayed. Whose fault is that? Mostly, they say, it is
Max Kaganovitch's fault.

There is nothing in the room to tell you who Max and Rosy
Kaganovitch were (a strange omission). The museum did, however,
let me ferret through their archives to find out.

Max Kaganovitch was a Russian-Jewish sculptor and art dealer,
who gave the French state his collection of paintings in 1973, five
years before he died at the age of 86. He emigrated to France in
1924, intending to become a great artist but becoming, almost by
accident, a dealer and gallery-owner instead.

He arrived in Paris penniless but realised that he could make
money by buying paintings from one gallery and selling them
to another. In the late 1920s and 1930s, it was possible to buy
impressionists and *fauvistes* for next to nothing. Kaganovitch
bought his Derain—a beautiful painting of Charing Cross Bridge—
for 1,000 francs in 1930. This would be the equivalent today of
€400 or £250.

After being stripped of his French citizenship by the anti-Semitic
Vichy regime in 1942, Kaganovitch and his wife, Rosy, and their
two daughters fled to Switzerland. He returned to France in 1945
and fought a long legal battle to reclaim his gallery on the Boulevard
Raspail from the Vichy sympathiser who had appropriated it.

Rosy, a Swiss student when he met her in 1927, died in 1960.

After retiring and returning to sculpting in 1968, Max gave his collection to the French state. He insisted, however, that the paintings should be kept together in one room; that the room should be named after Rosy and himself (what did his second wife think of that one wonders?); and that the collection should be treated as an annexe to the national treasury of impressionist paintings, which were moved into the Musée d'Orsay when it opened in 1986.

Museum officials say that the terms of Max's bequest make it difficult to give the paintings the prominent display that they merit. Many a city in France, or the world, would love and cherish such a collection. Max's bequest insists that they remain in Paris (apart from occasional trips on loan).

If you are tired of the usual trail around the Paris art galleries, we are happy to share our room on the back stairs of the Musée d'Orsay. Children and felt-tips are welcome.

■ Christmas in Paris
DECEMBER 2002

In Charles Dickens' story, "A Christmas Carol", Ebenezer Scrooge leans out of his window on Christmas morning and asks a loitering boy to purchase a turkey from the window of the local butcher's shop. Imagine trying that in London on Christmas Day 2002. Apart from the detailed advice that you might expect from any loitering 21st-century boy on where to store your turkey, how many butcher's shops are open on the 25th?

In Paris, they all are. It is my Christmas morning ritual to stroll out, whistling merry tunes from *Oliver!*, to collect the *appellation contrôlée* family turkey from the corner butcher. The bird still carries its head and a label informing you on which farm, and in which village, it grew up in in the poultry rearing area of the Landes, south of Bordeaux. One almost expects to be told its pet name.

In France on Christmas day, all food shops and food markets are open until lunch time. On Christmas morning, our local food market is always a dazzling spectacle of Dickensian plenty: a technicolour splurge of lobsters, crayfish, crabs, sea-urchins, tangerines and poinsettias. When the turkey is safely jammed into the oven, I go there to buy oysters and Brussels sprouts and cheese and bread.

There is another big advantage to spending Christmas in Paris. It starts late and finishes early. The great, holly-bordered British Christmas—robins with everything, page three girls in Santa hats and drunken office parties—starts in mid-October and straggles on into February. In France, Christmas is a quiet, family affair of gluttonous consumption, starting on the evening of the 24th. Everyone is back to work on the 26th.

And yet, and yet. Christmas is always a dangerous time for expats. Home-sickness, like the 'flu, can strike at any moment.

This is especially true in Paris this year—the first Christmas without Marks & Spencer. Even the British grocery shop started by Galeries Lafayette on the site of the M&S flagship store has thoughtlessly closed for renovations.

My wife was attacked the other day by an acute craving for mince pies. Having tried several shops without luck, she went to the posh Left Bank department store, Le Bon Marché, which has an excellent food department called La Grande Epicerie. There was a British Christmas section with mountains of Christmas puddings but no mince pies. There was an American section with heaps of cranberry sauce but no mince pies.

Close to despair, she stumbled on the German section, which had pumpernickel bread and—oh comfort and joy!—a pile of Mr Kipling's mince pies. (Maybe they should have been renamed Herr Kipling's.)

The paraphernalia of a British Christmas, once available cheaply at M&S, was not prized by expatriates alone. The French have a love-hate affair with the Christmas pudding—pronounced "le pouddeeng"—in particular.

One 25 December more than twenty years ago, I was working at the French news agency, Agence France-Presse. I brought in a home-made, whisky-soaked Christmas pudding sent to me by friends in Scotland. I placed it among the French delicacies assembled by my colleagues. It vanished in seconds.

Since returning to Paris, I have given M&S puddings as Christmas presents to people who have helped me. Some adore them. Some complain that their discriminating French insides will never recover.

Still, the demise of Marks & Spencer's missionary work for the British way-of-Christmas is a pity. Soon after M&S closed its European stores, a friend overheard a conversation between two young mothers in a Parisian playground.

Maman numéro un: "Isn't it terrible about Marks & Spencer? Last Christmas, I bought some bizarre things there. You pull them at either end, they explode and everyone has a present to put beside their plate."

Maman numéro deux (amazed): "Only the English could think of something like that."

■ Guitar Solo
JANUARY 2003

This is a story of patience, craftsmanship, the intolerance of Parisian neighbours and a £12,000 guitar which has to be played in a bathroom.

In the late 1970s, long before I knew him, my friend Olivier was a student at the Ecole Nationale de Musique in Paris. As a disciple of the Spanish classical guitarist, Alberto Ponce, it was Olivier's dream as a young man to own a Spanish guitar of the highest quality.

In a fit of whimsy, he wrote to one of the greatest of all guitar manufacturers, Ignacio Fleta in Barcelona, sometimes described as the Stradivarius, or Steinway, of the guitar. He received a polite letter in reply, saying that the company (now run by Ignacio's son Gabriel) would happily take his order. If he sent a letter of confirmation, his guitar would be ready in twenty years' time.

Fleta guitars have been prized by the greatest virtuosos, from Segovia to John Williams. They roll off the hand made production line in Barcelona at a rate of around twelve a year. Whether you are a famous musician or an obscure French music student, you have to join the queue. (When the weather is hot, which is not uncommon in Barcelona, production ceases because high temperatures affect the wood and quality of the workmanship.)

For a young man, twenty years seemed a lifetime away. Nonetheless, Olivier, from a mixture of amusement and stubbornness, placed his order. No deposit was required. What did he have to lose?

Life went on. Olivier got married to Martine. They had three sons, one of whom, Arthur, is a schoolmate and friend of our oldest son, Charles. (We first got to know Olivier and Martine Pilon after Martine and I ran the bouncy castle together at the school fete.)

Olivier, 49, is now a senior official in the computer department of the main French television channel, TF1.

Pressure of work and family forced Olivier to give up the guitar. He came back to it only in recent years. He bought an instrument in Paris, with which he was reasonably satisfied. But he never quite forgot his Fleta.

A couple of years ago (almost exactly twenty years after he placed his order) he persuaded a Spanish speaking colleague to ring the Fleta workshop. There was a long delay on the line as ledgers and files were consulted. "Yes," they finally said. "We have a record of Señor Pilon's order. There will be a small delay. His guitar is not quite ready. Call back in six months' time."

About a year later, Olivier and Martine were summoned to Barcelona to collect his guitar. It was, Martine recalls, "like adopting a baby". The handover took four days. When Olivier was finally accepted as a proper person to own a Fleta—and when he had produced £6,000 in pesetas—the instrument was presented to him, arranged on a fine silk scarf.

To my inexpert ear, Olivier plays it with great beauty. He points out however, that a guitar, and especially a great guitar, matures like a wine, partly with age, partly with playing. The player has to get to know his guitar and the guitar has to get to know its owner.

Olivier's attempts to introduce himself to his distinguished instrument were dogged from the start by the woman who lives on the floor above. Whenever Olivier played, she would thump with a stick on the Pilons' ceiling. When he stopped, she would continue thumping, revengefully, for as many minutes as he had played.

Olivier has had several tempting offers for his under-used Fleta. He could easily get twice what he paid for it. Not everyone, it seems, is prepared to wait twenty years for a new one. (Ah, the impatience of this modern, throwaway world.) He has refused all offers.

Recently, I am pleased to report, there has been a breakthrough of a kind. Olivier has discovered that, if he plays his world-class guitar in the bathroom, Madame Upstairs does not hear or does not care. She still thumps on the ceiling, but only when Arthur, aged twelve, does his music practice. Unfortunately, there is no space in the bathroom for Arthur's piano.

■ French Verbals – Regular and Irregular
JANUARY 2003

One of the curiosities of Paris is the eloquence of its beggars.

While travelling on the Paris Metro, it is a common event for one of your fellow passengers to launch into an elaborately constructed soliloquy. The other day, somewhere between Gambetta and La République on Line Three, a neatly turned out but depressed looking man in his mid-forties suddenly made, roughly, the following speech: "Good day, ladies and gentlemen. I am, I know, not the first to address you in this way and I will unfortunately not be the last. I would like to say, however, that despite what many of you may think, it is not through laziness that I come before you.

"It is not easy, for me at any rate, to have to solicit money from you in this way. It is not easy, if you are in the circumstances in which I find myself, in other words temporarily without a job, to raise enough money to put a roof over your head each evening, to eat, or even to keep yourself clean. I would like to apologise once again for inconveniencing you but to ask you, each one of you, to spare what little you may have to help me. Thank you ladies and gentlemen."

All of this sounded much better in the original French. I gave him a couple of euros (I thought his fine oratory merited some reward) but I was the only person in the carriage who did so.

My question is not, "why are the French so mean?" but "why are the French so articulate?"

Britain has recently been told that it has raised a generation of young people who communicate with grunts and incoherent bundles of clichés. Why is it that even French down-and-outs, even French footballers, speak so grammatically and so fluently?

During the 1998 World Cup in France, I interviewed a number of celebrated French footballers—Marcel Desailly, Emmanuel Petit, Lilian Thuram, even, briefly Zinedine Zidane—and was struck by how thoughtfully and coherently they spoke. No French footballer would ever be "aussi malade qu'un perroquet" (sick as a parrot) or "au dessus de la lune" (over the moon).

Even a gang of violent, multi-racial kids in an inner suburb of Paris, whom I met a couple of years ago (polite handshakes all round) expressed their aggressive alienation with great clarity and aplomb. Between themselves, they spoke in the bizarre word-reversing slang (*verlan*), which is the lingua franca of the violent suburbs but, for my sake, they were able to switch easily to standard, grammatical French.

France is not immune to the kind of verbal viruses which afflict the speech of young people in Britain. The words "voilà" (there you are) and "quoi" (what) litter the conversation of young French people. They are often yoked together to end sentences with a monotonous "voilà quoi" (just as the word "yeah?" now ritually ends English sentences).

Thus Winston Churchill, if young and alive today, would say: "We will fight them on the beaches, yeah?" General de Gaulle, if he was a young Frenchman alive today, would say "Vive le Québec libre, voilà quoi."

All the same, spoken French has not (yet) reached the level of the disintegration of spoken English. Why not?

I put the question to a number of French friends and also a couple of France's many sociologists. None gave a completely convincing explanation. They suggested that it might be something to do with the nature of the French language itself, which is more rigid than English. They suggested that the French family structure remained comparatively intact. French people still speak to one another at home, even over dinner. One French friend, educated partly in Britain, said that she thought that it might, paradoxically, be a product of the inflexibility of the French education system.

In French schools, teachers do most of the talking. When pupils are given a rare opportunity to speak, they are expected to have something coherent, and grammatical, to say. They are also drilled endlessly in grammar and made to parrot-learn poems and fables. All of this generates other educational problems (which I will come back to another time) but it does inculcate a permanent sense of the rhythm and structure of the spoken language.

Voilà quoi.

Death of a Good Samaritaine
MAY 2003

Once upon a time, if you lived in central Paris and you needed to buy a lawnmower in a hurry—or a puppy, or a mink coat or a concrete mixer—you knew where to go.

Samaritaine, the most eclectic and least fashionable department store in Paris—a Gallic version of Grace Brothers from *Are You Being Served?*—would sell you anything (diamond tiaras, pneumatic drills, piranha fish, ready mixed plaster, racing bicycles...).

Not any more.

Samaritaine reopened some of its art déco doors last week as a shopping mall devoted to designer labels and wealthy, foreign tourists. Another of the surviving landmarks of the old, unselfconscious, non-tourist Paris has vanished.

The store, once five separate buildings, now down to three, occupies a prime site on the Rue de Rivoli, five minutes from the Louvre and Notre Dame. Its slogan used to be: "Le Tout Paris vient à La Samaritaine" (All of Paris comes to Samaritaine). Its new slogan could be: "Le Tout Yokohama comes to Samaritaine."

Entering the old Samaritaine was like playing snakes and ladders. Each floor had several different levels, negotiated by short slopes of crumbling linoleum or by steep steps. To get from curtains to electrical goods, nominally on the same floor, you climbed a few stairs into showers and bathrooms, turned right and then strolled down a gentle but uneven slope towards hardware.

Samaritaine once employed 3,000 people, including some of the oldest, rudest and least helpful sales assistants in Paris (and therefore the world).

All of this, alas, is being swept away. One of the three remaining Samaritaine buildings was reborn last week, after eighteen months of renovation ("le relooking" in French) as an emporium for designer brands of clothes and perfume. When you walk into the new store, you are greeted by beautiful young women, all dressed in black and lime green, who say "bonjour" and smile.

The same fate is to befall the rest of the Samaritaine complex in the next couple of years. Until a couple of years ago, Samaritaine was, among other things, one of the biggest bookshops in Paris, a pet shop, a travel agent, a toy store, a hardware store, an auto accessories trader, a made-to-measure curtain maker and a garden centre. Much of this is already gone or going.

There is still a pet shop but you can no longer buy pets. You can, however, buy gourmet cat food and an Eau de Toilette for canines, called "Oh my Dog".

Three years ago, Louis Vuitton Moët Hennessy (LVMH), the world's largest and most successful luxury goods manufacturer, owner of 45 opulent brands from Christian Dior to Givenchy, bought a controlling interest in Samaritaine. The company already owns the top dollar Le Bon Marché department store on the Left Bank and two Japanese-thronged Louis Vuitton stores on or just off the Champs Elysées.

The part of the Rue de Rivoli where Samaritaine stands is resolutely downmarket but it is only a few hundred yards from the expensive tourist shops opposite the Louvre. LVMH is planning to shift tourist Paris a fraction to the east and convert Samaritaine into a powerhouse for its own, and other, luxury brands.

Samaritaine had been losing its customers—and loads of money—for years. Its traditional clientele has deserted to specialist shops or suburban shopping malls. (How, in any case, do you get a lawnmower, or a tank of piranha fish, home on the Metro?) In truth, most of Samaritaine's old customers—modest income, DIY families and maiden aunts—have also migrated to the suburbs.

Central Paris has become a land for the relatively rich, for young professionals and for tourists.

Samaritaine will survive in name but it has already died in spirit—another step in the gradual conversion of the centre of the French capital into an upmarket theme park.

■ In Search of Seurat – and Air
MAY 2003

To fill an idle, anxious hour the other day, I wandered over to the Île de la Grande Jatte: a place that I had long wanted to visit, even though I knew that it would be a sickening disappointment.

La Grande Jatte is a narrow island in one of the lazy meanders of the Seine, just to the west of Paris proper. In the 19th century it was a public park, a stretch of water-meadows and shady trees, which was a favourite place for Parisians to stroll and watch the boats and the river go by.

Several celebrated painters set up their easels on the island: Claude Monet, Alfred Sisley and most famously of all, Georges Seurat, whose enormous painting, "Sunday Afternoon on the Island of La Grande Jatte", became a poster on a hundred million student walls (including mine) in the 1960s and 1970s. The canvas, painted in 1884–6, is the high point (so to speak) of the *pointilliste* school invented by Seurat. Under a blinding white summer sun, a bizarre collection of fin-de-siècle Parisians—including a man in a top hat, a thuggish boatman with a pipe and an overdressed woman with a blue monkey on a leash—walk or loll on the river bank.

I once visited the painting itself, in the Art Institute of Chicago, but I had never been to the island. My advice is: please don't bother. The Île de la Grande Jatte was engulfed by the Paris suburbs some time in the early 20th century: it is now almost entirely occupied by football fields, tennis courts, modern offices, apartment blocks and the odd hotel and restaurant. As a pleasant joke against any art lover who passes that way, one of the streets has been named Boulevard Georges Seurat.

Paris has a reasonable claim to be the most beautiful city in the world but it is a city which fills the head, the belly and the eyes and neglects the lungs.

Until the late 19th century, Parisians could escape into the countryside which came right up to the city's edge. When Baron Haussmann and others presided over the rebuilding of much of Paris from the 1860s, they provided scores of small parks and gardens—there are 400 in all—but saw no reason to match Hyde or Regent's Park in London.

When the surrounding countryside was gradually covered in concrete and roads in the 20th century, few open spaces were preserved. Even the two great Bois on the edge of Paris—Boulogne and Vincennes—are crisscrossed with roads and provide only small islands of peace and greenery.

Just before he was elected in 2001, the mayor of Paris, Bertrand Delanoë, told me in an interview that he envied London only one thing: its great, green open spaces. He said that, if elected, he would try to carve out new recreational areas from disused, or underused, railway land.

M. Delanoë has already done much to make the 400 parks and gardens of Paris more accessible and useful. Close to my children's school is a small park which was once divided into three sections: two of which were banned to children. Now the fences have been taken down. Children can roam, and fight, at will.

But what of M. Delanoë's grander schemes? His plan to create a modest, twelve-acre park from railway sidings north of the Gare de l'Est in the 18th *arrondissement* should be finished by 2006. There was an even more ambitious project to turn 100 acres of disused tracks at the Porte de Clichy, north of the Gare St Lazare into the biggest single green space in Paris. This idea, it was quietly revealed last week, has been shunted into a siding. Most of the space is to be set aside for the Olympic Village which will be needed if Paris succeeds in its bid for the 2012 Olympics.

In the meantime, the Paris town hall has declared that this is "tree celebration week". First find your tree.

■ A Pigeon Fancier
JUNE 2003

For six years we have fought a hopeless battle against the pigeons that occupy the ledges outside our flat, making love, noise and a disgusting mess. We have netted off the window ledges, poked the birds with sticks and called them names. They have simply shifted from the main windowsills to a ledge beyond our reach.

The other day, the concierge of our apartment block stopped my wife and demanded to know why she was "still keeping pigeons". Margaret, not the kind of person you would normally associate with pigeon fancying, denied the charge. The concierge would not be put off. "I would like to inform you, madame," she said, "that it is strictly illegal to keep pigeons in Paris."

That, at least, solves a Christmas present problem. Where in Paris can I buy my wife a flat cap and a large wicker basket?

■ An Urban Rabbit Tail
NOVEMBER 2003

In the midst of the snarling eight lanes of traffic circling Porte Maillot, in western Paris, there is a public garden which looks remarkably like Teletubby Land. It has formal paths, lawns and shrubberies and even rabbit-holes.

Ten minutes walk from the Arc de Triomphe, at the heart of the busiest traffic junction in one of the most densely populated cities in Europe, there is a flourishing warren of wild rabbits.

As you sit in the jumbled, bad tempered lanes of cars waiting to drive up to the Champs Elysées or join the Paris ring road, you can see the rabbits skipping around a few feet from your wheels. The animals—black, brown, white or rabbit-coloured—are the descendants of pets dumped by Parisians over several decades.

At dawn one day last week, we—the photographer Alastair Miller, my nine-year-old daughter Clare and I—set out on a Parisian rabbit hunt.

We wanted a picture of a wild but sophisticated urban rabbit, with the Arc de Triomphe in the background. We saw plenty of rabbits, of different colours and sizes, but none that would pose in front of the Arc. Where is David Attenborough when you need him?

Shortly after we arrived in the traffic-girded gardens, we re-enacted one of the most celebrated scenes from the books of Beatrix Potter. Clare, armed with a carrot, was attempting to coax a large, black rabbit—a.k.a Pierre Lapin—out of the bushes. The park-keeper—a.k.a. Monsieur MacGregor—turned up on his miniature, red tractor pulling a miniature, red trailer. He shouted: "Don't feed those things. They're a menace. They've been dumped here by the cretins who live all around... They eat up all my flowers. We're soon going to kill them all..."

The word that the park-keeper used for "kill" was a very urban, French, non-Beatrix Potter word—"flinguer". The English slang equivalent would be to "to waste" or "take out".

Is this the end for the rabbits of Porte Maillot? Is *Watership Down* to be re-enacted in the midst of the City of Light?

Apparently not. Xavier Japiot, the man who runs the wild animals department of Paris Nature, the city's environmental agency, assured me that there is no plan to "waste" the Porte Maillot rabbits. In any case, they are just a sub-tribe of a much larger population of genetically varied rabbits—thousands of them—which inhabit the Bois de Boulogne and the grassy embankments of the ring road or Boulevard Périphérique.

Almost all of them are descended from pet rabbits evicted from apartments after they peed on the Persian rug once too often.

M. Japiot believes that members of the Porte Maillot colony come and go, by mysterious urban rabbit trails, from the Bois de Boulogne. "We trap some of them from time to time to keep the numbers down but there is no intention of exterminating them," he said.

How could such timid creatures adapt so happily to such a frenetic place—the equivalent of a rabbit warren at Marble Arch or Hyde Park Corner? "They have no predators and they feel as safe there as if they were on a real island," M. Japiot said. "Hearing and alarm calls are vital to rabbits in the wild. At Porte Maillot, the rabbits can hear little above the sound of the cars. They have adapted by making more use of their other alarm systems, such as drumming their feet."

Rabbits are the least of his worries, he said. Parts of the Bois de Vincennes are overrun by the progeny of ex-pet gerbils. Lakes and pools in the Bois de Vincennes, the Bois de Boulogne, the Buttes Chaumont and the Parc Monceau have colonies of abandoned tortoises and turtles. Some of them can be fierce and have been known to eat young ducks.

Ten different species of parrot have been identified flying around Paris in recent years. Animals let loose recently in the Bois de Vincennes include a prairie dog and an arctic fox. Several years ago a pair of piranha fish were found in the charming Canal St Martin, which wanders through eastern Paris into the Seine.

"In Paris, people will buy anything and dump anything," M. Japiot said. There is, apparently, no danger of piranhas breeding in the wild in France but don't trail your hand in the water the next time you take a Bâteau Mouche.

■ Manhattan-sur-Seine
NOVEMBER 2003

For a city whose trademark is a tall building, one of the most striking facts about Paris is its lack of tall buildings. Eiffel Tower apart, there are few skyscrapers in the French capital. They are confined to the northern edges of the city, the monstrous Tour at Montparnasse and a couple of brutal, high-rise plantations at the extremities of the Left Bank.

For the most part, the architectural style of Paris remains as planned 140 years ago by the Emperor Napoleon III and Baron Eugène Haussmann, the prefect of the *département* of the Seine.

In the 1860s, to the disgust of the novelist Victor Hugo and others, Baron Haussmann flattened much of what remained of medieval Paris. He carved out sweeping avenues and boulevards and imposed the pattern of eight-storey, stone apartment buildings which gives the city the pleasing unity of appearance which it has to this day.

Is all that about to change? To the alarm of some Parisians, the Socialist mayor, Bertrand Delanoë, is starting to show Haussmann-like urges. The city, already by far the biggest landowner in Paris, has been buying up immense amounts of property, ranging from apartment blocks to derelict railway sidings.

M. Delanoë, a popular and effective mayor, is also looking upwards. He has started to think aloud about lifting the ban, imposed in 1977, on the construction of tall buildings within the city boundaries.

The present rules ban new buildings taller than 37 metres (twelve floors) in the outer districts of the city and anything larger than 25 metres (eight floors) in the centre. M. Delanoë suggests a change to allow new outcrops of architecturally interesting buildings in the non-touristic, eastern part of the city. There would be no question of skyscrapers in the centre of town. The Île de la Cité would not become Manhattan Island.

The mayor argues that Paris, if it is to remain commercially and spiritually dynamic, cannot stay stuck in the 1860s. Under the present rules it would have been impossible for Paris to build the wonderful Guggenheim museum in Bilbao. "All the world's great architects are building in all the world's great cities—except Paris," he said.

Part of the mayor's concern is economic. Paris has a glut of elegant, old office space but a shortage of the large, open-plan, heavily wired offices which companies demand. As a result, French and foreign businesses are moving their headquarters to new tower blocks just outside the city boundary.

The city faces the prospect of becoming, commercially, "a suburb of the suburbs": a tourist's delight, the bastion of government, a residential area for the rich, but stripped of the vitality—and taxes—which should go with its status as economic capital of France.

M. Delanoë's ideas have, understandably, provoked a wail of protest, from residents' pressure groups, from the centre-right opposition on the city council and even from his Green allies. He was forced to concede last week that the height restrictions will remain untouched in a new city plan, to be formulated next year. In return, the mayor won approval for a consultation exercise: a series of public meetings to examine the pros and cons of tower blocks, maybe even a referendum.

The mayor's ambitions to re-shape the city are horizontal as well as vertical. He plans to create new parks and an Olympic Village for 2012 by reclaiming derelict railway land north of the Gares St Lazare, Nord and Est.

Paris, proper, covers a relatively small area, about six miles by six, not much bigger than London within the Circle Line. M. Delanoë is probably right. To preserve its character, accommodate new open spaces *and* create large quantities of modern offices, Paris, or parts of Paris, must eventually expand upwards.

Many of the places which define Paris—the Eiffel Tower, the avenues radiating from the Etoile, the Grands Boulevards—were opposed and hated in their day. A city is a living thing, which must grow and change, or become a kind of urban museum or theme park. Would a few, elegant high-rises destroy the most beautiful capital city in the world?

■ Café Society
JANUARY 2004

The scene is a modern, youthful French café near Les Halles in the centre of Paris.

You can tell that the café is youthful and modern. Old-fashioned French cafés are dazzlingly illuminated, like film sets; the barman often looks as if his father was a bulldog. This café is gloomy. There is no pinball machine. The barman looks like a film director. No-one is drinking very much.

A youthful, modern and intelligent-looking—terrifyingly intelligent—crowd assembles. They are not here by accident. They have to come to listen and to question. One Wednesday each month the café turns into a "political café." Anyone can wander in off the street. There is no entrance fee. A speaker is invited to talk on some pressing question of the moment.

As I survey the scale, and evident seriousness, of the crowd, I have a rising sense of panic. Tonight's speaker is—gulp—me. I have to speak in my far-from-fluent French for twenty minutes, *sans hésitation ni déviation*, remembering to roll my r's and distinguish my masculine nouns from my feminine ones.

The subject is Britain, France and Europe. Why are the British such poor Europeans? Why do the British and French not like each other? Why did *The Sun* represent Jacques Chirac as a worm on its front page?

I had accepted the invitation in a thoughtless moment, expecting to speak in a back room to a handful of earnest students. I was not expecting to have to speak into a microphone, in the café itself, to a room full of fiercely pro-European, young French civil servants, academics and executives.

The event was, as I told them, proof of the unbridgeable, cultural chasm between Britain and France. Was it possible to imagine sixty young Londoners gathering in a pub—or even a wine-bar—to hear a French journalist talk about the future of Europe? No, it was not. We have pub quizzes; the French have political cafés.

Recent subjects at other political cafés in Paris include "What is *laïcité*?" and "European economic policy in the face of the crisis of social-liberalism". The group which invited me sticks to European themes. Most of the participants were French but there were also Germans, Italians and a Greek.

The political café is a spin-off from the philosophical café or "café-philo", a French invention of the early 1990s, which has since become popular all over the world. A crowd gathers over a few drinks—or in France probably one drink—and discusses a subject like "How far is too far?"

A couple of years ago, I spent an evening in a café near the Bastille at a variant of the café-philo called a "psychological café". Participants were encouraged to describe problems in their personal life and invite comments from an intellectual agony-aunt.

France also has "cafés scientifiques" (gatherings where the scientifically minded can discuss advances in human knowledge) and "cafés artistiques" (ditto for developments in literature and the arts).

Does this all amount to a rekindling of the café society for which Paris was famous from the mid-19th century and from the 1930s to the 1950s?

Yes, but in a strangely formal way. Those old café societies were informal gatherings of like minded intellectuals, or just friends, for whom the café became a second home. No-one convened a meeting at Les Deux Magots in the early 1950s and announced that Jean-Paul Sartre would talk for twenty minutes on existentialism and opthological developments in the treatment of the squint. No-one convened a café-littéraire in the mid-19th century to allow the poet Gérard de Nerval to explain why he promenaded around Paris with a dead lobster on the end of a ribbon.

The phenomenon of the café politique and café philosophique shows how admirably interested young French people are in politics and abstract thought. It also shows how unclubbable, or unpubbable, some (not all) young French people can be. They need a formal occasion to bring them together.

I enjoyed the evening all the same. Despite many *déviations* and *hésitations*, I stumbled through. For a small fee, I am available to talk about French politics in the saloon bar of the Coach and Horses any time that you like.

■ Death of the Garret Room
FEBRUARY 2004

For several weeks, there has been an insistent banging and crashing from two storeys above our heads in our apartment in Paris.

On the seventh floor of our building, workmen are knocking down partition walls in order to combine two "chambres de bonne" (maid's rooms) into one small flat. Similar sounds can be heard across the city, as rents spiral and new regulations make it harder—though not impossible—for landlords to let tiny rooms with communal toilets, no hot water and, sometimes, no windows.

The chambres de bonnes are a Parisian institution. Almost all the old apartment buildings in Paris, constructed in the 18th, 19th or early 20th centuries, have a jumble of tiny, scruffy rooms on their seventh and eight floors, which used to house the domestic staff of the bourgeois families living in the posher flats below.

As servants disappeared (au pairs apart), the rooms were let to immigrants, students, artists, alleged artists, poor people, old people, families down on their luck, and romantic foreigners who liked the idea of living in a Paris garret. Many notable members of the political and cultural establishment of our age—from George Orwell to Madonna—have served their time in the ill-lit, freezing-in-winter, stifling-in-summer, attic cells of the grander streets of Paris.

The existence of different social strata within one building has been a characteristic of Parisian life for centuries. Poorer families would live in the roofs of fashionable town houses in the 17th, 18th and early 19th centuries. The appealing phenomenon of all-human-life at one address inspired the plots of novels from Victor Hugo, to Émile Zola, to Georges Perec and his *Life: a User's Manual*.

There are—or were—twenty chambres de bonnes in our own building. They resemble a living soap opera, with a constantly changing cast except for one or two principals who never leave. There is a thirty-something, jolly Iranian engineering student, who fled Iran ten years ago and could not continue his studies in France. He works on building sites and has just, to his great pride, purchased an enormous white van which is his entrée to the Parisian white van economy. There is a fifty-something, very tall, stately and sad Tunisian man, called Mohammed, who is separated from his wife and lives in one small room, sometimes with his two children. There is Concita, a seventy-something Catalan, retired concierge, who spends her summers in Paris and her winters near Barcelona. There used to be a very ancient and very smelly Chinese man with a wispy beard, who smoked large cigars. He was ejected a few years ago, to the relief of other residents. It emerged that he had not paid his rent for twenty years.

The parallel world of the chambres de bonnes has preserved an element of liveliness, and commercial variety, in all but the richest *quartiers* of the French capital. They have been disappearing for decades but, in the last couple of years, their demise has accelerated.

A boom in Paris rents means that small flats, created from two or three chambres de bonnes, are a profitable investment. New rules on minimum standards for rented accommodation, introduced last year, make it illegal to let any room less than nine metres square or 2m 20 high.

Finally, the heat-wave which killed almost 20,000 old people in France in the summer of 2003, took an especially high toll of elderly residents of airless attic rooms. Their tiny homes are now being sold off to property developers.

Frankly, many chambres de bonne were—and are—rooftop slums, unfit for habitation. Their passing may be inevitable but will erode what remains of the grittiness and quirkiness of the French capital.

Next month, Bertrand Delanoë will present a draft urban plan to guide the development of the city in the 21st century. It will address many issues already mentioned in this column—whether Paris should allow a few, distinguished, tall buildings; how to stop the haemorrhaging of small shops; how to prevent jobs and people migrating into the suburbs.

Above all, M. Delanoë says that he wants to preserve "social variety"—to prevent large parts of the city from turning into ghettoes for the wealthy.

The sound of banging and crashing in attics all over Paris suggests that is one battle which M. Delanoë has already lost.

■ A Trou Story
APRIL 2004

At the heart of the world's most beautiful city, there is a charmless, underground shopping mall and a jumble of tatty, airless gardens, haunted by drug dealers. The site would be an embarrassment to a provincial town in Bulgaria. For a city like Paris, the Quartier des Halles is a crime against urbanity; the most bungled piece of redevelopment in any capital city in Europe.

Here, in a space the size of twelve football pitches, once stood the elaborate, wrought-iron pavilions of the city's wholesale food-market. Les Halles were the city's belly but also its gritty, never-resting heart, littered with all-night restaurants and bars.

The market was moved to the southern suburbs in 1969 and the pavilions destroyed. There followed seventeen years of dithering, which turned a prime site in the heart of Paris into a wasteland and then a gaping chasm—"le trou des Halles".

President Georges Pompidou, a determined modernist, wanted to build a clutch of skyscrapers as a new business centre for the city. Nothing much happened. When Pompidou died in 1974, the new president, Valéry Giscard d'Estaing, scrapped the plan and promised—Ozymandias-like—"a monumental, architectural gesture" which would be a permanent reminder of his presidency. Nothing much happened.

Three years later, an ambitious, youngish, politician became mayor of Paris and scrapped Giscard's non-plan, largely because he detested Giscard. The new mayor, M. Jacques Chirac, declared: "From now on the architect-in-chief is me." Nothing much happened.

Finally, in 1986, the hole was plugged with an uninspiring series of gardens dotted with ventilation shafts for the shopping centre and labyrinthine Metro junction below. Eighteen years later, Les Halles is shunned by Parisians and tourists and colonised by young men in hooded anoraks. The Centre Georges Pompidou, 200 metres away, remains a great success; Les Halles is a waste of space.

The saga is not finished, however. The great and good Mayor of Paris Bertrand Delanoë has decided to rip everything up—including part of the shopping centre and the Châtelet-Les Halles Metro and RER junction, the busiest underground station in Europe—and start again. "We must invent a heart which is worthy of the city," M. Delanoë said. "Les Halles must become the symbol of the dynamism of Paris... somewhere that is visited by tourists in its own right, like the Centre Georges Pompidou, the Louvre and the Eiffel Tower."

M. Delanoë has chosen four competing plans. Residents of the area are being asked their opinion. A committee of city councillors will make the final decision in June.

All the plans look wonderful. Architects' plans always do. My favourite is the project put forward by a team led by the French architect, Jean Nouvel, which includes a vast "hanging garden"—a piece of open countryside suspended over a rebuilt shopping centre, with startling views over the Parisian rooftops to Notre Dame and the Eiffel Tower.

The Dutch architect, Rem Koolhaas (great name for an architect), has suggested opening out the road tunnel which bisects the site and turning it into a kind of glass canyon of shops. Instead of being buried under the park above, the shopping centre, underground station and swimming pool would be suffused with light admitted through a forest of colourful, four-sided, glass towers poking above the surface.

Whichever plan is chosen, residents of the area fear a rerun of a horror movie from the 1970s: the "Trou des Halles II", or the return of the chasm. Not this time, insists M. Delanoë. Everything will be done little by little. The shopping centre and railway station will stay open at all times. The main outlines must be finished by 2007 and the whole project completed by 2012.

That all sounds impossibly ambitious but M. Delanoë is a bizarre kind of politician. He tends to make things happen.

■ A Brush with the Police
APRIL 2004

After seven years in Paris, my wife says she is immune to the casual pick-up lines of French men, which she finds admirable in their way.

Parisian men, or some Parisian men, think nothing of approaching a woman on the street and inviting her to "come and have a coffee". No commitment is implied. It is understood that the woman can go for the coffee and refuse a follow-up invitation without risking insult or aggression.

Margaret was walking to her piano lesson the other day when she ran into a flustered, ill-dressed, fifty-something man with a pile of documents under his arm. When she gazed at the building behind him, he announced: "This is a police station." She asked if he had been paying his fines. He glanced at the documents under his arm and said, pompously: "No, I am a senior police officer. Do you want to come for a coffee?"

"No," said Margaret. "Tant pis (too bad)," said the policeman, gave her a naughty wink, climbed into his scruffy, illegally parked car and drove away.

France has twenty per cent more police officers per head of population than Britain. Now you know what they all do with their time.

■ Neighbour Wars
MAY 2004

A CD on sale in Paris comes with a free pair of ear plugs. The disc has yet to reach the charts but that can only be a matter of time. It is called "Vengeance: 17 minutes of hell for your neighbours".

The first track is the sound of a pneumatic drill. The second is the cry of a hungry baby. There are eighteen other tracks, including a dustbin truck, a marital row and a colony of amorous pigeons. The creators recommend that customers with noisy neighbours should set the CD on repeat at full volume and put in their earplugs.

The Parisian "neighbour wars"—of which I have written before—are hotting up. There has been a 200 per cent increase in legal battles between neighbours in the last two years, almost all concerned with noise.

I have mentioned my friend Olivier's problems with his very expensive classical guitar, whose gentle tones are not appreciated by the old lady upstairs. I described the plight of friends of friends whose cockerel—probably the only cockerel in Paris—had to be banished to the country after being found guilty of "tapage nocturne" (literally banging in the night).

Our own neighbourly quarrels continue, almost always generated by noise or water. Paris is a city of wonderful, old apartment buildings, characterised by thin floors and rotting plumbing. Our disagreeable "voisins d'en bas" (neighbours below) recently sent the concierge to tell us that we making an "infernal" racket.

It is true that my daughter Grace has taken up the piano, bringing the number of pianists in the household to four (everyone but me). On the other hand, we have to put up with the voisin d'en bas clattering his pots and grunting as he does the washing up, with the window open, below our bedroom, at ten minutes to midnight, every night. He sounds much worse than Grace playing "Le Petit Poney".

We invited twenty six-year-olds and a clown to the flat recently. When they emerged, en masse, on the landing in search of fairies or moonbeams, the disagreeable man downstairs screamed at them. How can anyone scream at a clown? Apparently, we should have informed him that we were having a party, even a party for six-year-olds on a Saturday afternoon.

Into this poisonous world, there stepped five years ago a young man called Atanaise Périfan. M. Périfan sounds like a character in a 19th-century French romantic novel, but he is a thirty-nine-year-old software entrepreneur and assistant mayor of our *arrondissement* of Paris, the 17th.

A decade ago, he organised a party for all the residents of his building. His wife said that no-one would come. She was wrong. Like warring armies declaring a truce, the neighbours came out from behind their armoured doors and spy-holes and talked to each other for the first time. "The eighty-five-year-old woman opposite, whom we had never spoken to before, is now a third grandmother for our children," M. Périfan said.

Five years ago, he started an association called "Immeubles en fête" (apartment block party-time) to spread the word. Last year, 150,000 Parisians joined in. So did 2,000,000 people in the rest of France and 500,000 in other European countries. The 2004 event takes place next Tuesday (25 May). Cities in all the 25 countries of the extended EU—including London in a biggish way for the first time—have signed up.

"The heat-wave in France last year, in which so many old people died lonely deaths in their apartments, showed how important this project is. It also showed how far we still have to go," M. Périfan said. "There is a tendency in the modern world for people to close in on themselves and also to become more aggressive. Why are there so many disputes about noise in Paris these days? Walls in Parisian apartments are thin but that was true twenty years ago or 100 years ago. Now, it seems, people find it harder to put up with one another."

M. Périfan is clearly a visionary genius but he has presented me with a dilemma. Should I organise a neighbours' party in our building; or buy a dishwasher for my downstairs neighbour; or take up the trombone?

■ Ruder than the French
MAY 2004

I thought that French waiters were rude until I went to Prague. I saw a bullet-headed Czech waiter terrorise a French family, who asked if they could have half a meal for a small child without paying the full price. "Is not possible," the waiter repeated over and over. "Is not possible. You better go now."

Whether this is Czech behaviour or post-Soviet behaviour I'm not sure but the phrase—"Is not possible"—seems to be the motto of all Czech restaurants, hotels and taxi drivers. Slovaks are bouncier than Czechs but their food is equally dreary.

There is a sign outside a restaurant in the splendid old city of Prague which reads, in English: "Traditional Czech meals. Six kinds of goulash."

■ A Star is Reborn
JULY 2004

A giant mosaic, with 650,000 pieces, is being broken up, restored and then reassembled in the heart of Paris this month. Once the second half of the work is completed next summer, the best known square in the French capital—and the scariest road junction in the world—will have recovered its long-forgotten, handsome, geometric pattern of green and pink.

To the fury of motorists, already deprived of their race track along the Seine by the annual intrusion of the "Paris beach", half the cobbles of the Place Charles de Gaulle, better known as L'Etoile, are being dug up and realigned for the first time in 57 years. While the re-cobbling shuts the inner half of the square until the end of August, the Etoile (star) is reduced—oh, indignity—to a mere roundabout, a circular four lane traffic jam.

The Etoile is normally an immense dodgem track, with ten or eleven lanes of cars spinning into and out of the twelve avenues which converge on the Arc de Triomphe. Drivers appear to observe no particular rule but, in truth, most of them obey, grudgingly, the regulation that traffic has priority from the right.

Since the Etoile lies at the centre of a triangle whose points are my home, my office and my daughters' school, I sometimes find myself plunging into the great automobile Jacuzzi three or even four times a day. Even after eight years and maybe 5,000 solo missions through the square, I still feel my hands gripping the wheel more tightly when I approach the Arc.

Hesitation is fatal. You have to barge straight into the traffic, however fast or thick, and—according to my game-plan—force your way to the centre as quickly as possible. When your exit approaches, you should start to spin out again, making as little allowance as possible for those trying to come on.

Bénédicte, my neighbour, has a different approach, both brutal and timid. She roars onto the square at 120 kph and stays in the outer lane all the way around. (She is not the only one.)

Oddly, in eight years, I have only once or twice seen a minor bump on the mother of all roundabouts and never a serious accident.

The great square is being re-cobbled to remove the dips and ridges which have accumulated since 1947. The stones are being cleaned on site and then re-laid. Little by little, the lost secret of the Etoile, overlain by decades of tyre-born grime, is being revealed.

The square is not supposed to be a uniform expanse of grey cobbles. It is supposed to be a giant 24-pointed star, with alternate pink points made from "porphyry" or "pink granite" indicating the twelve avenues, and green points made from naturally green-tinged granite, indicating the pavements in between. Grey cobbles fill in the gaps.

In the service of investigative journalism, I climbed all 240 steps to the top of the Arc to peer down on the work in progress. A star is being re-born; or rather an enormous, pink and green flower. When the work is completed next August, the view from the top of the Arc will be spectacular, for a few months at least.

The decision to re-cobble the Etoile, rather than cover it with tarmac, is part of an undeclared, urban counter-revolution: the re-conquest of Parisian streets by the "pavé" or cobblestone. It is often said that the student revolution of 1968 destroyed the Parisian cobbled street. The students pulled up whole boulevards of cobbles in the Latin Quarter on the Left Bank of the city and piled them into barricades or lobbed them at the riot police.

During the 1970s eighty per cent of the 10,000 miles of streets in Paris were paved with tarmac. The policy was partly anti-riot and partly pro-car. From the 1990s, the square, flat-topped, granite two-kilo (four-pound) pavés have started to creep back, much improving the looks of the city. Beauty requires pain, however. The furious honking of horns in the depleted Etoile this month is nothing compared to the chaos which can be expected next August. The outer ring of the Etoile will be re-laid, closing, one-by-one, the entrances to all the radial avenues, including the Champs Elysées.

■ An Unscheduled Stop
AUGUST 2004

The public address system on Paris Metro trains generates gruff, unhelpful remarks from some drivers and dry comments from others. I was in a train which stopped between stations the other day, an experience almost unknown in Paris. As we contemplated the tedious graffiti or tags on the tunnel sides (how do the taggers get to these places?), the driver said: "Ladies and gentlemen, we have stopped to admire the scenery."

■ A Hot Flush

OCTOBER 2004

Here is a story of hot flushes, neighbourly love and the dark, rotten secrets hidden behind the elegant facades of Parisian buildings.

The City of Light is also a City of Leaks: a city in which your neighbour's bathwater can suddenly and inconveniently appear in your bedroom or your own washing-up water can decide that its best escape route is through your neighbour's kitchen.

The plumbing in those wonderful six- or seven-storey 18th-, 19th- and early 20th-century, Parisian apartment buildings—even in the wealthiest *quartiers*—is almost universally decaying. And bizarre.

In eight years in Paris, our apartment has been soaked from above five times; we have leaked into the apartment below on at least four occasions. My office, next to the BBC office, in a modernish block not far from the Champs Elysées is regularly invaded by an unpleasantly brownish liquid from the flats above. Our upstairs neighbour has lived in our apartment building for forty years. He says that he has been flooded, or responsible for a flood, at least once a year.

There are two explanations for the leakiness of Paris. First, most apartment buildings are co-owned by a dozen or more different proprietors, who may or may not be also the residents. The structural maintenance of the building is supposed to be the responsibility of a "syndicat", or union, of the proprietors. Whenever large, costly maintenance work is needed, the syndicat decides to do the minimum patch-up job, rather than share the bill for proper repairs.

Our building, which is 94 years old and therefore relatively new by Paris standards, still has its original system of cold and hot water pipes and central heating. A century's problems have been solved by temporary repairs or complex pipe bypasses, which resemble the intramural horrors in Terry Gilliam's wonderful movie, *Brazil*.

The second explanation for the frequency of leaks is, in my

experience, the unreliability of Parisian plumbers, who are as rude, unhelpful and hard to find as Parisian taxi drivers.

Most Parisians, or long-standing residents of the city, have become philosophical about this state of affairs. By law, everyone has insurance against leaks. If you leak, or you are leaked into, you and your neighbour exchange amicable insurance declaration forms, rather like those which exist for small bumps between cars. The insurance companies then, in theory, decide who pays for the damage.

Often, however, this leads to labyrinthine, three-way arguments between your insurer, the leaker's insurer and your landlord's insurer about who is responsible for which bits of the repair work. We were leaked into by M. En Haut six months ago. Our insurance company is willing to pay to redecorate one bedroom. The loss adjustor says that our landlady's insurance, or possibly M. En Haut's insurance, must pay for the damage to the bathroom and another bedroom. We remain, just about, philosophical and on good terms with M. En Haut.

Others are not so reasonable. Our downstairs neighbour, M. En Bas, has never forgiven us for a leak three years ago, which led to an exchange of bilingual insults with my wife. We are more leaked against than leaking but M. En Bas seems to believe that we bore holes in his ceiling and stand over them with a watering can.

After another, pifflingly small, leak the other Saturday, he shouted at my ten-year-old daughter and told my wife that she was a "salope" (slut). (I was away.) Margaret gave as good as she got, alternating heroically between French and English insults (what the French call "noms d'oiseaux", birds' names).

She switched off all the water in the flat until the plumber could come on the Monday and evacuated the family to Normandy. When we returned on the Sunday night, we were perplexed to find that our toilet cistern had filled up with near-boiling water. Neither plumber, nor insurance loss-adjustor, nor M. En Haut could explain this unprecedented event.

Is our toilet individually central heated? Have we discovered a natural hot water spring in our toilet? Should we turn our bathroom into a health spa? Or is the plumbing of our building even more peculiar than we thought?

■ Metro Rage
NOVEMBER 2004

In an attempt to persuade Parisians to enter and leave Metro trains in a civilised manner, the city's transport authority, the RATP, has placed stickers with spoof dance steps on some of its station platforms. The stickers encourage those waiting on the platform to "stand still" until their "partners" aboard the train have safely "danced" past them. Some chance.

The RATP would be better advised to teach politeness to its staff. Metro workers frequently go on strike to "defend public services" but they have a bizarre idea of service to the public.

The other day, I bought a *carnet* (bunch) of ten tickets at my local station. The man behind the glass plonked them down on the counter. The Force Nine gale which mysteriously haunts all Metro station entrances, even on the calmest days, snatched up the tickets and blew them for several metres in each direction.

I asked for new tickets. I was told to get down on my hands and knees and find the old ones. I danced with rage. The man behind the glass ignored me. Maybe this is another type of traditional dancing encouraged by the RATP.

■ Café Society 2
APRIL 2005

Each morning for eight years I have been eating breakfast and reading the newspapers in the same café in Paris. I am now part of the drab furniture: "Monsieur John".

My order—coffee, fresh orange juice and a croissant—is brought to me without my asking. I am consulted by the chef, Alain, and the waitress, Cathy, on the great, unanswerable questions which face France and the world. What does Charles see in Camilla? More to the point what does Camilla see in Charles? Why are

Paris-Saint Germain, the capital's only professional football team, permanently rubbish?

There is nothing special about my café. It has head-splitting lighting and nicotine-coloured formica tables. It has toilets, opening straight off the main room onto holes in the floor.

My other favourite café in Paris is a truly scruffy place. It is one small room, with a cupboard-kitchen in one corner and a cupboard-toilet in another. I go there to watch Champions League games on cable TV.

The owner is a dapper, forty-something, half-Tunisian man, also called Alain. I once watched in astonishment and admiration as he refused to serve a group of twenty respectable young people on the grounds that a) he had never seen them before b) he would never see them again and c) he didn't feel like it.

For many months, I could not work out the sociology of Alain's regular clients, a multi-racial repertory company of depressive, bizarre, foul-mouthed people in their late fifties. I thought at first that they might have something to do with the mental hospital next door.

The truth dawned. They were taxi drivers, taking a meal break, and topping up their alcohol level, before heading back to the mean night streets of the 17th *arrondissement*.

According to a recent sociological study, conducted over ten years for the ministry of transport and tourism, French café and bar society is changing rapidly. The traditional café—metal bar, metal chairs, wooden service—is giving way to something more modern and woman-friendly, with soft armchairs, gentler lighting, low coffee tables, healthy menus and proper toilets.

Out of curiosity, I sampled one of these new places the other day. It was part of a chain called "Bert's". The English sounding name is intended to bestow an aura of cosmopolitan smartness. Whoever chose the title did not know that, to Anglophone ears, any café called Bert's ought to serve egg, bacon, two sausage and chips and scalding tea in chipped white mugs.

Bert's, which calls itself a "contemporary café", has mock-leather couches and low coffee tables. You have to serve yourself from tall fridges containing ready-made sandwiches and salads in plastic cartons.

If this—a sandwich bar with sofas—is the future of the Parisian café, French civilisation is doomed. Can you imagine Jean-Paul Sartre helping himself to a club chicken tikka sandwich from the fridge before joining Simone de Beauvoir on a mock-leather couch?

The sociological study by Monique Eleb and Jean-Charles Depaule traces the rise of different forms of café—music bars, gay bars, sandwich bars, tea bars, Irish and British pubs—as the capital's population has become wealthier, more cosmopolitan and more bourgeois-bohemian.

To these, one must reluctantly add the eight "Starbucks" which are now operating in Paris, serving coffee in paper cups to Japanese students who try to make one frappuccino last all afternoon.

All is far from lost. Paris is down to its last 1,700 traditional bars and cafés (compared to 10,000 a century ago) but that still means 85 cafés for each *arrondissement*. The city's union of bar and café owners reports that the erosion of traditional establishments has halted in the last few years.

Admittedly, the Bert's-type café—imposing a self-consciously youthful style for a well-heeled target audience—is flourishing. So is my unreconstructed and unselfconscious morning café, where the population of customers shifts hourly from street-sweepers to businessmen to mums-waiting-for-school-to-finish to shy tourists, to wannabe supermodels, to off-duty cops in jeans and leather jackets.

As Mme Eleb and M. Depaule's study points out, the true character of a bar or a café is made by, and belongs to, its customers, not its owners.

―――

I had an appalling experience in the park the other day. I lost my seven-year-old daughter Grace for ten minutes. I searched everywhere, calling her name. No sign of her.

Eventually, a sweet Indian woman, a nanny to another child, found her in a corner of the sand-pit where I had overlooked her. "You had better come quickly," the woman had told Grace. "Your granddad is looking for you."

A truly appalling experience.

■ One of the Greatest
MAY 2006

One of the greatest French theatrical artists of his generation has been forced to retire through ill-health. John Guez, the street artist, was a bit like a non-mute version of Harpo Marx. He had the same mixture of malice, child-like wonder and good-heartedness. He even looked rather like one of the Marx brothers (like them, M. Guez is Jewish).

I interviewed M. Guez eight years ago. He told me that he regarded himself as "part of the Maquis. Part of the Resistance against modern life, against the star system, against the world of fast food and the TV zapper... Every day I start with nothing. Every day, I force myself to perform better, to achieve something out of nothing. Every day is a victory over myself. I make a little money but my reward is to see the joy of others, and especially the joy of the children."

The other day, M. Guez telephoned me out of the blue. I went to meet him at a café near to his old stamping ground at the Centre Pompidou. Several months ago, M. Guez, 63, suffered a cerebral haemorrhage while at home. He was in a coma for some time. He has been left partially sighted and unable to perform, or as he used to say, "go out and play with the people on the street".

"That's all finished now," he said. "I am too tired to start again. I had a wonderful life. I met many wonderful people but..."

There have been no retirement tributes to M. Guez in the French press. Street performers come and go. No-one tends to notice their passing.

Le Monde, however, published a very eloquent and sophisticated "theatre review" of M. Guez a couple of years ago. His act was described as a "great lesson in democracy, in philosophical humour, in logic applied to art. You come away cured of something: of tiredness with life; of being too serious; of melancholy neurosis."

We went for a little walk to the town hall square. He showed me a scrapbook of messages that he had received from admirers including Danièle Mitterrand, widow of the late president, and

Bertrand Delanoë. Other celebrities who have befriended him over the years, after discovering him through his street performances, include the movie director Stephen Spielberg and the late French novelist, Marguerite Duras.

As we walked along, M. Guez occasionally showed flashes of his old skipping energy. His wit and bonhomie are certainly unimpaired.

He is retired, he said, but he would like to give one farewell performance. He would like to invite handicapped children to the Town Hall square and perform one of his impromptu versions of, say, a Shakespeare play. He would like the BBC to come and film it.

"Otherwise," he said. "I have a plan to open a patisserie. It would be like no other patisserie. Cakes would be free to everyone under the age of ten."

■ Making Paris Bigger
SEPTEMBER 2006

My family and I have been living in the shadow of the Arc de Triomphe for ten years. We have rarely bothered to climb the 288 steps to the top.

We did so on a bright, crisp afternoon the other day. The view of Paris was spectacular, more intimate and more interesting than from the remote peak of the Eiffel Tower.

In truth, nine-tenths of what you can see from the Arc de Triomphe is not Paris. Most of that splendid vista is—dread phrase— "les banlieues", the suburbs which lie beyond the Boulevard Périphérique, the murderous road which encircles Planet Paris like a ten-lane ring of Saturn.

The city of Paris is tiny. Imagine London within the Circle Line, plus a little bit of the South Bank. Paris proper occupies 105 square kilometres, compared to the 1,570 square kilometres of Greater London and the 889 square kilometres of the re-united city of Berlin.

Immediately beyond the Périphérique there is a patchwork of

eighty independent suburban towns or "communes", some of them wealthy and dull; most of them a vibrant tangle of factories, offices, motorways, superstores, bungalows and multi-racial housing estates. It was here of course that last year's riots began.

To make political or social sense of this jumble, there is no "Greater Paris" like the "Greater London" presided over by Ken Livingstone. There is an Île-de-France "region", but this is larger still and too far-flung and muddled to impose much sense of identity on its 11,000,000 people.

The psychological, and physical, barriers between the capital and its suburbs explain many of the racial and social problems of greater Paris. The historic city, beautiful but frozen in time, also suffers. "Old" Paris has been severed from the pep and creativity of its "young" suburbs.

Politicians, local and national, have discussed the problem on and off for years. Nothing has been done. Now, in a haphazard way, events and political decisions may be conspiring to create a de facto "Big Paris" over the next decade.

Plans are afoot for a series of enormous office blocks just outside the city, including one skyscraper at La Défense which will be almost as high as the Eiffel Tower or the Empire State Building. By 2012, more and more Parisians will be commuting to work in the banlieues, rather than the other way around.

A series of luxury hotels, with swimming pools and gardens, is mushrooming in the inner suburbs—and not just in the wealthier ones. Plans are also advancing for a new, circular suburban railway system, which will finally link the different banlieues. A new suburban motorway ring, the A-86, is nearing completion. At present, it is difficult to travel from suburb to suburb and often difficult—despite France's claim to have excellent public transport—to travel from the banlieues into Paris.

There have been two meetings recently of something new called the "Conférence métropolitaine de l'agglomération parisienne"— an attempt by politicians and planners to put a logical framework on this rather unFrench mishmash.

Nothing has been achieved, so far.

Roland Castro, a celebrated French architect and urban planner, former adviser to the late President François Mitterrand, believes that it is time to put aside forty years (at least) of selfish political quarrels and self-defeating divisions and create a "Grand Paris." This is one of the issues on which he plans to launch a polemical, independent campaign for the presidency next year.

The boundaries of Paris expanded steadily from Roman times. They have been frozen since 1860. In 1964, the old *département* of the Seine, a kind of Greater Paris which included the city and its near suburbs, was exploded into four separate départements, with Paris as a city-county to itself.

M. Castro argues that a new "Grand Paris" should be created within the pre-1964 boundaries of the Seine département, increasing the city's size tenfold and its population from 2,000,000 to 6,000,000. "Of course, there will be the usual opposition of the vested interests of politicians and the administrative techno-structure," he told me. "But this is an idea whose time has come."

He is right. Since France is France, however, there is no guarantee that anything will happen soon.

■ How Paris Really Works
JUNE 2007

Almost every apartment building in Paris used to have a permanently bad-tempered woman guarding the front door. They were once as much a part of the townscape as yellow cigarettes, *urinoirs* and elegant green buses.

In the 1980s and 1990s, thousands of concierges—it is now more correct to say *gardienne d'immeuble*—were replaced by electronic security devices and cleaning contractors. The owners of apartments decided that this was cheaper than paying wages (however small). They could also make money by renting or selling off the concierge's tiny flat or "loge".

As concierges or gardiennes became rarer, they became prized. Flats in the buildings where they survive sell for significantly higher prices. The drive to exterminate them has slowed down.

About 20,000 gardiennes (and occasional male *gardiens*) remain, compared to 70,000 or more in the 1950s. The profession seems to be a Portuguese monopoly but there are occasional, bizarre interlopers. The gardienne of the building where we live is a Bosnian-Serb Jehovah's Witness.

We bought a small flat nearby last year as an investment and as a possible bolt-hole for our retirement. We recently attended the annual meeting at which the "co-propriétaires" decide how to manage the commonly owned parts of the building. The main subject on the agenda was the firing of the concierge. The second main subject was whether to replace the concierge with an intercom system and a letterbox.

I have covered European summits, G8 summits, Anglo-French summits and US-Soviet summits. None has seethed so much with poisonous undercurrents as a meeting of Parisian "co-propriétaires".

There were seven people present. An electronic calculating machine was needed to judge whether we had a quorum. Under French law, major spending decisions by co-owners—such as whether to buy a new letterbox—must be made by people who own at least two-thirds of the floor space. The calculator was required to work out how many square metres were at the meeting. (The European Union's proposed "double majority" formula for taking decisions in the Council of Ministers seems elementary by comparison.)

Many interesting points emerged. Under the terms of a new law passed in 2003, 97 per cent of all the lifts in France will be illegal from next year. France being France, a loophole in the law allows, under certain circumstances, lift modernisation to be delayed until 2013. We gratefully voted to take advantage of the loophole. Since this was a decision NOT to spend each other's money, no elaborate quorum was needed.

Then there was the future of the concierge. She should have retired a year ago. She was given an extra twelve months. Now, she is asking to stay on longer. She does not want to move out of her "loge" to go home to Portugal. Our fellow flat owners fear—probably rightly—that she intends to squat there indefinitely, knowing that it is almost impossible under French law to evict an elderly tenant.

Heated argument broke out about how to handle the situation. Almost all the other co-owners did not want a new gardienne. We agreed with them that the old concierge should be asked to retire. We did not agree with them that the post should be scrapped.

The position would not actually be "abolished", one of the other co-owners pointed out sweetly. It would simply be "left vacant". Another person suggested that we, as non-occupiers, had no right to interfere.

Any large strategic decision, such as abolishing the concierge, must, by law, be taken by all the co-owners unanimously. We not only have a right to object. We have a veto.

One excitable man started scribbling little secret messages to us. "You are right," he wrote. Or: "It adds value to your flat". He did not want to quarrel openly with his neighbours. He wanted us to fight his battle for him. Eventually, he admitted publicly that he, too, had "reservations" about abolishing the gardienne.

In the best tradition of European summits, it was finally conceded that no big decisions could be taken. We were 100 square metres short of a quorum. The meeting had lasted two and a half hours. Battle will be rejoined in February.

■ Paris on Strike
NOVEMBER 2007

The Dunkirk Spirit—"we are all in this together"—is not something that appeals to Parisians. The rail and Metro strike, now entering its fifth day, has been received with a kind of sullen anger.

There is no cheerful banter, no camaraderie. On the Metro platform, everyone looks glum and ignores everyone else. On the car-clogged streets, selfishness rules.

Scenes from a transport strike.

An entire street of blocked cars blows its horns in frustrated chorus. A tiny, elderly woman appears on her first floor balcony. She screams down: "Imbeciles, shut up." The cars continue to blow their horns.

A packed Metro train arrives at a packed station platform. The crowd tries to storm the train before passengers can get out. (This is fairly normal Parisian behaviour but it has been worse than usual this week.) There is shoving and shouting and screams of: "We are not cattle." A fight breaks out. The train, one of the few still in service, has to be cancelled. Everyone ends up on the platform.

The new Parisian self-service bicycle hire service, Vélib, has proved a useful strike-breaker. In the early morning mist, before the avenues and boulevards fill up with immobile, hooting cars, Paris has come to look like Amsterdam or Cambridge. Unfortunately, in some parts of the city, there are not enough bikes to go round. This is a Parisian problem for which Parisians have found a typically Parisian solution: the bike chain. The bicycles stand in computerised racks. When you have finished with a bike, you put it back in the nearest rack and your hire-fee is charged automatically to your credit card. It is very cheap to hire a *vélib* for an hour; very expensive to hog one for a day.

On several occasions during this strike-scarred week, my seventeen-year-old son, a practised *vélibeur*, lifted a bike from an official rack and found that it had been chained in place. The vélib had been unofficially "reserved", without costing the other vélibeur a centime. Charming.

Parisians—and the Paris police—have been at their worst on the roads. On Wednesday night, I tried to drive a friend to the Gare du Nord. He had come from London on the first Eurostar from St Pancras in two hours and fifteen minutes. It took us ninety minutes to drive three kilometres from my office to just beyond Pigalle. He walked the last kilometre.

The traffic was even worse on Thursday and Friday. None of this was necessary. There are no box-junction markings in Paris. Parisian drivers refuse to accept that moving forward en masse and blocking large intersections is not a sensible way of driving. The southbound traffic jams the eastbound traffic; so the eastbound traffic jams the southbound traffic.

At the Place Victor Hugo in the 16th *arrondissement,* six streets and avenues converge. The traffic became so impossibly tangled on Friday night that not a car was able to move for ninety minutes.

One motorist telephoned the police. Shouldn't they consider doing something? "What do you want us to do?" the policeman said at the other end. "The whole city is the same."

Yes, but it need not have been. A policeman at each of twenty or thirty strategic intersections would have kept the city moving. I didn't see a single policeman on traffic duty all week.

Someone suggested that this was a deliberate ploy by the government to build up anger against the strikers. More likely, it is just the usual fecklessness of the Paris police.

The strike goes on...

■ A Meeting with George W
JANUARY 2009

Celebrity at last. My daughters are to appear in a film with George Clooney.

Strictly-speaking, they are not appearing in the film, which is, in any case, a cartoon. Their sweet voices will be heard, amongst a dozen others, for a couple of seconds, in the same movie as the voice of the coffee-loving smoothie.

Clare, fourteen, and Grace, eleven, are in the children's choir at the American Cathedral in Paris. From all the children's choirs in all the cities in the world, their choir has been chosen to sing a four line poem in an animated film of "The Fantastic Mr Fox", based on the book by Roald Dahl.

Other parts will be taken by Mr Clooney and Ms Cate Blanchett. The film is directed by Wes Anderson and is produced, naturally enough, by 20th Century Fox.

There is no telling where this might lead: stardom, riches, tidying their own bedrooms. I have already drafted their Oscar-acceptance speeches, including lingering references to the importance of their mother and father in their young lives.

Nor is this the first time that membership of the American Cathedral choir has brought them close to a smoothie called George. President George W. Bush attended a Sunday service at the cathedral last year. (I was sitting a few rows behind him. He has a very strangely shaped head, seen from the rear.)

As he left, the choir was already standing at the back of the church. My daughter Clare, dared by a friend, said "Goodbye, Mr President". He turned around, walked up to her, took both her hands, looked into her eyes, and said "You have a beautiful voice, my dear."

I never really liked President Bush until then.

▣ Eating Out
MARCH 2009

I went to eat in my favourite Parisian restaurant the other day and it wasn't there. My occasional lunchtime treat for the last twelve years (usually I eat a sandwich at my desk) had vanished overnight, another victim of the recession and changing French eating habits. The "patron" had been complaining for months that his trade was falling; that young French businessmen were unpatriotic and shunned long and detailed lunches; that his sons did not want to carry on after him.

In an attempt to boost the flagging restaurant business, President Nicolas Sarkozy has finally persuaded the EU to allow a reduction of the VAT on eating out in France. The changes will not take effect until next year. A lot of red ink will flow through the books of the French restaurant industry before then.

You can still, however, come across the occasional inexpensive gem in Paris. A friend took me the other day to a celebrated theatrical and literary restaurant near to the Luxembourg gardens. The restaurant, Au Bon Saint Pourçain on the Rue Servandoni, has cracked, uneven linoleum floors; only twelve tables; piles of books and literary reviews on shelves behind the diners.

The food is excellent, old-style, hearty, south-western French nosh, at no more than €30 a head for two courses and wine. This is the favourite eating place of, among others, the actress Juliette Binoche.

How is trade? "Terrible", said the patron. "All the publishers have moved offices. There are just tourist shops here now. No-one seems to eat lunch any more."

He has, however, solved the problem of generational succession which appears to have defeated the patron of my favourite eatery. His two North African chefs refused to work for his daughter on the grounds that she was a woman. He has, therefore, introduced them to their alternative future boss: his very tall, half-Senegalese son, acquired when he was in the French army.

■ How I Became a Snob
JUNE 2009

For the first time in my life, possibly only briefly, I have reached the pinnacle of Parisian chic.

The newspaper *Le Figaro* has published a list of what it calls the "panoplie du snob": a catalogue of fifty things which are at the furthest cutting-edge of in-your-face trendiness amongst the wealthy Parisian chattering classes.

Please note that "snob" is one of those words which subtly change their meaning when they catch the Eurostar. Something is "très snob" in French if it is a symbol of cool trendiness. It is what we would call, in English, "very chic"—a word which is no longer trendy, or "snob", in French.

Items on the *Figaro* snob list include English bulldogs, which are now apparently the mutt of choice for wealthy Parisians parading in the Bois de Boulogne on Sunday afternoons. The bulldog—or *bouledogue*—has supplanted the Jack Russell and the Labrador. Those breeds have become "trop populaires", in other words downmarket or *déclassés*.

Among the bulldog qualities admired by the wealthy French, *Le Figaro* says, is their "flegme so British". The word *flegme* refers to the dog's phlegmatic nature, not its phlegm.

I also learned from *Le Figaro* that the self-respecting rich French trendy in sunglasses would never wear a pair of Ray Bans. The shades of choice are now the Italian-made Persol (€185 a pair for the "aviator" model), as worn by Daniel Craig in *Casino Royale*.

Lacoste casual shirts are utterly *démodés*. They may still be fairly chic in London but not in Paris. To be "snob", you have to wear "un polo Fred Perry", part of the range of casual-wear launched by the last British man to win Wimbledon.

Exquisitely fashionable good taste also requires Parisians to drink "green tea" and the right kind of bottled water. Perrier, Evian and Badoît are for *ploucs* (yokels) or *beaufs* (chavs). The snob water of choice is Chateldon, which used to be drunk by King Louis X1V.

The height of cool in a select Parisian brasserie is to order a "café blanc". This has nothing to do with white coffee or even *café au lait*. It is a Lebanese drink made from warm water and the flowers of the orange tree. You can't yet order them in the Starbucks outlets which are advancing like a green weed across Paris. It probably won't be long. By then "white coffee" will no longer be "snob".

Parisian cultural "snobisme" is highly perverse, it appears. The trick is to claim to adore artistes who were, until recently, regarded as hopelessly old-fashioned or just hopeless. The top kitsch cultural icons of "le snobisme nouveau" include Arielle Dombasle, the actress and singer of modest talent who is married to the philosopher, Bernard-Henri Lévy. Another is the deceased French comic movie actor, Louis de Funès, a kind of diminutive Gallic John Cleese.

Why does any of this transform me into a trendy? I do not wear Fred Perry shirts or Persol sunglasses or drink warm water and orange flowers or own a bouledogue. I cannot abide Arielle Dombasle (but do think that Louis de Funès is quite funny).

Le Figaro lists two other "snob" traits. It is now apparently utterly oafish behaviour to turn up at a Parisian dinner party with a bunch of shop-bought flowers or a box of *marrons glacés*. The annoyingly cutting edge thing to do is to present your host with a few roses, or even an entire herb plant, "from my little garden in Normandy".

At the same time, the humble parsnip, or *panais* in French, has become an exotic vegetable prized by Parisian food bores. Parsnips were long regarded in France as fit to be eaten only by horses and the English. They have now become, according to *Le Figaro*, "top of the hit parade of forgotten vegetables, with a very subtle taste reminiscent of the artichoke".

I happen to have "a little garden in Normandy" where I grow not only roses but parsnips. For the first time in my life, until the restless wheel of fashion moves on, I am not only chic, but "snob".

■ Picasso Comes Home
MARCH 2010

Jean Cocteau, poet, playwright, friend of Marcel Proust, Pablo Picasso and Edith Piaf, was also an occasional artist. His drawings, often erotic, frequently on ancient Greek themes, are sought after but not hugely valuable.

Shortly before Cocteau's death in 1963, he gave an interview in the old studios of the BBC. Before he left, he painted on the wall a large, lovely, non-erotic Picasso-like drawing of an ancient Greek head and lyre. He did so, he said, to thank the BBC for having been the voice of freedom in France from 1940–44.

When the BBC moved soon afterwards, they chopped out the section of plasterboard containing the Cocteau drawing, placed it in a frame and hung it in the new offices. For the last thirteen years, I have shared that office and shared the pleasure of seeing the Cocteau on the wall. It has come to be known to some members of the the Beeb's bureaucracy in London as "the Picasso".

Last month, the BBC moved offices for the first time in nearly four decades. They agreed to bring me—and the Cocteau drawing. I was able to get up the stairs, just, but the drawing, eight feet high by six feet wide, was too large.

Calamity. The new offices feel naked without the Cocteau. This week an attempt will be made to haul the immense drawing up five floors by rope from the building's back yard. With luck, we will have our "Picasso" back.

———

I was walking past the lovely, ceremonial gates of the Interior Ministry on Saturday when the policeman on guard duty gravely held up his hand to stop me. I waited for a big, black, ministerial car to sweep by. A small, blonde boy on a tricycle pedalled calmly out of the broad gateway. Another small blonde boy on a bicycle pedalled in. The sons of Brice Hortefeux, the interior minister, were playing not at cars but at limousines.

———

My daughter, Clare, was invited to lunch by a school friend who has an excitable relationship with her mother. After the usual angry exchanges, the friend stormed out, saying: "Maman, vous êtes une salope."

Clare, who has lived in France from the age of two, was shocked. She was shocked not because her friend had called her mother a rude word, but because she had used the formal *vous*, rather than the familiar *tu*. It was as if a teenage British girl had said to her mother: "Mrs Smith, you are a slut."

PART TWO

Normandy

We bought our little house in Normandy to give the children space and fresh air. They have now, sadly, grown out of it. They don't mind making the occasional state visit but they would much rather spend Saturdays with their Parisian friends. Margaret, my wife, loves the quiet and the hill walks but she is equally happy in Paris.

To me, Normandy has become home. It reminds me of the countryside where I grew up on the borders of the Peak District in the 1950s and the 1960s. My garden is my auxiliary lung and my decompression chamber. The village micro-politics have taught me much about rural France—and about France.

Our house is 160 miles west of Paris in the Suisse Normande (which looks much more like Derbyshire Normande or Herefordshire Normande). Our hamlet has eight full time residents; all of them local; almost all retired. We have come to be accepted well enough. "At least," our neighbours say, "you are not Parisians."

Behind the hamlet, there are thick deciduous forests full of beech and oak trees, deer and wild boar. The landscape around the village is a rare island of small, hedge-bordered fields within the increasingly hedgeless and ranch-like Norman countryside. There were two dairy farms when we first came twelve years ago. The fields are now used for beef and cereals by bigger farms in neighbouring villages.

In August 1944, the hamlet was the scene of a brief skirmish between the Germans and the British. One disused building just below our house has a lazy V-shape because it was partially squashed by a British tank and then rebuilt at an angle to widen the road. On the edge of the hamlet, a retired postman, and ex-OAS terrorist, lives in a caravan. History in Normandy, as in the whole of France, is "buried in shallow graves".

■ Cold Comfort Ferme

DECEMBER 1998

He looks too frail to be a farmer. He looks like a character from a Thomas Hardy novel: a dreamy, hunched young man, born by mischance into a life of rural drudgery. Despite his outdoor life (a life in which he has no use for doors, as we will see) he looks pale and sickly and depressed. He smiles a lot, mostly apologetically.

Jean-Michel is our neighbour: a dairy farmer in the hill village in Normandy where we recently bought a small house for weekends and holidays. My conversations—everyone's conversations—with Jean-Michel tend to be limited to a few words about the weather (or since this is Normandy, the rain) and whatever minor atrocity he has committed that day (for which he is always sincerely sorry).

Jean-Michel is a menace; a rural sociopath; an agricultural down and out. He is transplanted from *Cold Comfort Farm* alive, but not especially well, in the French countryside; a French Eddie Grundy. He seems always to be balancing on the edge of a new disaster, which is, presumably, why the only other active farmer in the village calls him, despairingly, "l'acrobate".

"Il est là, l'acrobate?" (Is he there, the acrobat?) asks André, the other farmer, coming to our gate, as if he is convinced that Jean-Michel must be hiding in our garden. Usually it is because Jean-Michel's long-suffering but free-spirited cows have escaped again and are eating André's much greener grass.

Jean-Michel's home is a scene of pre-medieval squalor, in which the kitchen floor joins seamlessly with the farmyard. I've never been inside but I've often seen inside: Jean-Michel never shuts his door, even at night, even when it is -8C outside.

Here, he lives with a mysteriously urban and gentle-seeming woman—a relatively new addition to his life—who is viewed suspiciously by the locals (all fourteen of them). She is known as "la copine": the girlfriend.

Small wonder that Jean-Michel's animals wander. His fields are full of unappetising weeds. Their boundaries are marked by pieces of string, reinforced by electric fences he forgets to switch on. He has a tendency to get up later than dairy farmers are meant to. Towards the end of the morning, the cows become impatient, and uncomfortable, and make their own way down to the milking parlour.

On cold, rainy mornings when he does remember to get up, Jean-Michel herds the cows through the mist in his battered white Renault 4. He proudly told me that he had 28 milking cows—by no means a small herd by French standards.

They are huge beasts of the increasingly rare Norman race, which are being driven out by the black-and-white Holsteins that have conquered the dairy world. (Authentic Norman cows have prettily indistinct brown, white, and grey markings, like Holsteins which have been through the wash too often.)

Unlike their owner, Jean-Michel's cattle seem healthy and content. The milk they produce goes to make Camemberts in the shiny factory down in the valley, which churns out 10,000 cheeses a day. Some stubborn gourmets insist that true Camembert should be produced from only the Norman breed of cows but that rule had to be abandoned years ago.

Jean-Michel is a local boy, formerly a farm labourer. His career as a farmer—he took the tenancy only two years ago—is doomed to be short-lived. The career of such a hopeless farmer might have been doomed, in the long run, at any place or at any time. But Jean-Michel's activities are threatened by other factors: the forces of modernisation and hygiene, tourism and market demands, and European Union rules, which are reshaping the French countryside, for good or bad.

The cow-sheds and milking parlour of Jean-Michel's farm—nearer to our house than his and two feet deep in freezing, liquid manure—have been condemned (quite rightly) as failing EU-imposed hygiene standards. Within a year, Jean-Michel will be ousted; his land and EU milk quota will be let to another farmer, perhaps to the competent André (who owns nothing but standard-issue Holsteins).

In the past thirty years, 1,300,000 French farms have disappeared in this way; there are about 700,000 left but another 200,000 are expected to go in the next two decades. Hence all those cheap French country houses.

When Jean-Michel goes, our village, which has lived principally from agriculture for more than 1,000 years, will be down to its last farm. The cow-muck encrusted roads, which Jean-Michel is supposed to scrub but does not, will become clean roads. Self-willed Norman cows will disappear. Tourists—the likes of us—will arrive in greater numbers.

Jean-Michel will, doubtless, go on the dole and be a much happier man. The village will, like several other post-agricultural villages within walking distance, become tidier, prettier, but still and unreal: without liquid manure or soul.

■ Cold Comfort Ferme 2
JANUARY 1999

All politics is local and there is no politics so human, and so dirty, as local politics. Literally dirty, in the case of the tiny Norman village where we spent the New Year holidays.

Since I first reported on the activities of our neighbour, Jean-Michel, the world's most incompetent dairy farmer, the story has moved on, comically, but also tragically.

The village roads have sunk even deeper under liquid cow-manure. Jean-Michel's neglected farmyard has over-spilt like a foul-smelling volcano, sending a dark, sticky lava-flow down the steep lane towards the notional centre of the hamlet. At the insistence of his mysteriously respectable girlfriend, Jean-Michel, 27, has abandoned his doorless hovel in the path of the lava flow. He has moved into her bungalow in a village six miles away (making him the world's only absentee dairy farmer and milking times even later and more haphazard than before).

Jean-Michel's tractor, always a temperamental machine, now works only in reverse gear. It lumbers out of the Norman mist, like a steam locomotive working tender first, usually towing some piece of rusting farm machinery that has been precariously chained to the front bumper. The unwashed Jean-Michel sits facing backwards, glancing irregularly over his shoulder to check for oncoming traffic.

And now comes the tragic part. A person unknown, most likely in revenge for some, or all, of the above misdemeanours, has poisoned two of Jean-Michel's many dogs. Eeyache and Rikiki were friendly dogs, adored by our small children. The village is quieter and poorer for their passing. Other dogs in the large and constantly changing pack surrounding Jean-Michel were more threatening. But the two who ate the poisoned meat—deliberately left for them, Jean-Michel is convinced—were harmless, floppy creatures. They died in agony. Who could have done such a terrible thing?

There are only eight full-time residents of the village, twenty when the weekend and holiday homes fill up as they did over the New Year break. The only other active farmer in the village, the neat and efficient André, despises Jean-Michel, but André is a gentle, humorous man who would not poison an animal deliberately. There are also our chief local benefactors, Michel and Madeleine, who work in the town twenty miles away during the week. They adore, and would do anything for, good food, animals and small children. Since they had more or less adopted the clumsy, half-blind Eeyache, they are definitely not suspects.

By prior arrangement, the gentle Michel and I jointly cornered Jean-Michel to complain that the liquid manure was now several inches deep on the roads, which made going for a stroll or stepping out of one's car less pleasant than it should be. Jean-Michel admitted that he was a "cochon" (pig) but promised nothing. "Who poisoned my dogs, that's what I want to know?" he said.

Why did he not go to the gendarmes, I asked. He laughed: "People complain to the gendarmes about me. How can I go to them?"

Ah, the pleasures of a quiet week in the country.

As we were wading through the road outside to pack the car to leave, Jean-Michel wandered up with a piece of grubby paper on which he had written the telephone number at his girlfriend's house. "The next time you are coming," he mumbled apologetically, "call me in advance. I'll try to do something about the road..."

Turning over the piece of paper, we found that the number was scribbled on the back of an official laboratory report on Jean-Michel's milk. On 24 June 1998, his cows got surprisingly high marks. He must, secretly, be doing something right.

■ Geronimo

MAY 1999

Geronimo is free. But maybe not for long.

Geronimo is a horse. He belongs to our neighbour, Jean-Michel.

All autumn and winter, he kept the horse—actually his father's horse—chained in a draughty, manure-choked stable. The poor horse became more and more depressed and distressed. Horses always look depressed. Have you ever seen a horse smile? But Geronimo was very depressed.

Many people complained. We complained. The mayor of the commune complained. Hikers, seeing Geronimo's distress, complained to the local branch of the French equivalent of the RSPCA. Nothing happened, although Jean-Michel invariably promised that something was just about to happen.

Imprisonment was, partly, Geronimo's own fault. He is a huge chestnut stallion with a hatred of other male horses and a tendency—like all Jean-Michel's animals—to wander. To try to supplement his income by breeding foals, Jean-Michel had, last September, brought in another stallion and two mares to join Geronimo, and his concubine, Elisa.

The big horse could not cope with this influx and started to assault all the newcomers. He was placed in solitary confinement.

In the next hamlet, there lives another dairy farmer, who is the complete antithesis to Jean-Michel. Bernard has built up and modernised his holdings so successfully that he can afford to indulge his hobby—flying a tiny, canary-yellow light aircraft. He has built a landing strip in one of his fields and keeps the plane in a barn.

One of the many atrocities attributed to Geronimo is to have wandered the mile or so down to Bernard's farm and grazed in the middle of the runway when the plane was in the air. Bernard had to divert to an airfield ten miles away.

Our tiny village—eight dwellings and a mobile home on the hills south of Caen in Normandy—is getting busier as spring turns to summer. Having owned a house in the village for almost a year now, our sense of the history, sociology and feudology of the place, and the wider commune to which it belongs, is becoming richer and more confusing.

Apart from ourselves, all the weekend visitors have a family connection with the village. Patricia, for instance, visits her late grandmother's house, where she spent her childhood summers. She is now a thirty-something mother and a personnel officer with a big firm in the Paris area. She remembers a time—only twenty years ago—when there was no running water in her granny's house and "mémé" did all her washing, with most other villagers, at a communal wash-stone beside the stream in the valley bottom.

The village roads are getting busier for another reason. It is birthing time for Jean-Michel's herd of twenty dairy cattle. Since his idea of fencing is an old piece of blue string, all his animals come and go as they please. Jean-Michel still forgets sometimes to milk his animals, until they come down off the hill to complain.

Once, we arrived in pitch darkness just after 10 p.m. A figure staggered up with a torch strapped to his hat. It was Jean-Michel going to fetch the cows for milking. How was he, I asked? "Ça vache," he replied, in his usual cheerful-depressed way. This is a cerebral, French dairy farmer's joke.

These events apart, there have been mystifying signs recently that Jean-Michel is trying to clean up his act. He has repaired fences and ploughed fields. His tractor no longer works only in reverse gear. Most of all, Geronimo is no longer chained in the stable. Jean-Michel has created a stout electrified enclosure, just for him.

What is going on?

Our neighbour, Michel, as ever, provided the explanation. The village has been expecting, week by week, the annual state visit of the matriarch of the chief landowning family. She is Jean-Michel's landlady. There have been many complaints about his activities. His lease is due for renewal.

Hence the sudden burst of good husbandry. Unfortunately, no-one has told Geronimo that he has to be on his best behaviour. He spends part of each day staring menacingly over an unkempt hedge at another field where the rest of the horse herd grazes. He spends the rest of his time galloping up and down his enclosure, restoring his muscles after his winter in jail.

Clearly his plan is to escape and put the new stallion to flight. To do so he has to leap over two hedges, a muddy track and a caravan. No problem for a horse that has already defeated an aircraft.

■ Jour de Fête
JULY 1999

The commune is buzzing like never before. The roads have cars (something seldom seen here in the plural). There are trucks pulling horse-boxes. There are tractors and trailers, laden with purposeful lumps of wood. Unexpected people are wearing unexpected clothes.

Our next-door neighbour, a sour man who is the assistant mayor of the commune (one small village and four hamlets), is wearing a straw cowboy hat and a smile. André, the elderly farmer down the road, has replaced his usual manure-coloured, woollen hat with a blue baseball cap: he looks instantly as if he could be farming 10,000 acres in Kansas instead of 120 acres in Normandy.

It is the day of the *fête du village*: an annual festival of pony-jumping and sausage-grilling and an opportunity for everyone to clear the rubbish out of their attics and replace it with the rubbish from other people's attics.

The fête takes place in the field beside the village hall, surrounded by freshly mown fields and the wooded slopes of the Normandy hills. The precise name for the village hall is the Salle Polyvalente, which means many-sided room or room-with-many-uses, sounding both poetic and bureaucratic at the same time.

There are twenty stalls in the sunshine, arranged in surreal still-lives of glittering and garish obsolescence. One stall displays two Barbie dolls (half-undressed), a pair of Wellingtons, a rusted typewriter, Johnny Hallyday's greatest hits (volume eight), two tubs of fibre-protection agent, a collection of miniature brandy and Calvados bottles (empty), a broken accordion, and an axe-head without a handle. Small wonder that the French gave us the word fête and the phrase bric-a-brac.

Another stall's principal offerings are dog-eared Jean Plaidy novels and a roll of barbed wire. The two women in charge come from Southampton. They have a house in a neighbouring village.

A poster advertises animals for sale. "Un doberman (pur race). Hamsters (20 francs). Chatons à débattre (kittens by negotiation)". Very convenient: you presumably buy the hamsters and the kittens to feed the Doberman on the way home.

I studied the crowds at the fête carefully. (The word "crowds" is relative, but the commune does have something to celebrate this year. The 1999 census showed that the population has risen in the last nine years, from 300 to 319.)

I studied the festival-goers to test a theory that I have.

There is an exhibition in Caen, twenty miles to the north, which has irritated the French-hating section of the British press. The exhibition makes the perfectly reasonable point that the culture of England, and Britain as a whole, has been shaped partly by Normans. The English like to think of themselves as Anglo-Saxons, the exhibition says, and the Normans of 1066 as alien invaders. In truth, 933 years on, we are as much Norman as we are Anglo-Saxon.

Anyone who has visited Normandy will have been struck by the "Englishness" of the countryside, the churches, the villages. I think the resemblances go further. My study of the crowd confirmed my view that Normans, en masse, although friendly and charming, are not an especially handsome people. They are rather un-French. They are, in point of fact, rather English-looking.

My eye was distracted by the mounted head of a goat. Judging by its running nose and clouded eyes, it died of pneumonia. The man running the stall, who had a beard rather like the goat's, insisted that he killed the beast himself. It was a wild mountain goat from the Mont Blanc massif, he said. It could be mine for only 400 francs (£40).

"I was obliged to kill it," he said sadly. Why? Did it attack him with murderous intent? Did it eat his home-grown lettuces? "No," he said, "It was butted in the arse [*tapé dans le cul*] by another goat and crippled. I was obliged to kill it out of compassion."

That explained the surprised expression on the creature's face.

It came down to a choice between buying the goat or an old, two-seater school desk for 100 francs which would be ideal for my two young daughters to sit side-by-side and steal each other's felt tips. I was greatly tempted by the goat (what a story to be able to tell) but, in the end, logic triumphed over romance and I bought the desk.

■ Cold Comfort Ferme 3
OCTOBER 1999

Autumn in Normandy is a season of muddy fruitfulness. The apples are falling. The pears are ripening. Our village is threatened once again by a lava flow of liquid manure and mud from Jean-Michel's farmyard.

Jean-Michel has had an industrious summer. He cut down a tree and he moved a caravan. In most other respects, life on his farm remains the same. Jean-Michel, a one-man counterpoint to the romantic view of la France Profonde, seems to derive little pleasure from his pastoral life.

Evening milking is generally so late that, even in the height of summer, the cows stagger home to their field in pitch darkness. Jean-Michel is sincerely fond of his animals—which also include a rabble of dogs and horses—but often treats them carelessly. His fields are so infested with tall weeds that he recently spent twenty minutes searching for a lost calf in a half-acre enclosure.

During the summer, life appeared to be catching up with Jean-Michel. His tractor finally disintegrated. The heaviest machinery on his farm is now a bicycle. Menacing men in suits arrived in vans marked with the names of suppliers of agricultural feed. Other bizarre and disturbing things happened, too. Jean-Michel's dogs got bored and decided to round up the neighbour's cows. The mayor, in person, came to protest. Jean-Michel was, as usual, absent.

Our children came into the house one day to say that they had seen an eight-year-old boy driving a car, very fast, with Jean-Michel in the passenger seat. We dismissed that as an exaggeration.

The next day a white car was parked outside Jean-Michel's farmyard. A boy was at the wheel, looking at me defiantly. His father—a friend of Jean-Michel's—emerged from the cowsheds and climbed into the passenger side. The car sped off down the narrow lane and round a tight bend. As we had suspected, our children had been exaggerating. The driver was not eight years old. He was at least nine.

But there is new hope for Jean-Michel: a civilising and warming influence has entered his Cold Comfort world. Her name is Marie. She is about twenty years older than Jean-Michel: a gentle, tiny, wiry, distinctly urban woman in her late forties, with bright red hair.

At first Marie was an occasional visitor. Now she is playing a bigger and bigger part in running the farm. Sometimes, when Jean-Michel has disappeared, she drives the herd to milking, single-handed—dwarfed by the fifteen huge brown-grey-and-white, blotched cows of the beautiful but vanishing Norman race. She has failed to acquire any suitable agricultural clothes; she wades cheerfully through the foot-deep muck in the farmyard in leather boots and tight black leggings.

Marie has a silent, rather crazed-looking son of about Jean-Michel's age. He, too, works on the farm, wearing a jumper that wishes you, in English, a "Happy Christmas".

The village people tolerate Jean-Michel (most of the time) but refuse to have anything to do with "la copine". They make a point of not knowing her name.

For this reason alone, I have made a point of speaking to her. We have become almost pals. She is an intelligent, sweet, hard-working woman. She adores our small children. It turns out that she is an auxiliary nurse in a psychiatric hospital, where she works four nights a week. Why she would wish to bring home her work and form a relationship with Jean-Michel is an unfathomable mystery.

Little by little, Marie is trying to make the farm work. She had Jean-Michel and her son cut down a dead tree to sell for firewood. She persuaded them to harvest and sell the fruit from the scores of cider-apple trees that stand out (just) above the weeds in Jean-Michel's fields. Last year the apples rotted on the ground.

A large, ugly but luxurious caravan recently appeared right in front of our house, spoiling our view of the weeds and the hills and forests beyond. Jean-Michel promised me that it would be gone within fifteen days, as soon as he could borrow a tractor. That was six weeks ago.

My wife is not pleased with this blot on the landscape. I tried to explain that it was probably another sign of Marie's benign influence. Commuting five miles, uphill, on a bicycle to work as a dairy farmer was not practical. They needed the caravan, I said. They were working country people. What right did we week-ending city dwellers have to make them shift their temporary home?

The other day, Marie gave us some plums from yet another previously neglected tree. Our five-year-old daughter decided, in return, to leave a felt-tip drawing in her caravan. My wife went with her. They made a discovery that devastated my unanswerable argument. Marie and Jean-Michel are not living in the large, plush caravan. They are using it as a store for dog food.

◼ Cold Comfort Ferme 4
NOVEMBER 1999

There are two farms in our village. Within a couple of years, more's the pity, there may be none.

Jean-Michel continues to stagger from crisis to crisis. His latest plan is to pack up his cows and his dogs and broken tractors and move to the South of France to escape the Norman rain and his debtors. Since he finds it awkward to organise two milkings a day, this may not happen soon.

The second farm resembles a scene from a children's wooden puzzle. It is the kind of farm you seldom see these days, even in France. There is a neat yard with bad-tempered chickens and wandering ducks and rabbits in hutches and countless cats and dogs. There are orderly apple trees in the fields and vegetables in the cottage garden.

Our two-year-old daughter, Grace, likes to visit this farmyard at least twice a day. She has seen several generations of fluffy ducklings grow—in four months—to awkward, teenage duckdom and then, abruptly, disappear.

This farm belongs to André and Solange. André is a short,

taciturn, humorous man, with a shapeless hat, the colour of dried cow manure. He drives his cows to milking with the words "au boulot ("get to work"). Solange is a cheerful woman in her fifties. Both were born in the commune; neither has travelled much beyond it.

André and Solange despair of Jean-Michel, as much as the other residents, and occasional residents, of the village. In truth, they have more reason to complain than most. When Jean-Michel's cows escape, it is André's grass they eat; when Jean-Michel's dogs get bored, it is André's cows they chase and nip.

None the less, André remains heroically indulgent of his eccentric neighbour. For months now, Jean-Michel has stayed in business only because André has lent him an ancient, but working, tractor.

Since the summer, André and Solange have employed an honorary occasional farm hand, our son Charles. Charles is a typically urban, late 20th-century child, fascinated by video games and television. He went along one evening to witness the milking and became as hooked on the complexities of supplementary feeding, cow management and milk temperature as he is on Batman or Super Mario.

He now claims to be able to recognise the twenty Holstein milking cows individually, without looking at the large orange number identification tags on their ears. ("Why are all these cows for sale, Daddy?" asked his five-year-old sister, Clare, as we watched the cows queuing for their turn at the milking machines one evening.)

It was on this visit that Solange told us the latest crop of ducklings was so plentiful that she had one bird left over. We snapped it up. The reputation of Solange's ducklings extends for miles around. They are promised, from hatching, to specific customers, rather like children with their names down for public school.

Another neighbour, Madeleine, a living cookbook of ancient Norman recipes, informed us how to roast the duck in the traditional, simple Norman way. Stuffing made from the gizzards and liver, with plenty of parsley, onions and breadcrumbs; served with duchesse potatoes and a "generous" wine, preferably a Bordeaux. The duck was indeed delicious, its meat as red, almost, as beef.

Leaning over a tubular fence, watching Charles milk the cows the next day, I thanked Solange for her duck. She said, wearily: "Only two more years." Two more years of what? "Two more years until we retire." What will they do when they retire? "We are going to travel. André and I have never been anywhere much. We have the cows to milk twice a day. It is expensive to get anyone to replace us. When we retire, we have always said we will travel."

Where to? I imagined that she might say to America, or Asia or Africa or even to Britain. "To France," she said. "We're going to visit the whole of France. They say that it's very beautiful." She giggled.

I knew that they were coming up to retirement but did not know it was so soon. I mentioned what Solange had said—and Jean-Michel's vague plans to emigrate to the South—to Madeleine's husband, Michel. As an authentic farming village, our village is a local rarity. Most of the other villages near by have become retirement homes or dormitories for people working in Caen.

If Jean-Michel goes and André and Solange retire, their land—both of them are tenants—will almost certainly be absorbed into one of the bigger farms. The village will become more like the picturesque, mud-free, flower-box-infested village on the next hillside, inhabited entirely by widows, save for one widower.

Michel, who works in the Citroën factory in Caen, and has lived in the village all his life, except for ten years in the French navy, agreed that it would "change everything" if the farms disappeared. Gazing at the stream of liquid manure and mud flowing down the road from Jean-Michel's farm, he said: "It would be a shame. However, one has to admit that there would be conveniences as well as inconveniences."

■ Geronimo 2
MARCH 2000

Geronimo has gone. For more than a year, the great, shaggy, brown, mournful, delinquent stallion was the nearest neighbour in our village. For Grace, no day was bearable without half a dozen visits to "Momo" in his lonely field: to give him windfall apples in the autumn; or secret extra helpings of hay in the winter; or just to say hello and stroke his ugly muzzle.

Geronimo's crimes were many. He had fought with other horses; he had stepped over Jean-Michel's collapsing fences and invaded other farms; he had knocked another stallion into a neighbour's vegetable patch, killing the horse and several square metres of lettuce, beans and cabbages (causing a feud which lasts to this day).

Ultimately, Geronimo did the impossible; he proved there were limits to Jean-Michel's carelessness. Finally, after pleas for clemency—from ourselves among others—Jean-Michel created a small electric-fenced pen for Geronimo near to our house.

There the big horse stayed, alone and unkempt, through the hot days of summer and the apple-munching days of autumn. The great Boxing Day hurricane flattened a large tree in his pen but Geronimo survived, unharmed. And then, abruptly, he was gone.

We feared the worst. Jean-Michel's experiment with minimum-care agriculture has not been going well. For months, Jean-Michel and his unlikely friend, Marie, have had no machinery larger than a bicycle. Before that, a succession of cars and tractors had appeared and rapidly disappeared.

The word in the village is that Jean-Michel's days as a tenant dairy farmer are numbered. André used to help him, but has given up in despair. He told me, with a shrug: "Jean-Michel va prendre le car-ferry" (ie is going to vanish). The "proprietor", a shadowy figure who lives in Paris, has grown tired, it is said, of the mistreatment of her ancestral hectares. Jean-Michel's farmyard, it is rumoured, is to be rebuilt into holiday homes. The fields are to be planted with trees.

Had Geronimo been sold? Had he been locked up again? Had he escaped and been injured? Or worse? No, Marie assured us, he was fine. He was grazing once again with the rest of the horses "là-bas en haut" (literally, down there, up there).

Many things in Jean-Michel's world happen, or are supposed to happen, "là-bas en haut". The caravan placed at a drunken angle in front of our house "for a fortnight" and still there eight months later, is due to be moved "là-bas en haut". The village roads, centimetres deep in the liquid manure boiling out off Jean-

Michel's farmyard, will be fine as soon as he constructs new buildings "là-bas en haut".

On a bright, cold evening, Grace and I set off up the field track in search of Momo. We climbed over, or under, a series of vaguely strung electric fences. We struggled through sloughs of mud. Eventually, we came to a firm plateau, with beech forests on one side and a great panorama of the Norman hills on the other. The fences forming the fields had dissolved, creating a kind of miniature prairie, where cows and horses, instead of deer and buffalo, roamed at will. All around, there were vehicles in advanced stages of decomposition—brown tractors, white vans—an elephant's graveyard of Jean-Michel's many vehicles.

Geronimo recognised us immediately and trotted over to have his muzzle stroked. He has six equine companions "là-bas en haut" as well as a tame bull and several young cows. He is presumably happier, even though he looks as miserable as ever. There is something of Eeyore in Geronimo. Maybe he has heard the depressing rumours that he is to be replaced by trees.

■ Cold Comfort Ferme 5
JULY 2000

The sun is breaking through the Norman clouds and our village looks more than usually lush and green. As Jean-Michel has no tractor he can no more trail the liquid manure from his farmyard along the lanes. His only piece of heavy machinery is a misshapen blue Renault 5 with no rear seats so he can carry hay. The roads are miraculously clear.

All should be set for a wonderful summer, except that dark deeds are afoot in the Norman hills. Two crimes, one banal and unsolved and one disturbing and unreported, have blighted our pastoral idyll.

When we are in the village, we visit the horses in Jean-Michel's dead-tractor-strewn fields above our house every day, sometimes twice a day. Grace regards the animals as part of her extended family.

There is Geronimo; there is a big, light-chestnut mare called Elisa; there is a black mare with a foal; there are two small, brown mares and two frisky adolescent stallions. Grace has given her own names to some of the horses. The two ageing, brown mares, are—or were—Sharon and Tracey.

A few days ago, Sharon, or Tracey, was found dead in the field: not just dead but horrifically mauled. Most of her face was torn away.

Jean-Michel has been greatly upset by her death. Usually, whatever befalls him, he carries on in a state of cheerful, muddled indifference. The old chestnut mare, actually called Jupiter, had belonged to Jean-Michel since his childhood. He learnt to ride on her. Jean-Michel and Marie give different explanations for the death. She believes the old brown mare was attacked, by someone or something.

No predator in Normandy is large enough to do such damage to a grown horse. There are deer and wild boar in the forest beyond the horses' fields but nothing carnivorous bigger than a fox. There are no packs of wild dogs in the neighbourhood. Marie believes Jupiter was killed by a person, or persons, unknown.

Jean-Michel scoffs at this theory. He blames Geronimo. The big stallion is the softest horse in the world with humans but has a string of previous convictions for assaults on other horses. He believes Jupiter fell and was injured during some kind of horse-play, possibly while resisting the unwelcome attentions of Geronimo. Her face, he explains, must have been torn away later by carrion crows or by small predators. Hmm.

Marie's theory—an assault by humans—is the more disquieting but the more plausible. I suspect Jean-Michel knows as much.

But who would attack a horse in this way? And why? Eighteen months ago, someone left poisoned meat for Jean-Michel's many noisy but harmless dogs: two died.

Jean-Michel owes many people money. Plain white vans with menacing-looking young men often call for him and find him, as usual, missing. Would someone—shades of *The Godfather*—half-sever a horse's head over a village feud; or more likely a quarrel over money? Maybe they would.

The other blight on our rural tranquillity was a burglary at our home. The thief, or more likely thieves, parked outside the house in broad daylight with a van and trailer and removed a cooker, a fridge, a vacuum cleaner, a television, an iron, a child's electric piano and a coffee machine.

Jean-Michel saw the van and a young man with red hair but assumed (reasonably enough) that he was working on the house. He is convinced he had seen the man before.

The local gendarmerie brigade made a big, one-day show of investigating this major crime (there are few burglaries in the area). They took fingerprints and footprints and asked for the names of all people who had worked on the house. Then they did nothing. Two months after the event, they have yet to interview the chief witness (Jean-Michel) or any of the people on the list.

The relationship between the gendarmerie and rural people in France is an odd one. I was brought up in an English village with a locally born village policeman who knew where and when every apple had been stolen (mostly because they were stolen by his son). The gendarmerie is part of the French military and a caste apart: a strangely unaccountable, unpredictable and sometimes alien presence in the French countryside.

I asked Marie if she had reported the horse's strange death to the gendarmerie. She looked at me as if I was not just foreign but half-witted.

■ A Mushroom Hunt
NOVEMBER 2000

We went hunting for the trumpets of the dead. It is not a task to be undertaken lightly. To find the trumpets of the dead, you need sharp eyes, stout boots and knowledgeable neighbours.

The trumpets of the dead lurk in sodden banks of rotting leaves at the edge of the forest. They resemble truncated body parts of alien creatures. They sound like something invented by JRR Tolkien or perhaps JK Rowling ("Harry Potter and the Trumpets of the Dead").

But *les trompettes des morts* are mushrooms; queer-looking

mushrooms but, despite their unappetising appearance and gothic-horror name, safe to eat. Safe is not the right word. They are wonderful to eat.

Madeleine was pessimistic about our chances of finding trumpets of the dead. We were two or three weeks late, she said, and mushrooms of all kinds, once plentiful in Calvados, in the forests, in the fields, by the roadside, had become depressingly scarce.

Weed-killers and chemical fertilisers may explain their disappearance from the fields. Madeleine could not explain their rarity in the forests. "Everything is different now," she said. "Nature is being ruined. Nobody seems to care."

Madeleine, who is in her mid-fifties, is a walking encyclopaedia of country lore, from mushroom habitats to ancient recipes for rabbit pâté. Her concern for her beloved Norman countryside may be exaggerated, or premature.

Compared with a similar stretch of rural England, the Calvados hills are delightfully unspoilt: the bird life is rich and varied, from buzzards to swifts; there are roe deer and wild boar in the forests; you can walk for miles along the country lanes without seeing a car, even in summer.

On the hill-tops, the pattern of agriculture (chemicals apart) has barely changed in decades. Dairy cattle roam between hedges and woodlands. There have been many cases of Mad Cow Disease in the *départements* to the east, west and south but only one in the whole of Calvados.

How long can this last? As you approach our village from the main road five miles away, you can see the tide of modern agriculture and weekend-home prettification advancing up the hill. Around the village below ours, almost all hedges have been ripped out to make Nebraskan cereal fields. In a couple of years, the village will probably be swamped by neatness and modernity. An advance column of weekenders from Paris has already arrived. Ourselves.

Despite her pessimistic mushrooming forecast, Madeleine and Michel drove us to one of their secret spots in the forest, two miles from the village. If the boar hunters were in the forest, Michel warned, he would not allow us to enter. French hunters sometimes have strange notions of what a wild boar looks like.

The forest was clear. We walked up a long-distance public footpath or "Grande Randonnée". If you walked to the end of the path, you would be in the Pyrenees that straddle the Spanish border, 500 miles away. Steep, dank, mossy slopes rose on either side of the track, with towering beeches and oaks on the bank tops. Madeleine and Michel shook their heads.

We were too late, it seemed. There were a few spindly, white-yellow, inedible mushrooms; no trompettes des morts. Madeleine learnt to distinguish between a free meal and sudden death as a girl, on a farm near Bayeux. The knowledge was handed down to her by an elderly woman in the village. Now the old wisdom is dying, she says. Lots of country people shoot rabbits and wild boar; few know where to look for mushrooms.

Michel is also a countryman but he was terrified of mushrooms until he married Madeleine. The first time she took him mushroom-hunting he made her eat her fungi alone. He waited 24 hours before he tried one himself. (About thirty people die of mushroom-poisoning in France each year.) Now Michel is almost as keen a mushroom prospector as his wife.

Food, of all kinds, is their passion. They think nothing of driving thirty miles to a particular street-market to buy the right kind of Baie Saint Michel mussels.

Abruptly, Michel found a grey-black, wizened trumpet of the dead. A few moments later, three of them appeared at Madeleine's feet. After that, there was a steady stream of sightings. We would stare at the grey leaves on the banks for minutes and see nothing; then someone—not usually me—would look at the same spot again and find a couple of trompettes des morts.

We found thirty altogether, enough to dry in front of the wood stove and eat as an hors d'oeuvre the next day. We also found two other kinds of delicate, frilly, edible mushrooms, which Madeleine identified as *girolles d'hiver* and *pieds de mouton* (sheep's feet). (Harry Potter and the Sheep's Feet? Not quite right.)

Then Madeleine noticed a group of large, more traditional-looking, orange-blotched mushrooms, *coulemelles*, by the roadside. We added those to our basket and drove to their house to celebrate with a bottle of "Norman Champagne" (seven-year-old *poiré* or pear cider) and homemade chestnut brownies.

There can be few more perfect ways to spend an autumn afternoon, so long as the mushroom population survives. Gather ye trumpets of the dead while you may.

■ An Historic Moment
APRIL 2001

When the evening milking ends tomorrow, our village in Normandy will cease to be a working, agricultural community for the first time in at least 1,000 years. Readers of previous columns will be sad to learn that our farming neighbour, the chaotic, eccentric, lovable Jean-Michel, went out of business last month. This is nothing to do with foot-and-mouth or BSE or any of the other plagues ravaging the European countryside.

Jean-Michel was a victim of his own fecklessness and lack of resources. He is far from a perfect case history but his demise also illustrates the difficulties facing small, traditional farms in the early 21st century, despite the cant pouring from the urban and suburban press in France and Britain about the need for "ecological" and non-intensive farming.

Jean-Michel had twenty milking cows at the height of his activity. Towards the end, things got more chaotic and desperate than usual. At least ten of these beautiful large cows of the Norman dairy race, with brown-grey swirling markings, died in unexplained circumstances.

He claims they were poisoned with powdered glass. On previous occasions, there is some evidence that two of his dogs and an old brown mare were attacked and killed by his numerous enemies (mostly creditors). This time, no-one in the village believes the powdered glass story. The truth is that Jean-Michel, even by his insouciant standards, had let go of the rope; or had been forced to let it go.

Money problems obliged him to take a part-time job on another farm. As a consequence, he failed to grow any winter feed last summer. He planted, too late, a field of maize, still rotting on the stalk six months after it should have been harvested.

Whatever the cows died of (BSE has been ruled out) malnutrition is likely to have been a contributing factor. Jean-Michel loved his animals: he would not have mistreated them or neglected them deliberately. My belief is that he hoped he could get away with grazing them all winter on the lush Norman grass and a little bought-in hay. He could not.

In any case, the Camembert cheese factory in the valley was threatening not to send its milk truck any more because of the foot-deep swamp of liquid manure in Jean-Michel's farmyard.

By coincidence, the only other farmers in the village, André and Solange, retire this weekend. After they milk "Chocolat" and "La Bretonne" and their other cows for the last time tomorrow night, our little group of eight dwellings will become, like other flower-infested villages hereabouts, a sort of retirement-dormitory-weekending community with no true economic activity of its own. André is utterly unsentimental about this change. "After forty years staring at cows' arses morning and night, we deserve to look at something different," he says. André and Solange plan to travel: first to see France and later to Britain. They will live in the farmhouse, which they own, and keep a few ducks and hens but otherwise their retirement fund is enough for them to survive modestly.

But is it not a shame that his well-run farm is not being taken over as a going enterprise by a younger farmer? André shrugged and whistled. Under new regulations, French not European, his neat farmyard would fail to meet the requirements for a "new" farm. "These days, before you start out in the dairy business, you have to have a bathroom and toilet for each cow," he said.

André and Jean-Michel were both in their different ways (the orderly and the chaotic) ecological, "non-intensive" and anti-productivist. They did not rip out hedges or use aggressive feeding methods or pour chemicals on their fields.

The rented land of both farms has now been taken over by bigger farmers in neighbouring villages. Manure will doubtless be replaced by chemicals. Dairy cows will be replaced by beef cows and cereals and maybe, in the long run, trees. This is the classic pattern seen all over France as small-scale agriculture is gradually squeezed out, despite the lip-service to "family farms" paid by successive French governments.

In 1965 there were three million farms in France; there are now 600,000 and falling.

Despite the fashionable talk about the need for human scale and non-intensive farming, the BSE and foot-and-mouth crises will drive more farmers out of business, in Britain and France.

There is an odd, urban hypocrisy at work. Yes, we want environmentally friendly, "traditional" farms (preferably a series of petting zoos which mysteriously produce meat without killing animals). We also insist on food at mass-production prices and, of course, we do not want to pay farmers any subsidies.

Jean-Michel now has a full time job on a farm ten miles way. He is still keeping a few beef animals on scattered fields which belong to him. Geronimo, his lovable, wandering horse, has been sold to another farm. His new owner hopefully knows how to build fences to keep him from trouble.

■ An English Country Garden
AUGUST 2001

English visitors say that my garden looks rather French. My French neighbours insist that it is "typiquement anglais". "Ah les anglais and their lawns," they say, as if large stretches of grass are a waste of space, better devoted to seven different varieties of leeks or courgettes.

In truth, I did not set out with any national model in mind: I inherited a lovely, complicated, maze-like garden created by the old lady who previously owned our house. I cleared spaces for the children to run and for vegetables to grow: the result is part cottage-garden, part suburban-lawns-and-borders.

The fascination for me, as a gardening foreign correspondent, is to learn how to grow things in a different country. The challenge, as a weekend gardener, is how to keep my garden watered and weeded (and eaten) when we live—most of the time—in Paris 160 miles away.

I have learned a great deal from a countryman and retired car-worker, who has a genuine cottage garden of the kind I remember from the English countryside in the 1950s: he has no space for grass just a jumble of flowers and vegetables. The one thing that distinguishes my Norman neighbour, Michel, from the village gardeners whom I remember in England is that he judges the success of his vegetables—and selects his varieties—almost entirely by their taste. He cares nothing for looks and little for yield. To him, the proof of a garden is the exquisiteness of the vegetables on his dinner plate.

Michel is also an all-organic gardener, not because that is fashionable but because he has always done things that way. (Would that this were also true of commercial French growers. An EU study published this week found that French fruit and vegetables are among the worst in Europe for excessive residues of pesticides.)

My Norman garden is my third. My first, in the 1970s, was in Lancashire. When I walked out on it on a summer's day in 1978, to go to a new job in Paris, I felt like I was abandoning a wife and children.

My second, in the late 1980s and early 1990s, was in Georgetown in Washington DC: a truly urban garden, which spilled onto, and even into, the pavement. (One night we were woken by the sound of two men brawling as they rolled in my largest flower-bed. I was about to shout at them to leave my begonias alone when my wife sleepily reminded me of the Washington murder rate.)

Otherwise, growing in the semi-tropical climate of Washington was a delight. With minimum effort, I had an explosion of colour, mountainous clumps of herbs and Russian sunflowers twelve feet tall (which the tourist buses used to stop to admire). My garden was eventually included in the prestigious annual Georgetown Garden Tour as a token "small garden" among the rolling acres of the Washington aristocracy.

Now, in Normandy, the only vandalism in my flower-beds is caused by occasional incursions by neighbouring cows. I have a south-facing garden of well-drained clay, terraced high above Michel's garden next door: a grower's delight.

The season is shorter than it was in Lancashire. The last frosts are in mid-May; the first in late October. However, when plants begin to grow, they grow like fairy-tale beanstalks. The

Norman summer combination of warmth and almost constant damp is horticulturally explosive. We have just eaten our first outdoor tomatoes of the season (a new variety to me, called Super Marmande, as muscular-looking as a body-builder but delicate to eat). They were planted in mid-May, only eleven weeks ago. In some places in the south of England, it may be possible to have tomatoes red and ripe out of doors by early August. In Lancashire, even in the hot summers of the mid-1970s, it was impossible.

I also have an inherited vine (variety unknown) growing on the south-facing front of the house, which provides, with slight care, scores of bunches of small but sweet and succulent mauve-coloured grapes by the end of August.

My garden is strictly organic. My bible is the same book that I used in the 1970s, the then recently published Lawrence D. Hills' *Grow Your Own Fruit and Vegetables*, published by Faber and Faber but now, I think, out of print. Mr Hills was a great—and eloquent and witty—evangelist for organic gardening long before it became fashionable or trendy.

In the last two years, I have (peeping over the garden hedge) judged the comparative benefits of the Lawrence D. Hills method of growing potatoes against the traditional Norman method.

Michel digs in liberal amounts of well-rotted farmyard manure early in the spring, then he makes dibber holes and punches the seed-potatoes down into them. I follow the Hills technique: I dig foot deep trenches, which I half fill with manure or compost, cover with a little soil, lay out the seed spuds and cover with earth.

In most respects, Michel's vegetable garden is superior to mine: it has more variety and a better continuity of plumper produce. But my Hills-method spuds are, I have to report, much better than Michel's: earlier, better-cropping, more resistant to the blight ("la maladie") which is endemic in Normandy and—the clinching French argument—better-tasting.

I use a red-skinned variety called Desirée, partly because that was my mother's first name, partly because I used to grow them in Lancashire a quarter of a century ago. I use much the same method—again recommended by Mr Hills—for the outdoor tomato, courgette and cucumber beds, putting a large block of trodden compost and manure six inches down to give them a reserve of moisture and nutrients to get through dry spells when I'm away in Paris and unable to irrigate. I have also successfully grown peppers outdoors this year using the same method. I only wish I could do the same for the lawn, which frizzles up in the Norman sun if I'm away for more than a week at a time in early summer.

In the name of sentimental continuity between my gardens, I grow not only Desirée potatoes but Russian sunflowers (which reach only a miniature eight feet tall in Normandy) and large clumps of the Busy Lizzies which are the staple of all Washington gardens. (The winters are so severe in DC that perennials are difficult to keep going.) The tropical colours of the Impatiens used to look just right in the southerly light of Washington. They grow very well in Normandy but—as in Britain—look wrong: much too showy, too intense.

What else, apart from the importance of choosing varieties for taste, have I learned from the Norman gardeners? Michel and Madeleine, who looks after the flowers, are great believers in collecting their own seed. They also swear by the importance of planting with phases of the moon. If you have no choice but to plant at the weekends, this is an impossible piece of country lore to follow.

In one respect, if no other, I have discovered that British gardeners have been doing it wrong—and back-breakingly wrong— for decades, maybe centuries. I bought an English-type spade, short with a horizontal section at the end of the shaft, when I started gardening in France three years ago. The spade broke after a couple of weeks. I replaced it, somewhat nervously, with a French-type spade, with a handle up to my chest and no cross-piece at the end of the shaft.

Digging was transformed: less exhausting, less back-breaking. If you travel to France this summer, forget the crates of wine and beer. Buy a few French vegetable varieties and a long, French spade.

■ Rural History Lesson
MAY 2002

A sad, and predictable, change has come over our small village in the Norman hills in the last twelve months.

Where blotchy, brown and white Norman dairy cows once peacefully grazed on the green and weed-infested Norman grass, there now stand acres of wheat and maize. The half-derelict cow-sheds once used by Jean-Michel now stand wholly derelict and mournfully empty.

Jean-Michel went bust a year ago. After hanging around for a while doing odd jobs, he has left the area. The other dairy farmers in the village, André and Solange, retired at about the same time. These were the last farms to survive in our hamlet, which once had eight.

Their land has been taken over by two young, larger-scale farmers in neighbouring villages. One farmer grazes beef cattle; the other has ploughed up Jean-Michel's nearly wild grassland and planted many hectares of subsidy-attracting cereals. According to elderly, local people, much of this ground has never been ploughed before. With the help of chemical fertilisers and pesticides, it seems to be growing excellent wheat.

André and Solange are thriving on their retirement, funded partly by the government but mostly by their own contributions into a farmers' retirement scheme. As dairy farmers, they milked their cows morning and night for thirty years. They had a rare day off when their adopted daughter, born in the French Pacific islands, stood in for them. Until last year, André and Solange had never ventured outside Normandy in their lives. I bumped into a dapper-looking André the other day. He and Solange had just returned from driving to Prague.

Much of this is inevitable. There were over two million farms in France 30 years ago. There are now fewer than 700,000 and falling. The question, in Britain as well as France, is where this process should end.

The peasant-scale agriculture which survived in France up to the

1980s was evidently doomed. It would, however, be a miserable fate for the French countryside—socially, environmentally, aesthetically—if everything went the way of the great cereal-growing belt, 100 miles wide in places, which now surrounds Paris. Here there are immense fields of wheat larger than anything that I saw in Iowa or Nebraska or Kansas.

Although successive French governments from the 1960s to the 1990s paid lip-service to small and family farms and the mystic soul of La France Profonde, they pursued in Brussels a policy of ever more intensive agriculture. The last French government changed all that. It took a muddled and never properly implemented step towards the encouragement of medium-sized, environmentally-friendly farms.

In recent years, Brussels has allowed EU governments to "tax" rich, highly subsidised farmers, by taking away part of their aid and giving it to less intensive, smaller farms. Previously, eighty per cent of EU subsidies in France went to twenty per cent of farms (many of them the big cereals farms around Paris). Only Britain and France took advantage of the new EU rule.

Now it is just Britain. The new centre-right French government has just abolished the "Robin Hood" farm tax.

Little surprise there. President Jacques Chirac and the largest French farmers' union, the FNSEA, dominated by the big, cereal-growing interests, have always been mutually generous supporters of one another.

During the presidential election campaign, Mr Chirac made a speech attacking Lionel Jospin's government for failing to prevent the disappearance of family farms in France. Now the government that President Chirac controls has scrapped a policy intended to do just that.

Quelle hypocrisie, Monsieur Chirac.

■ Pas Dans Mon Backyard
FEBRUARY 2003

Our favourite walk from our house in Normandy takes us into a hidden valley where a friendly black horse grazes and then up a muddy track onto wooded hills. The track, which must be hundreds of years old, is like a sloping tunnel between high hedges. You emerge, after a few minutes of wheezing and gasping through semi-darkness, to a mind-clearing view over the winding green valley of the River Orne.

In ten years' time, if a group of local politicians have their way, our muddy, sloping track will disappear beneath a four-lane road with embankments, viaducts and interchanges—a motorway in all but name. The *département* of Calvados plans to spend €280m to drive a fast road through the Orne valley and the Suisse Normande, massacring the most beautiful stretch of countryside in lower Normandy.

Of all the *communes* (broadly-speaking parishes) to be riven by the new road, the worst mangled will be ours: Culey-le-Patry, a string of villages and hamlets on the hills just south of the town of Thury Harcourt.

If the new road is built, our main village, standing on a hill-top, will be hemmed in on three sides by lorries travelling between Brittany and the Loire valley and the channel ports at Ouistreham and Le Havre.

Of course the villagers are up in arms. Some are, at any rate. Others welcome the new road because they believe it will bring jobs to the area and reduce the steady toll of deaths (nineteen a year) on the over-crowded road which runs through the valley of the Orne.

Even the pro-roaders in Culey have been startled to find, however, that the chosen route takes a huge detour to avoid the tourist centre of Clécy, and clambers all over our commune with the help of five enormous viaducts.

The other evening, I was one of sixty people in the village hall to hear a presentation by Jérôme Lépy, a calm young man who runs an association opposing the road. It turned into an evening of high rural drama.

The villagers, and even the mayor of the commune, had been led to believe that the route chosen by the Calvados council was provisional. They could have a final say in the road's course and push it away from the village. M. Lépy argued, convincingly, that they—and the mayor—had been "rolled in the flour" (tricked). One plan, showing a bundle of options, had been presented to the association of local mayors. Another, with a single, selected route, had been approved by the Calvados council.

A lesson in the workings of French bureaucracy and French democracy.

The mayor—a charming, gentle, tall, retired farmer, whose own family land will be divided by the road—stood up to denounce M. Lépy as a Jeremiah. He had it in writing from the Calvados council that the route of the road was still "flexible". The mayor went to fetch his letter. It turned out to be phrased in deliberately misleading bureaucratic terms but to say, in effect, that the route of the road could now only shift a hundred metres here or there.

Stupefaction in the hall. "It's not so. It's not so," the mayor said. "I stick by my letter. I still believe in my letter."

The room dissolved into a dozen private arguments. One of my neighbours, "Le Petit Michel", a short, talkative man with red hair, favoured the road. "France can't be a museum for tourists," he said. "We need other work here. We can't eat the landscape."

A woman behind me hissed: "But it's not Los Angeles here. We don't want the American Dream in Culey-le-Patry."

As foreigners, outsiders and second homers, we accept that our own concerns carry little weight. Le Petit Michel has a point (although it is not certain that the new road will bring jobs).

After the meeting, the mayor came to me and said: "You know, if this road is built, you can drive here all the way from Paris without seeing a traffic light."

Yes, I said, but I would not need to come all the way from Paris to find a house one mile from a motorway. La Suisse Normande was a national treasure, which could only be ruined once.

"Don't worry," he said. "I will have this roa
sure that it comes through the forests up the
disturb just a few pheasants."

"Up there?" I said, following the direction
that's where I live."

■ April is the Prettiest Month
APRIL 2003

In Normandy, April is the prettiest month. The apple trees are coming into flower. Primroses and cow-slips gleam along the road verges and beside the few hedgerows which have not yet been grubbed out as dairy farming succumbs to cereal murder.

Above our own hawthorn and holly hedge, we can admire the top of our neighbour Michel's cherry tree in snow-white blossom. It shines more dazzlingly than ever this year. Among its upper branches dangle eight compact discs, turning in the wind and glinting in the sun.

This is an ancient Norman ruse (at least as ancient as compact discs) for scaring away sparrows and preventing them from eating the tiny cherries as they form. (Sparrows, in case you've never seen them, are nondescript, small brown birds which were once common in Britain.)

The CDs were free samples which a friend of Michel's found dumped in a dustbin. Michel calls it his "arbre qui chante" or singing tree. He is looking forward to eating cherries this year.

Michel and Madeleine are already retired (he from a job as shift foreman at the Citroën transmission plant in Caen; she as caretaker of several blocks of flats). Like many French people of their age, they have benefited from generous early retirement rules, created to free jobs for young people. As the French population ages, this system is under challenge.

Michel and Madeleine's garden is a jumble of flowers and vegetables in classic cottage garden fashion. You used to see similar gardens, with no demarcation line between flowers and veg, when I was growing up in the rural north of England.

Normandy most country gardens are still organised, or ganised, in this way.

Michel and I are in friendly horticultural competition which he generally wins. This is partly because he is a much better gardener than I am. However, I suffer from the handicap of living 160 miles away most of the time, which makes watering and planting at precise times a little awkward.

My only victory over Michel so far has been my onions. He told me that all his attempts to grow onions in the rich, pebbly soil of the Norman hills had failed. Last year, I produced onions the size of large oranges, which have lasted—including some triumphant gifts to Michel and Madeleine—until now. This year, he is growing his own.

A constant source of amusement to Michel and Madeleine is my heroic attempt to create a lawn from the scruffy field which I inherited five summers ago. Rural Normans have little time for lawns. This may seem odd since they live in one of the finest grass-growing areas on the planet. In Normandy, it seems, grass is too plentiful to be treasured.

Norman gardens do have grassy areas, usually dotted at mathematical intervals by bushes or fruit trees. The concept of a neatly cropped lawn which you sit out on is regarded as an English eccentricity. Gardens are for working in. "C'est comme Wimbledon," Madeleine said when she saw my slightly improved lawn last summer—and then screamed with laughter.

The other day when messing with my sward—seeding a patch here, moving a lump of turf there—I found what looked like a flint arrow head. I mentioned my discovery to Claude, the shy man who looks after the grounds of the largest house in the village. He told me that workmen who had levelled a piece of earth next to our house last year had found a cache of Palaeolithic tools—dozens of them. They rapidly buried them again to prevent their work being interrupted by an archaeological dig.

So our little hill-top village—on these two pieces of evidence—has been inhabited for at least 7,000 years, from flint arrow heads to compact-disc bird scarers. Imagine my excitement when, lifting a piece of battered turf the other day, I found, three inches deep, a large, time-blackened coin. I rubbed it vigorously, expecting a Louis d'Or or maybe even something Roman.

It was a two-euro piece, which, even without resort to carbon-dating, I can confidently date as approximately sixteen months old (or less).

■ The Saint in the Hedge
MAY 2003

I must have walked past the place a hundred times. My wife, more observant than I am, had spotted the little shrine inside a hawthorn hedge, but had thought little of it. Road-side shrines are common in our part of Normandy.

It was not until our next door neighbour, Madeleine, began to take our nine-year-old daughter to visit the tiny shrine, situated nowhere in particular, beside a quiet lane, 400 metres from our village, that I went to look for it myself.

Deep inside the hedge is a wooden box a foot high, with a pointed roof, like a miniature dog kennel or a bird house. Inside there is a brown wooden carving of the Virgin and Child. In front, there is a pile of flowers—wild flowers and garden flowers—brought as offerings by local pilgrims, mostly by Madeleine and her grown-up daughters and now by my daughter, Clare.

Madeleine visits the shrine—she calls it "La Sainte Vierge"—secretly and defiantly. Her husband, Michel, is a Jehovah's Witness (an uncharacteristically jolly Jehovah's Witness). He disapproves of his wife's lingering Catholicism. Madeleine never goes to mass but few French Catholics do these days. When she visits the hedge shrine, she tells Michel, rather grandly, that she is making a "tour of the village".

There are two other shrines in our commune: more elaborate affairs, grottoes made of stone, encasing white plaster figures of Mary two feet high, surrounded by plastic and paper flowers and sometimes by real ones. Why should a commune with 300 people—maybe 600 in the early part of the last century—have three shrines to the Virgin? Why are they still visited and remembered when the church in the main village, a mile from our hamlet, is mostly unused?

The last parish priest left more than twenty years ago. We are now part of a group parish, with three priests covering what used to be 35 parishes. Even in Normandy and Brittany, relatively more faithful than the rest of the country, Catholicism, as an organised, participating religion, is dying slowly. According to the poll published last week in *Le Monde*, 62 per cent of French people still identify themselves as Catholic (67 per cent in 1994) but only twelve per cent say they go to mass regularly (fourteen per cent in 1994).

The vacuum has been filled—up to a point and especially in rural areas—by new faiths and dotty sects. The Jehovah's Witnesses are especially strong in rural France.

And yet the small Catholic shrines flourish. The hedge shrine near our village was, according to local memory, built by a young man just before he went to the trenches in the 1914–18 war. By building a shrine to Mary, he hoped to survive. He did.

After his death, the shrine was kept up by local people. A couple of years ago, one of Madeleine's married daughters noticed that the original statuette of the virgin was broken. She replaced it. The box was recently rebuilt by Bruno, a middle-aged teacher who was brought up by his grandmother in the village. He is now a secular, left-voting, successful professional who lives in Paris and comes back to the village once or twice a year. He and his sister, Patricia, another Parisian professional, always visit the hedge shrine.

An association called Oratoires has been created in France to help to preserve local shrines. On its website—www. amisdesoratoires.com—the organisation argues that such places are, in a minor key, as much a part as the religious heritage of France as medieval cathedrals. It calls for a national effort to recognise and conserve them.

This seems to me to miss the point. If local people lose interest in such shrines, they have no reason to exist.

The devotion to "oratoires" is, partly at least, a devotion to local tradition; a way of remembering the way things were. They are Catholic shrines but they are also a link with something much older, something pre-Christian. They have become—or maybe always were—shrines to local memories, a way of celebrating, and worshipping, Mary as a local deity, someone in the hedge up the road, not in a church seven miles away.

■ Killers in the Forest
JANUARY 2005

The weather in Normandy has been absurdly mild and bright. The other day I walked through the ancient beech and oak forest which runs for fifteen miles along the ridge of the hills just behind our house.

With no leaves to filter the sunshine, the lichen and moss on the bark of the giant trees shone like stained glass. The magic of a forest walk in January! The tranquillity of a weekend in the Norman hills!

Within twenty minutes I began to fear for my life. In the distance but growing nearer, I heard the characteristic sound of the French countryside in winter: the mournful, medieval call of hunting horns and the crack of high-performance hunting rifles.

The killers were loose in the forest.

I have nothing, in principle, against hunting. In the case of Tony Blair versus the *Daily Telegraph*, the English Countryside and Fox Hunting, I am, on the whole, on the side of the *Telegraph*. French hunters, though, are a shifty, aggressive and irresponsible bunch. They drive plain white vans and dress in paramilitary uniforms, like a sort of Bosnian Serb militia. They leer menacingly at passers-by. If you say "bonjour", they stare and do not reply.

In my experience, genuinely rural French people do not hunt very much: "la chasse" is a preserve of middle-aged men from small towns and the suburbs.

With extraordinary, and depressing, frequency, the hunters shoot one another. Sometimes they shoot walkers or cyclists. Occasionally they hit an animal.

As the sound of horns and rifles drew nearer, I imagined myself starring in one of the short dispatches which you find on the French news wire, AFP, each weekend at this time of year. "A man of 55 was mortally injured by a hunter during a boar-hunt yesterday...

Just as an animal was breaking cover, the hunter heard a noise in the bushes and fired. The rambler, hit in the femoral artery, bled to death before help arrived..."

There have already been twenty human deaths since the boar-hunting season began in October and 254 hunting deaths in the last seven years. For some reason this death toll is regarded as acceptable. The hunting lobby is politically powerful. Armed lobbies usually are.

The present centre-right government has been busy dismantling the legal safety-catches on hunting which do exist: such as the ban on hunting in twilight and the "hunting-free day" on Wednesdays introduced by the previous Socialist-led government.

The pro-animal and pro-rambler lobbies, although gaining in strength, have no illusions about their immediate prospects. Olivier Rousseau, president of the Association pour la Protection des Animaux Sauvages, sent an empty cartridge case to every member of the National Assembly this month. He asked them to support his idea of a Sunday ban on hunting to allow walkers and nature lovers to enjoy the countryside without fear of gun-shot wounds. "There is no chance of winning this battle yet," he says. "In rural France we live in an armed dictatorship, the dictatorship of the hunters. But there are many more walkers and nature lovers than there are fundamentalist hunters and, one day, we will prevail."

To escape the Norman hunters, I took a detour along a road, meaning to cut back through the forest later. By the time I approached my turning through the woods, it was growing dark. The hunters were still hooting and shooting. Two of them, in khaki jackets and caps, stood at the entrance to the path, holding their rifles.

It is against the law in France to shoot near a road or a public foot-path. The hunters frequently ignore the law, which is only enforced after they happen to shoot someone. In any case, boar hunters use rifles capable of hitting a target two kilometres away. So what does "near" a footpath mean?

"Is it safe to go through?" I asked. They looked at each other and smirked. "You can risk it if you want to," one said. I carried on along the road, making a two-mile detour.

Later, I checked the AFP dispatches. Three people had been shot in hunting accidents that weekend, two hunters and a rambler: an excellent bag even for France at this time of year.

■ Pas Dans Mon Backyard 2
JANUARY 2005

On the edge of the forest a couple of kilometres from our house, there is a lonely crossroads. If you pause, on foot or in a car, you gaze over ridge after ridge of green hillsides and woodlands.

Two years ago, the Calvados council decided that this magical spot should be buried in concrete and bitumen and road-signs and roundabouts and viaducts. The little crossroads was to become a complex interchange on a four-lane road, built to motorway standards.

The plan to build a fast road through the valley of the Orne has provoked a fierce and fascinating quarrel. The dispute is quintessentially local but also universal. Battle-lines have been drawn but not always where you would expect them. Villages have been set against towns; village against village; family against family.

Our own commune was to be desecrated by embankments and slip roads and three large viaducts. Michel and Madeleine were appalled, but resigned. "Everything will be ruined," they said. "But what can we do? In France, when 'they' decide to build a road, 'they' build a road. It may take ten years or fifteen years but the road will be built. Nothing here will be same again."

Other local people seem to take an almost perverse delight in the despoliation of the countryside. One talkative neighbour in the next hamlet is a passionate member of the pro-road faction. "Of course the countryside is important. But you can't eat the countryside," he says. "We are not an Indian reservation. We don't want to sell beads. Tourism is not everything. If we don't get the road, we will lose all our factories and jobs. We will become just a garden for Parisians and tourists."

Despite my neighbours' fears, "they"—ie the local powers that be—have not had it their own way. Thanks to two laws on local consultation passed in the last decade, there has been a "débat public", or public inquiry, with open meetings and an interactive internet site.

The inquiry, a perfect model of local democracy, rejected the idea of a dual carriageway or "quatre voies" through the Suisse Normande. It suggested that a fast, four-lane road should be built up to the edge of the valley from the south and another from the north. In the twelve beautiful miles in between, the existing D-road (i.e. B-road) should be upgraded.

This seemed like a judgement of Solomon that all sides could accept. In December, the Calvados council went along with the recommendation. All seemed settled.

A few days ago, "they" struck back. Two small towns to the south of the valley insisted that they must have a four-lane road all the way to the coast and the national motorway network. The mayor of one of the towns, who is also vice president of the Calvados council, announced that "upgrading" the existing road must, and would, mean a dual-carriageway.

Opposition groups fear that they have been tricked. Once the fast roads are built north and south of the valley, "they" will insist that they have a right to join up the dots. Hostilities, complicated by shifts in local politics, have broken out all over again.

Since the original scheme was announced, the Regional Council for the whole of lower Normandy has shifted from right to left. The Calvados council remains centre-right. The new leadership of the Region, which would have to pay half of the €300m cost, seems unconvinced by the arguments for a fast road.

I am definitely anti-road but I accept that the decision belongs mostly to local people. When asked my opinion, I say that I hope that France—in this and countless other planning decisions in the next decade—will not repeat Britain's, and especially England's, mistakes.

Unlike suburbanised, concretised and bitumenised south and central England, much of the French countryside has preserved its beauty, its wildlife and its flora. The annual carpets of wild primroses are already appearing on the verges of la Suisse Normande. Cowslips are a few weeks away.

Do local people really want to throw all that away?

▪ Rural History Lesson 2
MAY 2005

This is the story of a white bullock called Alain, who is the last link in an unbroken line of cattle stretching back at least a thousand years.

Alain is a large, white Charolais steer (in other words a bull with no balls) who belongs to a neighbour, Marcel. Christened by another neighbour, a retired postman who adores animals, Alain is an immense, dopy creature, who rarely moves. He stands in his field and stares at passers-by in the sullen manner of all cows and most teenagers.

When he retired from dairy farming, Marcel retained a few beef animals to keep himself busy and to qualify for a hill farming subsidy from the European Union. He has been selling the cows off gradually. Alain is the last one.

Since we came to the area, cereals and pesticides and weed-killers have advanced year by year from the valley bottoms higher into the hills. They have driven out hedges and cows and especially—sadly—the tricoloured, white, brown and black, Norman breed of dairy cows which helped to make Calvados one of the greatest milk and cheese-producing areas in the world.

Our village is typical of the region; and of France as a whole. The myth, often propagated in the British press, that France is still honeycombed with tiny "inefficient" farms living on EU subsidies, is absurd.

In Calvados alone, 400 farms disappear each year. The number of dairy cattle in the *département* which gave the world Camembert and Livarot is falling by 10,000 animals a year (forty per cent down in the last twenty years).

By my reckoning and local researches, our village has been a farming community since William the Conqueror lived down the road in Caen. It has been a village of some kind since the Stone Age.

Cows—resident cows, belonging to villagers—have lived here for ten centuries at least. Leaving aside the shifting population of young cows from other villages—mere bovine tourists—Alain is the village's last cow.

The other evening as I strolled down the lane with my daughters, we found Alain standing beside the "gate" from his field to the "main road". Both terms are relative. The gate consists of four strands of barbed wire on sticks. The road has an average of one car every thirty minutes.

Alain was unusually agitated, for him. There were young cows frisking in the next field. As we turned away, he took a huge leap—probably the most strenuous piece of exercise he has ever undertaken—and landed painfully astride the barbed-wire gate.

I ran, equally an unusual exercise for me, to warn Marcel. He is the least friendly of all our neighbours. He never smiles except when, in his capacity as deputy mayor and chairman of the commune's "festivities committee", he presides over a fireworks display or sausage grilling. Then Marcel wears a straw cowboy hat and a grin. We call him the Chairman of Fun.

Marcel was extremely grateful that I had informed him of Alain's plight. If he had escaped onto the road, he could have caused an accident, for which Marcel would have been responsible. "Usually, he is very calm. He gives no trouble," he said, propping up the gate and switching on an electric fence, which was previously only decorative. "The other cows must have excited him. In any case, he will be going in July. He's my last one, you know."

Yes, I knew.

Alain is Marcel's last cow, after seventy years of farming, man and boy. He is the village's last cow, after 1,000 years of "inefficient" agriculture: i.e. farming with hedges, without chemicals and on a human scale.

■ Travels with Donkeys
AUGUST 2005

One of the peculiarities of rural France, heavily dependent on tourists, is that many things close down in late summer, when the tourists arrive. I defy you to find an operating riding-school or pony-trekking centre in lower Normandy—which is classical French horse country—in the first half of August.

Having promised a horsicultural holiday to my daughters and their cousins from England, I was in deep trouble. I had fallen at the first fence; the stable door was closed; all the horsey types had bolted.

In the small print of the local attractions guide, I discovered what I thought was my salvation: "Donkey trekking", it said, "Accompanied or unaccompanied".

I hired three donkeys for an afternoon.

Donkeys have a poor reputation. They are said to be slow, stubborn, lazy, uncomfortable to ride. My wife warned that we would spend the whole time tugging on a rope with a static ass on the other end. No, I said, donkeys are now all the rage in France, Look on the internet. Scores of people—and donkey fan clubs—bray the therapeutic advantages of getting close to donkeys. The French have even invented a name for it: "asinothérapie", the calming influence of donkeys. There is also "asinomédiation"—the teaching of social skills and other virtues to children and teenagers through contact with donkeys.

Besides, I said, donkeys are part of the history of Normandy. From the early Middle Ages, they were used to bring the region's most famous products, milk, cheese, apples and cider, to market in the towns. There is a recognised "Norman" breed of donkeys, grey and larger than usual, almost as big as a mule. Even the name "Calvados", according to the official website of the *département*, is thought to be a corruption of the Latin for "bare donkey's back".

And so we were introduced to our donkeys: Okie, Olympe and Offenbach. The last two were large grey donkeys of the Norman race. The first was smaller and browner.

Their owner was a man with a drooping Asterix moustache. Belligerent facial hair of this kind has become universal (among men at least) in rural France. The fashion was originated by the small farmers' leader and McDonalds-basher, José Bové.

Donkey trekking was simple, the Bové look-alike explained. Up to a maximum of two children could go on a donkey's back. An adult must lead each animal. Pulling made them uncooperative. Gentle persuasion was best.

Each adult must carry a ski-stick to place in front of the donkey's nose to discourage running away on downward slopes. There were two red flags to warn cars on public roads. We were also given a large sheet of aluminium paper which, failing all else, could be waved behind the donkeys' bottoms if they refused to move.

It took us 45 minutes to reach the top of the first slope, even with the help of the aluminium, the donkeys' owner, and his wife and son. Once the animals had accepted that they could not loaf in their field all day, they moved reasonably well, on the flat. They detested hills, up or down.

Walking with donkeys through the high-hedged tracks, centuries old, you could imagine yourself in the Middle Ages. Emerging onto the ridge-tops was an exhilarating experience—even with children complaining that donkeys are less comfortable than bicycles. We could admire the rolling light-brown countryside of Calvados, supposedly one of twenty (out of 96) départements in France to avoid an outright drought this year. Tell that to my lawn, or to my tomatoes.

A two-hour trek took the best part of four. The calming influence of donkeys was not apparent to me, my wife or her sister or her husband. The animals refused to go down the final slope to their own home. Patience, like the grass in my lawn, wore thin.

After much heaving and cursing, one of the animals suddenly put on a spurt. The others followed.

"Did you use the aluminium sheet?" I asked.

"No," my wife said grimly. "This." She held up a stick.

Next day, we heard that two of our donkeys had run away from home. They ran?

———

Walking up to our village one day, I was given a lift by our local wood merchant in his crumpled blue van. The wood man is equally crumpled—in his seventies, short and bent. He looks like a Sicilian Godfather but is the sweetest of men. He had a metal detector in the back of the van. "Looking for treasure?" I teased him.

"No," he said. "If you cut an old tree around here, you have to use the metal detector first... If you hit a piece of metal, the power saw is f...ed in the air and you are f....d in the air with it."

Our part of Calvados was the scene of intense British-German fighting in August 1944. Any tree more than 61 years old is likely to be honeycombed with bullets and shrapnel.

■ A Country Home
AUGUST 2006

Something new is happening in the once frozen world of French rural real estate, at least in Normandy.

There used to be two clear markets, which hardly overlapped. First, there was the domestic and local market for modern, bijou bungalows—"pavillons" in French—invariably painted pale peach, with orange roofs. Then there was the market for "old stones with possibilities" (roof preferable but not essential). This was partly a Parisian weekenders' market. Mostly it was the preserve of British immigrants and holiday homers.

Over the last year, in lower Normandy, the genres have become confused. The pale peach bungalows are still spreading like bindweed. At the same time, French people, even local French people, have begun to discover the delights of restoring old stone buildings. Within a couple of miles of our house there are half a dozen abandoned, or under-used, former farm cottages or smallholdings under reconstruction this summer. All the owners are French.

As a result, the supply of cheap, rescuable buildings onto the local real estate market is beginning to dry up. A new market is emerging, aimed almost exclusively at the British. It might be called the "hovel market".

We took a friend, vaguely interested in acquiring a Norman retreat, to see a tumbledown which had appeared in a local estate agent's window. At the beginning of the summer, it was advertised ecstatically: "For the lover of nature. Rare. To be seized. €33,000." By the end of August, the description has been toned down to "possible two room house, €27,500", in other words about £19,000.

The building consisted of a small stable, ten feet by ten, with a corrugated iron roof. Twenty yards away, there was another set of crumbling old walls, with no roof. The land in between was owned, inconveniently, by two other people. Neither has any plans to sell. There was a possible "garden" three feet wide in front. Nothing behind. There was no view, except onto a house on the other side of the lane: a bijou, peach-coloured bungalow with an orange roof.

As we contemplated the possibilities and complexities of this divided site, the owner of the bungalow came to investigate. "You are not going to live in *that*, are you?" he asked grumpily.

Er, no, probably not. However, Monsieur Grumpy should not count on no-one ever buying it. What could you hope to acquire in a pretty part of rural Britain for £19,000?

In truth, there are still hundreds of empty or tumbledown properties in rural France, abandoned as the farm population has fallen from over 3,000,000 to under 500,000 in the last forty years. Many of these properties, ranging from pretty little cottages to Sleeping Beauty châteaux—cannot come to market because they are jointly owned by squabbling siblings under France's bossy and complex inheritance laws. If one family member refuses to sell, nothing can be sold.

Think twice before buying a hovel without-a-view, however. A change in the inheritance law went through the French parliament this summer. It takes effect in January. The new law allows a quarrelsome, property-owning family to take a two-thirds majority vote to sell off an unwanted piece of property. Expect an avalanche of first time offers.

■ Feel Good Facteur
JULY 2007

The children call him "Postman Patrice". I call him the "feel good facteur". He is one of the most relentlessly positive and enthusiastic people that I have ever met. *Facteur* means postman in French. Thus, the "feel good facteur". Get it?

His real name is Christian Sabri. He is our postman in Normandy.

He retired this weekend after travelling the same 63-kilometre route through the hill villages of Calvados for 32 years. Rain or shine, summer or winter, M. Sabri was always as bright and charming as his yellow La Poste van. He is retiring at the age of sixty, only eight years older than France's "young", new and equally enthusiastic president, Nicolas Sarkozy. (All public servants in France retire at sixty, except for politicians. They go on forever.)

I chatted to M. Sabri about the changes that he had seen in the Norman countryside since 1975. His answers were not quite what I had expected. "There are more people now than when I started, many more," he said. "But they are not country people. They are town people, who live in the country... Everywhere you look, there are new houses going up or old ones being restored. When I started my rounds, the countryside around here was full of ruined houses. Not any more. At one time, it was only the English who would buy a house without a roof. Now the French, too, have found a taste for old stones. They may not be country people but they want to feel that they are living the country lifestyle."

M. Sabri's observation about the new flood of "urban" residents in rural France—commuters or internet "remote" workers—is backed by national statistics. Ten years ago, France was still worrying about the "desertification" of rural areas. Now the countryside is gaining 60,000 new inhabitants a year. More than eight million French people say that they are actively considering a move from the town to the country. The third biannual "fair" for urban would-be emigrants to rural France was staged in Limoges at the weekend.

Some of the most remote country areas—in the centre of France and in the unfashionable north-east—are still losing population. Everywhere else is being re-colonised, especially the so-called "rurbain" zones within thirty miles of big towns.

All this is inevitable and positive in its way, but also depressing. The same thing happened decades ago in the more densely populated European countries: Britain, Germany, Belgium, the Netherlands. It is better that the countryside should be mildly surburbanised rather than simply abandoned. And M. Sabri agrees. Up to a point. Irredeemably positive though he is, he mourns the passing of the traditional, rural France that still existed in the mid-1970s.

There are six farms remaining in the commune where we have our small house. M. Sabri could list the names of all the active farmers to whom he delivered mail in 1975. There were 25 of them. "When I started, everything was still cows and hedges and apple trees and people working in the fields," he said. "Now it is mostly cereals and machinery. You can drive around a whole day and see no-one in the fields at all. In the early days, people had time to chat. At sausage-making time, I had to eat a little piece of sausage at every farm. Now people are friendly but always in a tearing hurry."

The changes began, he remembered, in the late 1970s when there was an official drive to "redraw" the boundaries of small fields. Calvados was once famous for its maze of ancient hedgerows. This was the "bocage" country which caused so many problems to the allied armies in the summer of 1944. Some of those ancient hedges remain. Perhaps eighty per cent have been rooted out to create bigger and more efficient fields.

"That's progress," said M. Sabri, the feel good facteur. "Or perhaps it's not progress. Things change. Though they don't always get better."

■ My French Son
AUGUST 2007

The extraordinary characters that once adorned our small constellation of villages are vanishing one by one.

Maybe, like rare butterflies, they cannot adapt to the creeping tide of suburbanisation. Year by year, the pale peach bungalows advance southwards from Caen. Little by little, the authentic colour of the countryside is washed away.

Bernard Gosselin was a charming, gentle, intelligent man, whose life began in high drama during the battle of Normandy in 1944. His life ended equally dramatically this summer.

M. Gosselin, whom we have met before, was a successful dairy farmer until he retired last year. One of his great passions was flying. He had two light aircraft. The first he built from a kit and painted bright yellow, like Norman butter. Bernard converted an absurdly sloping field into an air-strip, complete with wind-sock and airport signs. He would fly on still, bright mornings and afternoons, after milking his cows.

One of Bernard's other great passions was the local history of the Second World War. This is not surprising. He, himself, was part of it.

In July 1944 Bernard was born in the grim, square farmhouse which stands just over my garden hedge. The battle of Normandy was raging twenty kilometres to the north. The only civilian doctor in the area had been injured in allied bombing. Bernard's parents, Albert and Emilia Gosselin, were distraught. Their three previous children had died in infancy.

Unable to find even a midwife, Albert Gosselin appealed in desperation to German troops who were drinking in the bar in the main village of the commune. To his horror, M. Gosselin found that the carousing Germans were from the SS, Hitler's infamous praetorian guard. Less than a month earlier, soldiers from another SS division had massacred all the men, woman and children of a village in central France.

The SS ninth division doctor, Bernhard Runge, had been amputating the limbs of wounded soldiers until the day before. He agreed, nevertheless, to deliver the French baby.

Almost all local people willingly forgave the Gosselins this act of enforced collaboration. A few of them never did.

Twenty-eight years later, in the spring of 1972, Bernard Gosselin was sitting on his tractor ploughing a field. A tall, elderly man with curly, grey hair approached and flagged him down.

Bernard recounted the story to me three years ago, for an article on the 60th anniversary of D-Day.

"He said: 'Is your name Bernard and were you born in July 1944?' I said: 'yes'. I had already recognised the German accent and my heart was racing."

"He asked me: 'Do you know who I was? Do you know who I really was? I was the SS. I was the wicked SS.'"

There began an unlikely 25-year friendship between the two men—a spiritually troubled ex-Nazi, who had been a minor defendant at the Nuremberg war crimes trials, and a successful

Norman dairy farmer. The friendship ended only with Dr Runge's death in 1997 at the age of 93.

Every summer until 1994, when he became too ill to travel, Dr Runge would spend several weeks living in the Norman hills with the man that he called "my French son".

Bernard Gosselin's life ended this summer a few miles south of the house where he was born. He took off in his small plane from a local airfield and was seen to turn back, as if he had mechanical problems or had been taken ill. He crashed before he could land.

Bernard always took a special interest in allied airmen who were shot down over our part of Normandy. He helped three years ago to arrange a visit by the family of a Canadian fighter-bomber pilot who is buried in the churchyard in the next village.

Bernard Gosselin now lies in our village cemetery beside the Commonwealth War grave of Flight Sergeant MKH Wilson of the Royal Australian Air Force. Flight Sergeant Wilson came all the way from Brisbane to die when his aircraft, brought down by flak, crashed near our village on 14 June 1944. Three weeks later, just over the hill, an SS doctor delivered a French baby...

■ A Wife-Swap Shop
AUGUST 2008

Our nearest town in Normandy is a sad little place which has never fully recovered from the summer of 1944. In June of that year, it was pointlessly bombed by the British. In August, it was partially burned by the SS.

Sixty-four years later, shops and restaurants are struggling to survive. The population is ageing and glum. Excitement, other than month-old films at the municipally-owned cinema, is hard to find.

A few days ago work began on renovating a long-closed shop on the town's main square. Would this be yet another estate agent to sell houses without roofs to the British? Or something more interesting?

An elaborately hand-written red and white sign appeared in the window. The sign read: "Ici bientôt, Club Echangiste." Opening here soon, Wife-Swapping Club.

"Clubs Echangistes" are an accepted part of the entertainment industry in the wicked big cities of France. Paris has more than sixty of them, including one near to our apartment in a notoriously dull part of the capital. This club, a converted hotel, advertises itself "for couples only... car-parking available, air-conditioning in some rooms, Thai-themed evenings and other special events, smart-dress essential." The smart dress is required only when you arrive.

Wife-swapping doubtless occurs in small towns in France but an officially proclaimed wife-swapping club—next to the Notary's office, a few steps from the town hall—seemed too good to be true. On closer inspection, the red and white sign in the tiny shop front added the following details. "On peut apporter son mari, son chien, son âne, sa belle-mère". (You can bring your spouse, your dog, your donkey, your mother-in-law.)

A separate sign read: "Fully booked until 20 August."

Was this meant to be a satire on the submerged sexual curiosities of rural life? An oblique attack on the evil of big cities? I asked the man who was painting the inside of the shop. He shrugged. He denied, straight-faced, that he was responsible for the sign. "It's meant to be funny, I think," he said.

Yesterday, a new sign had appeared next to the other ones. "Through pressure of demand, we will open on Sunday. After Mass."

———

Such oddities are part of the inexhaustible charm of France. Here is a more graceful example.

I was travelling on a train the other day from Clermont Ferrand to Paris, trying to compose a difficult letter to a friend whose mother had died. I looked up as we passed an abandoned wayside station.

On a derelict grain silo there was a large blue and white advertising banner which read: "On n'est pas seul. Il y a des Mots." The word Mots had a capital M. We are not alone. There are Words.

Was this part of some kind of poetry-by-the-lineside exercise by the state-owned railway company, the SNCF? Apparently not. Just the work of an individual, or a group of people who wanted travellers between Clermont Ferrand and Paris to know that they were not alone.

■ Lament for a Lost Landscape
APRIL 2010

A long stretch of ancient hedgerow—maybe 300 metres, maybe 200 years old—has been torn out close to our village this spring. The mutilated roadside now looks like a gum with no teeth in it. As a result, the farmer from the next commune, who rents the land, will be able to plant another couple of rows of triffids. Triffids are what we call the tall, ugly stalks of maize which have progressively invaded the Calvados countryside in the last decade. The maize is grown for cows to eat. In Normandy the maize has gobbled up the cows—and the hedges. Just over half the dairy farms in some of the finest dairy country in the world have disappeared in the last fifteen years (including both the dairy farms in our village).

Lower Normandy used to be celebrated for its hedges—the "bocage country" in which tiny fields were enclosed by lateral woodlands as thick as castle walls. Most of the "bocage" has long gone. In the 1970s the French government encouraged farmers to swap, and then join up, their jumbled scraps of land. The hedges were torn out to make bigger fields.

In recent years many of the remaining hedges around the enlarged fields have fallen to the cereal killers. Our tiny hamlet was an island of relative, hedge-enclosed beauty when we bought our house twelve years ago. The destruction of a first long stretch of hedge suggests that our immunity is over.

Triffids are not the only invaders. There are new blotches of bright colour shining in the Calvados countryside this spring: not primroses and cowslips but fresh constellations of pale peach or cream "pavillons", which may be visible from the moon.

The suburbs of the city of Caen, twenty miles to the north, are scattering bungalow seeds which are taking root in what was, until a few years ago, deep countryside.

There are no peach bungalows in our hamlet yet but a score of them have been built in the main village, just over a mile away. When the hedges go, can bungalows be far behind?

PART THREE

The Education System

When we moved to Paris, we took the decision to plunge our two children, then aged nearly seven and nearly three, into the French education system. Bilingual or international schools were available but we shunned them. Or rather, it was my wife who was convinced, and convinced me, that this was the right route to take. International schools can breed rootless kids who, far from acquiring broad horizons, come to hate their host countries. French schools, Margaret said, would give our children French friends and make them feel part of the country that they lived in.

She has been proved absolutely correct, even though dealing with French schools and French teachers has not proved easy for her—or me. The children (we quickly gained a third child, born in France) have done well in the French system. They have made French friends. We—an unexpected bonus—have also made French friends through meeting the parents of our children's friends.

Observing French schools and French kids has—alongside my Norman connection—given me more insight into France and Frenchness than a host of "sources" in the world of official politics.

As for the nature of the French education system, I will let the articles speak for themselves. The French, especially right-of-centre politicians, would have you believe that French schools have become a sink of undisciplined, post-1968, anything goes, learn-what-you-like sloppiness. This is silly and a classic example of the French trying to reform the myth rather than the reality.

The days when French children sat in rows and intoned the same lessons at the same times from Cannes to Calais have (if they ever existed) long gone. But the system remains, if anything, a little too obsessed with the rote learning of facts, definitions and theories.

■ A Kiss from Teacher
JANUARY 1997

We had, as a precaution, gently terrified Charles with tales of the formality of schools in France. The children, we told him, sit and walk in geometrical precise rows, just like the orphan girls in the Madeline books. They are obliged to learn long and complicated lessons by heart. Their manners are impeccable. The teachers are strict, though kind. But mostly strict.

His new school looks precisely the part: an austere, educational factory in nicotine-coloured concrete, occupying the length of a Parisian block. Two-year-olds are fed into one end and eighteen-year-olds emerge from the other. Charles, who is seven next month, seemed uncharacteristically subdued on his first morning.

Almost nothing, it turned out, was as promised by his parents. Sybille, his class teacher, greeted him like a favourite nephew. First a big hug, then a kiss on the cheek, not a peck, but a long, intimate, sloppy embrace. Charles was amazed. This had never happened in Putney.

He and his classmates do sit in rows, but rather jumbled rows; they do learn some things by heart, mostly poems. They also do a great deal of singing and learning by touch and play. Their manners are not impeccable. Once released from their lessons, they are very pushy and sharp-elbowed. But they are, after all, little Parisians.

Charles loves his new school, even though he has no more than a few words of French. His proudest moment was when the school-approved dress-maker finally sent his navy-blue school smock, which is worn at all times by primary boys and girls. It makes him look somewhere between a Tsarist peasant and a chic hairdresser.

His little sister, not quite three, who attends the pre-school or *maternelle* department on the ground floor, is not so convinced. She loves the interminable singing but is irritated that no-one can understand her previously perfectly acceptable talking. She cannot talk French, she has decided, because she does not have French teeth.

One morning, Clare became so disillusioned that she wandered off to try and find her big brother, who at least has English teeth. After a hue and cry, she was intercepted trotting happily along the upstairs corridor. Her mother was later ticked off for having a child who had wilfully got herself *perdue* in this way.

We are adjusting our stereotypes to coincide with reality: the school's bewildering alternation between officiousness and inefficiency, formality and warmth is, it seems, *typiquement français*. Rules and lists and forms proliferate but, unlike Germany, not all need to be obeyed all the time.

Before moving to Paris, we had changed our minds several times about what to do with the kids. An international or bilingual school would have been easier for them. But children who go to such schools (however well run) can have the worst of both worlds: they are torn from their familiar surroundings and friends but they never truly belong to their new country.

We were recommended to try a particular French school— Catholic, therefore private, but heavily state-subsidised and following the state curriculum—which is used to taking English-speaking kids. Friends who have already been the same educational route warn that our children will learn not just to speak French, but how to be French.

But the intense Frenchness of the French education system is beginning to be criticised in France. Although a fine system in many ways, the critics say, the emphasis on a cultural education for the whole child is a disadvantage in the modern, globally competitive world. It turns out, they say, a nation of literate and argumentative people, full of self-esteem but with little sense of enterprise, except, maybe, how to get the last seat on the bus.

Better, the critics imply, that France should be churning out a new race of computer nerds, like the US, or accountants, like Britain. I wonder. After two weeks, Charles still adores his school. He has a few more words of French. But is he learning how to be French yet?

I was passing the time on the long walk to school the other morning by speculating on possible Franglais street names. The Rue de Remarques? The Rue de Noises? This previously gentle little boy looked at me pityingly and gave me a sharp, Gallic elbow in the ribs.

■ A Rabbit for the Weekend
MARCH 1997

For Charles, social acceptance in Paris was having a rabbit as a house-guest. "Black", the rabbit in question, belongs to Charles's class of seven-year-olds. Like some floppy-eared King Lear, he spends his weekends with a different child in turn. It is the greatest of honours to receive him.

Our children will shortly have spent three months, or one whole term, in their French school. In all this time, Charles had never been awarded the custody of Black (whose name is Black, not Noir).

Last Friday evening Charles's teacher announced that, after a few ups and downs, largely because of language problems, he was starting to "do very well" at school, especially with his writing. She presented his mother with the reward: a black rabbit in a dropping-strewn cage, which she had to carry, averting her nose, one mile back to the flat.

At every third step, the cage door lurched open but, fortunately, Black had the good sense not to risk escape through the Parisian traffic.

Doing well with his writing does not mean that Charles is shaping up as the new Baudelaire (yet). His French, though building steadily like a second skin behind his English, is still rudimentary. Those words that he does know, he pronounces beautifully, with the guttural roll that no adult, native Anglophone can ever quite capture. But he still puts the words together without verbs, like a toddler learning language for the first time.

Clare, his three-year-old sister, is more resistant to French, although she no longer insists that she will never speak the language because she is not equipped with French teeth. Instead, she demands, "Why don't they speak normal?" Even she is absorbing French unconsciously. She delights in pronouncing her name in the way that her teacher pronounces it, not Clare but "Clarrreachh".

In England, Charles was taught to form his letters in pencil with careful spaces in between. The fact that he is now "writing well" means that he has finally come to grips with French joined-up copper plate and leaky fountain pens. French children learn to read and write later than British children but skip the baby-writing stage completely.

Charles's class spends an inordinate amount of time (whole mornings it seems) doing "dictée"—copying the teacher's handwriting from the blackboard or an exercise book. They are never asked to compose anything from their memory or imagination. At his school in London, Charles was always being given difficult, and often very interesting, creative writing tasks. But he was never sufficiently drilled—so it seemed to us—in the mechanical business of letter-formation. We were told that this would come naturally.

From the age of five, he wrestled, in huge, uneven letters, with projects such as the Spanish Armada, the Second World War and the history of theatre. The transition from pupil to *élève* was, therefore, awkward. For weeks Charles's efforts at joined-up writing looked as if Black had walked across the page with ink on his paws.

His teacher put forbearing remarks like "courage" and "continue" at the end of his work. Finally, it seemed, both she and he got bored simultaneously and agreed that he would now make an enormous effort to write as neatly as the other pupils. After that, his exercise book came home with elegant, small writing, full of whirls and curls that a fastidious British twelve-year-old would have been proud of.

Madame's remarks were "Bravo" and "Splendide". All of which points, in its own small way, to disparities in the French and British approaches to education. "French children don't seem to learn very much," remarked Charles on one occasion. For children of his age, the curriculum comes down to the five r's, reading, writing, arithmetic, art and (in Catholic schools like his), religion.

French primary schools, though not as regimented as they once were, still exist in the era of drilling and rote-learning beloved of the anti-modernists in the education debate in Britain. It would be wrong to say that individuality is discouraged. It is a warm and happy school. But conformism is definitely encouraged.

Even at the older levels, right up to the *baccalauréat*, the emphasis in French schools is on absorbing facts and pre-packaged concepts. Little creativity, or imagination, or independent thinking, is demanded. This old-fashioned approach, which is sometimes portrayed in Britain as belonging to a golden age, is now criticised by some in France as a trap and a betrayal.

In the most recent global league tables French education— especially in maths—comes out pretty well. But French children lag in science and especially computer science. Although formally excellent, the critics say, French schools fail to generate young people with the adaptability, creativity and flexibility of mind to cope with the demands of the modern world.

Some critics blame the school system for the high levels of youth unemployment in France (which probably has far more to do with the high social costs of employing anyone at all).

We are reserving judgement. On the whole, we believe Charles has benefited from the French approach. We feared he was losing his way in his British school. It encouraged his imagination, which needed little encouragement, but neglected some of his basic skills, which did. The French concentration on fundamentals has made him more physically adept, and more focused, in the space of three months.

On the other hand, we fear that, as he gets older, once he has conquered his copper-plate and his French, he may get bored. Some middle way between British creativity and French rigidity must be possible: is there not a Eurocrat in Brussels with spare time to harmonise the two approaches?

In the meantime, Charles's teacher says that he is now conforming so well that he can have Black for the weekend whenever he wants to. Fine: but guess which member of the household ended up cleaning out the cosseted and much-beloved creature's cage?

■ Toto the Snail Has Hay-Fever
SEPTEMBER 1997

France is a country of immutable rhythms. The grapes are being harvested, conkers are falling, unheeded, from the trees, children are back at school and the education minister is threatening to reform the French education system.

The new school year has started with another ritual debate: are school satchels too heavy? French school-children, like bag-ladies, tend to carry all their possessions with them. The chic item this autumn, for boys and girls alike, is the wheelie-satchel, which resembles the overnight bag popularised by flight attendants.

Charles has been advised by his school-friends that when you reach the heights of his new class—CE1, or the second year of primary school proper—it is no longer cool to wear your satchel on your back. If your parents refuse to provide you with wheels, you must carry your huge bag in your hand, with the correct degree of pained insouciance.

Now that he has moved up one class, the iron grip of the French education system is beginning to tighten on Charles. School for seven- and eight-year-olds consists of the five r's: reading, writing, arithmetic, religion and running around the playground. There is little art and no geography or history.

Reading starts later in France. Charles already reads perfectly in English. But in French he and his French classmates remain at a basic level. "Toto the snail has hay-fever." (Lucky Toto, you might say, if it saves him from being eaten in garlic.)

The school day is composed mostly of copying from the blackboard, and dictation to improve the pupils' handwriting, spelling and grammar. Creative writing is unknown. Project work exists only on the religious lessons, where Charles and his classmates are studying the life of Mother Teresa. (Diana, Princess of Wales, whose fatal car accident occurred a half mile from the school, also received an honourable mention from the teacher.)

Charles goes to a Catholic, and therefore private school, but one under contract to the state and generously subsidised, in return for obedience to the national curriculum. The time when education ministers knew exactly what each child in France was studying at each hour of the day is long gone. But much—almost certainly too much—remains controlled from the centre.

The French attitude to the French education system is like the British attitude to the British justice system; a simultaneous belief that it is the best in world and riddled with failings. The most common criticism is that the emphasis on the basics, and the reliance on rote learning, produces minds which are literate, well-informed but lacking in initiative and creativity.

A survey last week suggested that some schools were not even delivering the basics very well: it found that one in ten young French people presenting themselves for induction for national service could not read properly. The other criticism is that the system is over-administered, too centrally directed and too much under the chalky thumb of the teaching unions. In other words schools in France are run for the benefit of bureaucrats and teachers, not pupils.

This, in essence, is the view of Claude Allègre, the son of a teacher, a former university professor and administrator, and now the Socialist minister for education, research and technology. Even before the left won the general election in June, M. Allègre announced that his ambition was to "get the fat off the mammoth" of the French education system.

He plans to reduce the number of directorates in the vast education ministry from nineteen to ten and to transfer surplus officials to university and local school administrations. The aim is to promote local and regional decision-making and to give teachers more sense of independence and initiative.

M. Allègre is one of most interesting members of the new government; a jovial, irascible man who, unusually for a French politician, or politicians anywhere, speaks with both humour and common sense. Though not young—he is sixty—M. Allègre is one of the most new-Labourish of ministers in Lionel Jospin's government, and the closest personally to Jospin himself.

In the space of a couple of days, he criticised the high level of absenteeism by teachers in state schools and their habit of awarding themselves training days in term-time, even though they have the shortest teaching year in the EU. Within a week of the *rentrée des classes*, a senior teacher at one of the snobbiest state lycées in Paris informed his pupils that he would be away for two weeks on a pottery course.

The teaching unions screamed at M. Allègre, but the subtext of his remarks was clear. Unlike other education ministers—especially Socialist education ministers—he would not be held in the corporatist vice of the cosy relationship between the education ministry and the education profession.

Plans are being made to arrange a meeting in Paris shortly

between M. Allègre and his British counterpart, David Blunkett. One can imagine the two men getting on well, even though, in some respects, they are facing in opposite directions. Mr Blunkett is pursuing the movement towards basic disciplines and accountability in British schools and away from the looser, and more imaginative, approaches which became common in the 1970s and 1980s. M. Allègre's aim is to reduce the Paris-controlled, curriculum-led, predictability of French education and to allow schools, and teachers, more freedom.

Both men could be right. In theory, France and Britain could converge on an approach which preserves the best of both systems: encouraging more creativity in France and more drilling in the basic skills in Britain.

Charles did not thrive in a British system which plunged him into creative writing projects (The Ancient Egyptians; the Blitz) before he even knew how to form his letters properly. In France his powers of concentration and his hand-writing have been miraculously improved. But he is beginning to be unimpressed by the health problems of Toto the Snail.

■ My Son, the Author
APRIL 2000

Charles, aged ten, has written a book. To be precise, he is the co-author of a book, with sixty of his French schoolmates.

It is doubtful whether anyone will ever read the book, which is the gripping sixty-page story of a modern boy who stumbles back in time to live with the master builders of medieval cathedrals. Harry Potter need not tremble. Steven Spielberg has yet to bid for the rights to *Hardi Compagnon* (Brave Companion).

No matter. Charles and his friends had enormous fun in the space of two weeks free of parents and siblings, writing the book and illustrating and publishing it in classically French soft covers. A copy of the book now resides, alongside those of Sartre and Maupassant, in the Bibliothèque Nationale.

Uprooting entire school classes and sending children away

from home for one or two weeks—*classes découvertes* or "classes of discovery"—is one of the better peculiarities of the French education system. Some schools have *classes de neiges* or ski classes combined with lessons. My son's Parisian school sends away two groups of children aged nine and ten to the island of Belle Ile off Brittany each spring for *classes d'écriture* or creative writing classes.

The pupils have their ordinary lessons in the morning and, with the help of a children's author in residence, invent, write and publish a book in the afternoons. How much of the book is actually "written" by the children is open to question. The final draft is, suspiciously, well-turned and grammatically precise. None the less, the ideas, characters and many of the words are the children's own.

This firework display of creativity is all the more striking because it is almost the only creative work that Charles and his classmates ever do. In his previous English school, at the age of five or six, he was expected (absurdly) to write little essays in which he had to "imagine that you are dandelion" or "pretend that you are a child living through the London Blitz" or maybe it was "imagine that you are a dandelion living during the Blitz". All of this before he could spell or even form his letters reliably.

In three years in his French school, Charles's hand-writing has blossomed; his technical knowledge of French has soared. But his creative writing has been restricted to an occasional sentence or poem.

There are many things in favour of the discipline and the clarity of the French education system; but it also tends to be, at once, over-laden with facts and yet strangely abstract; over-intellectualised and yet distrustful of individual children's minds.

Thus the French state curriculum treats the French language like an expensive aeroplane. Trainees are not allowed to take out the language for a spin until they have proved that they understand the controls and even the theory of flight.

Although the curriculum has been "lightened", pupils aged nine or ten spend hours on the regulations and sub-regulations of French grammar and—far less justifiably—the theory of grammar. French is a more complex language than English. There is, I suppose, no alternative to slogging through the different endings of the "future simple indicative of verbs of the third group" until they are lodged in your skull.

But the curriculum also demands that those aged nine or ten should understand, or at least rote learn, the mechanisms of the language and how to deconstruct sentences and put them back together again. Charles and his classmates spend many hours learning the "functional decoupling of circumstantial complements". ("Warning," his grammar book says, helpfully, "there may be several circumstantial complements in one sentence.")

In effect this seems to be a very complex form of "parsing", or breaking down sentences: a practice already regarded as old fashioned when I was at school in the middle of the last century (and a practice that should surely be outlawed under the European Convention on Human Rights).

The two weeks in Belle Ile were intended to give the children a sense of how their imaginations and the painfully acquired rules could work together. It was, however, typical that they were not allowed to actually write anything individually themselves. It wasn't so much a first solo flight with the language as a trip in a jumbo jet in which they were allowed to sit on the pilot's lap.

Charles got a lot out of the trip all the same. He seemed much more grown up when he came back. Outside classes of this kind are part of the maturing process. They also teach social skills and self-reliance. They are a more sensible substitute for boarding school: a two-week inoculation of independence rather than the whole six or seven-year disease.

The children were taught how to eat quietly in restaurants. They were taught to look after their clothes. In sum, they are taught how to be French. The adult helpers descended periodically on the children's rooms and, if they were untidy, subjected them to a series of graded "tornadoes": if one locker was untidy it was emptied on to the floor (a brown tornado). If all the lockers were untidy, they were all emptied on to the floor (a black tornado); if they were hopelessly untidy, all the clothes were thrown out of the window...

Such classes are a great rite of passage in France. The other parents, waiting on the railway station platform for their children to return, swapped misty-eyed reminiscences of their own "classes of discovery".

Unfortunately, it seems that classes away from home are becoming less common. Younger generations of French teachers are less willing to take on the responsibility.

I asked Charles what he thought he had discovered in his classes of discovery. After serious consideration, he said the most important thing was learning "to put up with my friends for two weeks". I suspect that may serve him better in life than the functional decoupling of circumstantial complements.

■ A Police Call
JANUARY 2003

My five-year-old daughter's school class was visited a couple of days ago by what she describes as a "nice, fat policeman with a gun".

He was not looking for evidence against me: he was making the rounds of Paris schools to explain what the police do and how small children should keep out of danger. My wife was rather shocked that, in the cause of safety, he should have brought his gun into a class of five-year-olds. On the other hand, a French policeman without a gun prominently suspended from his hip would, in the eyes of French children, not have been a proper French policeman.

Through the filter of Grace's young mind and selective memory, we have had a string of different accounts of what the policeman told them. He said that he "used his pistol for shooting robbers". He told them "never to walk out from behind a car". He told them that the "police were our friends". He told them "always to close the door, when we go to the lavatory". He told them that "grown-ups do not have a right to be nasty to children."

Fair enough, except that Grace now refuses to be punished in even the mildest way. When I separated her from a screaming match with her sister, she informed me: "You can't. The fat policeman told us that you have to be nice to children..."

■ Another Police Call
APRIL 2003

Police visits to schools, chapter two. I explained how impressed my daughter Grace had been when a policeman, complete with gun, visited her kindergarten class in Paris a few weeks ago. Her elder sister, Clare, aged nine, and her school-friends, have now been visited by a *brigadier* (sergeant), no less.

Clare has had trouble with the Paris police in the past. She went on a bicycle proficiency course when she was seven and ignored all the stop signs. The policeman in charge asked my wife whether "Mademoiselle numéro huit" (Miss Eight) was educationally subnormal. No, she replied, calmly, she had simply spent most of her life observing the traffic in Paris.

On this occasion, the brigadier came to address Clare's class on road-safety and school playground racketeering. He also told them that they should be kind to their pets. Failure to respect the rights of animals was punishable by two years in jail, he said.

Silence. Then Louis, the naughtiest boy in the class, put up his hand. "Including goldfish?" he asked. Yes, said the brigadier, "including goldfish".

Louis made a confession. When he and his family had been setting out on a cruise last summer, there was no-one to look after his goldfish, "so I threw them out of the window". "That was not very respectful of animals," the unsmiling policeman said. "However, my own parents are just as bad. They had the same problem with their goldfish and they flushed them down the toilet."

■ Saturday School
SEPTEMBER 2003

After six years in France, we have finally come face to face with one of the great French exceptions and oddities: Saturday morning school.

Six and a half years ago, we plunged our son—then nearly seven—into a French school, even though he could hardly speak a word of French. Our cruelty has paid off. Charles has done well in the French school system; he is bilingual; he has French friends; he has been exposed (to his great enrichment) to the inner workings of the French juvenile, and adult, mind in a way that would have been impossible in an international school.

Last week, we did something even more cruel. We moved him from one Parisian Catholic school to another (half a mile away) at one day's notice. After six years in the same institution, he and we had decided that it was time for a change, new horizons, a new challenge.

For months the school we approached insisted that it would probably have no vacancies. Last week, on the day before the new school year began, they offered Charles a place.

Overall, he seems pleased with his new school but he finds two things upsetting. He is banned from wearing any of his extensive collection of "baskets" (trainers) and the new school—unlike the last one—has classes on Saturday mornings. "No more late, relaxed Friday nights," he moans. "No more 'grasses matinées' (literally fat mornings, or long lie-ins) on Saturdays..." I also have a selfish moan of my own. Saturday morning school will enormously complicate family weekends in my beloved house and garden in Normandy.

Why do the French do it? Why does a nation obsessed with "le weekend", a nation of second home owners, the nation of the 35-hour week, preserve the cultural oddity of Saturday morning schools (usually matched with half-days or free days on Wednesdays)?

The institution has been gradually dying. It also shows remarkable signs of life. A Great Debate on Saturday school rumbles endlessly among parents, teaching unions, politicians and child psychologists. The debate bounces, in a very French way, between abstract theories, sound arguments, and self-interest masquerading as the public interest.

Many French school districts have abolished Saturday school. Hundreds of primary schools, and one million children, switched last month to a new four-day system, with both Wednesdays and Saturdays free but shorter summer holidays. Some private (i.e. mostly Catholic) schools have abolished Saturday classes at the insistence of parents; others cling to them.

Two years ago, the mayor of Paris, Bertrand Delanoë, tried to scrap all Saturday classes at state schools in the capital. He was defeated by the teaching unions, mostly because free Saturdays would have meant longer terms and shorter school holidays.

It turned out that many of the teachers who campaigned against the plan work in *maternelles* (kindergartens), which had already, unofficially, abolished Saturday classes as well as keeping their long holidays and Wednesdays off. Obstinate tots who turned up for school on Saturdays were discouraged from trying it on again by ruses such as being left in their raincoats all morning. (This is what the more militant French teaching unions, now planning an autumn of discontent, call "defending the principle of public education".)

There are *some* arguments for Saturday morning school. Child psychiatrists say that children study best in the mornings. Working on Saturday, and keeping Wednesday afternoons free, gives them an extra morning's learning. Where Saturday school has been abolished, surveys suggest that the people who most regret the change are the children themselves. "On Saturday morning I now end up going to the 'hyper' (supermarket) with mum," one child complained. "Before I was with my friends."

A French diplomat with children at Charles's new school is convinced that it maintains Saturday classes as an unspoken means of selecting parents. "The school's attitude is that your child should come before your weekend. If you are the kind of parent who puts the weekend first, you are not the kind of parent they want."

I, of course (cursing horribly under my breath) willingly put my son's education before my lawn and potatoes.

■ Sic Transit...
JUNE 2004

My theme is classical education, in the French style.

At academically demanding schools in France, it is fashionable to study Latin or German, as well as English. When Charles, aged fourteen, changed schools last autumn, we were informed that he would not be taken seriously unless he studied all three.

A few weeks ago Charles's Latin class was told by their teacher—a rigid woman of a certain age—that they had to extend their knowledge of ancient culture by making, individually or in groups, a model of something Roman: a house, a fort, a ship, a chariot. Models that scored more than ten out of twenty would be placed on display at the school.

What an excellent idea, I thought. The French education system, although admirable in many ways, does not always prize initiative or creativity. Here was a teacher who wanted to expand her pupils' minds.

Charles chose to make a model of a Roman baths, on his own. He preferred not to join a group, having had awkward experiences working in groups with French children in the past. (He had the, perhaps unfair, impression that the others let him do all the work but managed to snatch all the credit.) Charles did the research, finding ground plans and pictures of a Roman baths in Pompeii on the internet. That must have taken at least ten minutes.

Would I help him with the model? I was trained on Airfix spitfires from the age of seven and constructed one of the finest model railways in east Fulham in the 1990s. He knew that I would jump at the chance to get glue on my fingers.

I spent a sunny day indoors cutting up cereals packets to make the walls of the baths and, ingeniously, snipping the ends off cotton buds to use the plastic sticks as marble columns. We found lichens on an oak tree to simulate the Mediterranean flora in the baths' garden. I used real sand to make a sand pit for the gymnasium and—with the help of my ten-year-old daughter, Clare—simulated mosaic floors with felt-tip pens. I finished the walls in a pleasant shade of pink, which we happened to have left in one of those stub-ended samples jars which you can buy in decorating shops.

The finished model was, though I say it myself, not bad. It looked like a cross between an adobe supermarket in Albuquerque and a second home near Avignon. It had, however, the correct layout, with separate cold and hot pools for both men and women. (Mixed bathing was frowned upon in ancient times.)

I even made a little statue by cutting the head of a plastic cowboy, sticking it to a child's bead and painting the whole white. I waited confidently for my high mark from the teacher.

She rejected the model as "trop bricolé" (too home-made). Wasn't that the point? She objected to the pink walls as un-historical. The walls of Roman swimming pools were grey. How did she know? She held my miniature statue up to ridicule before the entire class. She demanded more substantial pillars than cotton bud sticks.

Back to the glue and paint-pots. I reconstructed the columns using wooden tubes, bought from a hardware store and then painted white. They looked like 1950s untipped fags but otherwise not bad. My wife and daughters painted the walls a pale grey (with pink showing through).

Charles proudly presented his teacher with the finished Roman baths (to which his contribution had been minimal). Her face froze. "Don't want it," she said. "Still too home-made." Eight out of twenty. Not selected for show.

The models which won her favour were mostly constructed from expensively-bought kits. One of the kits—an intense injustice—had been bought by the teacher herself and given to a group of her favourite pupils.

Here, then, is the explanation of the decline of French creativity in the last thirty years: no "Blue Peter" culture; no childhood training in making the Eiffel Tower out of coat-hangers.

Even Charles's French school-friends agreed that he (or I) had been robbed. As a protest, they converted his Pompeian baths into the post-Vesuvian version by pouring flour over the model, stamping on it and throwing it out of the school window.

Sic transit gloria mundi.

■ September – the Cruellest Month
SEPTEMBER 2004

September is here again, the cruellest month for all parents of school-age children in France. After a hard-earned holiday, watching the rain-clouds circling over Normandy like stacked aircraft, you come straight back to a school examination, set by sadistic teachers.

This is an examination designed to test the ingenuity and patience, not of the children, but of the parents. The exam paper takes the form of an extensive, abstruse list of "fournitures scolaires" (school equipment), which the child—to avoid teacherly rage—must possess on the first day of school.

In theory, education is free in France. In practice, primary schools provide nothing but bare walls, desks and a teacher. The parents must supply everything else: pens and pencils, of course; gym clothes, naturally; but also the textbooks, the exercise books (of precisely stated dimensions and characteristics) the plastic exercise book covers (in specified colours), the ink, the paper, the sticky-tape, the rolls of wire, the paper-plates, the shoe-boxes, the scissors, the paint-brushes, the paint, the painting paper, the tracing paper, the paper hankies and the glue. Lots of glue. French teachers are addicted to glue.

My ten-year-old daughter Clare needed 48 items to start the final year of primary school in Paris last week, including three different kinds of loose-leaf paper, eighteen exercise books of four different specifications and five plastic exercise-book covers (blue, red, yellow, green and transparent).

Grace, aged six, had a marginally shorter list of much greater complexity, including pink and orange exercise book covers (extremely rare; now stocked only by the most specialised dealers) and a pencil-case with two pockets, "both capable of housing a 20 cm plastic ruler".

Every year there is a fuss in the French press about the length and cost of the school lists. Every year, parents' associations protest and suggest that it would be much cheaper, and simpler, for schools—even school districts—to buy all this stuff in bulk. Nothing changes, except that every year the lists grow longer and more fiendish.

I have a notion (maybe not entirely fanciful) that the teachers in each school convene a coven meeting at the end of each year to draw up the list of fournitures scolaires for the next. At this meeting, the teachers put on their pointed hats and then scan stationers' catalogues, several years out of date, to identify the most outlandish items.

"First teacher: We should ask for two exercise books for practical work in big format... Second teacher: Hee, hee, hee, yes, but with the bigger squares and with 96 pages, no more, no less... Third teacher: Ho, ho, ho, yes, and we should specify that the size must be 24 cm by 32. Fourth teacher: Yes, yes (wiping tears from eyes) but only, in the non-spiral-backed version..."

My daughters' school offers a service in which they supply you (for a large fee) with all the equipment required in a brown cardboard box. We have been down this cowardly route in recent years but found that the equipment in the box does not match the list. We have ended up, at the last minute, searching *le tout Paris* for the last "cahier de travaux pratiques, grand format, grand carreaux, 96 pages, sans-spirale, 24 x 32".

This year, therefore, we devoted the last Friday of our holidays to a trip to a hypermarket near Caen in Normandy, with a floor-space three times the size of the Vatican. This shop claims to have the cheapest and most comprehensive range of fournitures scolaires in the nation.

After three hours of searching the football-pitch-length aisles, and fighting off other equally desperate mamans and papas, we emerged with a supermarket trolley full of gear (cost €268.77). However, we did not have the six exercise books with alternate blank and ruled pages, in small format, non-spiral; we did not have the pink and orange exercise book covers; and we could not find Grace's pencil-case with two, separate pockets over 20 cm long.

It took trips to three other shops to locate the exercise books and covers. Finally, I located what appears to be the last double-barrel pencil case in France. It said "Harry Potter" on the side and carried a picture of Hedwig, Harry's owl. In triumph, I presented it to Grace. "No good," she said. "It's a boy one. Only boys in France have Harry Potter pencil cases."

Has anyone out there got a twin-bore pencil case? Must be 20 cm long and pink.

■ Dictating the Future
DECEMBER 2004

To be dictated to by one's children is the fate of most parents.

The other night I asked Charles to read out two moderately complicated texts in French. I scribbled down the words as accurately as I could, ransacking my fading memories of school lessons in the 1960s to unmask the subjunctive verbs and satisfy myself that all adjectives and participles were on speaking terms with plural and/or feminine nouns.

One of the many joys, or terrors, of French is that words can be spelled in different ways according to how they are employed or where they fall in the sentence. The words continue, treacherously, to sound much the same.

When I handed in my exam papers, I was quietly smug. Not for long.

Charles marked my work with the sadistic eye and vicious turn of phrase of his *professeur de français*. I had committed, he said, several "barbarismes" and many "horreurs".

In the first dictation, I scored ten out of twenty; in the second eleven out of twenty. In other words, I barely reached the pass-mark for the *baccalauréat*, the French equivalent of A level. I consoled myself with the knowledge that French children often get minus scores.

The dictation or "dictée" has long been one of the pillars of the French way of education. A teacher reading out a text for students to copy is still the model of what some in France—including the education minister, François Fillon—believe that education should be. Even at university level, first degree courses frequently consist of lecturers reading out lists of theories and facts.

M. Fillon said recently that it was time for the madly innovative French education system to go back to the basics. In a circular to school districts, he said that there should be more dictées, especially for children in their early teens.

This seemed like telling a heroin addict to take more drugs. From the age of five, to the age of sixteen, French school-children are given one or two dictées a week. My wife, Margaret, recently signed up for an advanced French course at the Sorbonne. The centre-piece of the week's work for her class of Japanese, Chinese, Taiwanese, Vietnamese, Estonian, Ukrainian, and a few Anglophone students, is the dictée.

The Japanese and Chinese students are brilliant at the dictations but cannot string two words of verbal French together. Margaret speaks French pretty well. Her dictée scores err on the low side of ten.

The sheer complexity of French grammar and variable spelling means that the dictée occupies a much greater place in the national consciousness than the spelling test in America or Britain. BBC TV has recently launched a successful spelling programme. Next month the France 2 TV channel will reach its 19th national final of the dictée championships, the "Dicos d'Or".

The programme is one of the most popular of the television year. Millions will tune in once again next month to try to write down "zinnias nonpareils à l'abri des moucharabiehs" (unrivalled zinnias in the shelter of balconies).

So why is the education minister M. Fillon complaining? Until thirty years ago, dictation was a daily exercise in French schools. Since then, there has been a cautious trend towards requiring children to write creatively, as well as copying down what teacher says. Only a cautious trend. The national curriculum still dictates that there should be lots of dictées and abstract lessons in the theory of sentence construction.

Employers, as they do in Britain, complain that children are leaving school unable to write clearly. Some teachers believe that more creative writing is the way forward. M. Fillon, and the traditionalists, want to put the clock back.

It is a typically French argument but also a universal one. Which is more important? Grammatical accuracy or creativity and imagination? Both, surely. The first should serve the second; the second is not possible without knowledge of the first.

My youngest child, Grace, aged seven, was recently given a copy of a reproduction of the original Babar the Elephant book from the 1930s, with the French text printed in ornate hand-writing. She loved the book but, on a second reading, complained, with a shocked expression, that it was "full of grammatical errors". Sigh.

■ Egalité, Fraternité, Hypocrisie
JUNE 2006

Does experience teach you anything? Is happiness preferable to the truth? Why is the French higher education system, theoretically devoted to equality, an elitist, hypocritical mess?

Almost all seventeen- and eighteen-year-olds in France wrestled with the first two of those questions, and questions like them, when the dreaded philosophy examination started the *baccalauréat* season last week.

The third question is mine. But it is not just mine.

Many of the 517,000 kids taking the "bac" this month were on strike until just over a month ago. They were protesting against a government plan to make it easier to hire, and fire, young people.

Fair enough. It was an ill-considered law in many ways. I had a problem with the protests all the same. I tried to make my point, fruitlessly, to some of the charming kids on the streets. Why protest about something new when so much of what is old and entrenched in the French system is stacked against you?

The same argument is made, much more eloquently, by the President of the Sorbonne university in Paris in a book published this month. Jean-Robert Pitte's book (Fayard, €12) is called: *Jeunes, On Vous Ment!* (Kids, they are lying to you!)

Let me try to condense M. Pitte's 130-pages into a few lines.

In France, nation of equality, liberty and fraternity, state education is free and open to all, with no selection. The primary and secondary education systems—through which my own three children are progressing happily—have many problems (which system does not?) but it broadly works.

Higher education in France is a disaster, unworthy of a developed nation. A few thousand of those 517,000 kids taking the bac this month will push their way through into the elite, well-funded, non-university system called the "grandes écoles" or other, equivalent, well-regarded business schools.

In theory, these kids are the crème de la crème. In reality, they are clever, yes, but also the kids of the crème: children of well-off or highly motivated parents who can afford to let them spend another two years at school (until the age of twenty) in "preparatory classes" for the grandes écoles. Graduates of these institutions have the pick of jobs in France, in both the public and private sector.

One in three of the kids taking the bac this week are sitting a "professional" form of the exam, which may, or may not, help them to go straight in to jobs, from farming to hairdressing.

Almost all the rest will fall, like lemmings, into the general university system.

In French universities there are no state loans but the fees are very low. Everyone who passes the bac is guaranteed a place. You can, more or less, choose whatever course you like.

Result: catastrophe. Because the fees are low, the level of teaching is low, with little teacher-student contact. The students are herded into giant amphitheatres where they blindly take notes. The notion that there is no selection is an institutional hypocrisy. Around forty per cent of students—more in some subjects—are thrown out after the first year.

Vocational studies, such as medicine or law, are well respected but the first year failure rate is even more crippling: over sixty per cent in some universities. In other subjects, even if you graduate, your chances of finding a job are poor. Employers have a low opinion of ordinary university degrees in France, especially in the general, arts subjects to which tens of thousands of students flock.

M. Pitte makes three or four main recommendations in his book. Fees should be increased—with government subsidies for the needy—to give universities more money. Universities should be allowed to select their students. The entry classes for the grandes écoles should be moved from schools to the universities to boost their prestige.

These are all sensible suggestions. They have all been rejected, not just by other university administrators, but by student organisations as impossibly reactionary and "liberal" (the French code word for unFrench).

Student unions, and many teachers, are blindly devoted to the fake equality of the present system. Most senior politicians, left and right, are products of the elite grandes écoles and have no interest in universities.

In 1968, Alain Peyrefitte, the education minister, said that the French university system was "like organising a shipwreck to find out who could swim". "Reforms" made since then have put more passengers on the ship and burned the lifeboats.

Does experience teach you anything?

■ Do it Yourself
JUNE 2007

My spare time and our flat have been laid waste by barbarian invasions.

First the Vikings colonised the kitchen table. Then Joan of Arc arrived to boot the wicked English out of France.

It is school project time.

The last time I became involved, I was deeply humiliated. My son and I built a Roman baths out of cereal packets and cotton buds. We painted it Barbie pink because someone assured us that was the colour of the buildings in Pompeii. The finished structure resembled an adobe supermarket in New Mexico but was, otherwise, rather good in a Blue Peter kind of way.

There is no Blue Peter tradition in France. My son's literal-minded Latin teacher declared the building "sui generis" (unusual) and "non grata" (useless). We scored eight out of twenty. My son's friends threw the model out of the school window.

Just before Christmas, my older daughter, aged twelve, was commissioned, with two friends, to build a Viking ship. By Odin and Thor, this time we would show them.

My daughter and her friends read the runes of the internet and produced an avalanche of information on "drakkars" and "long ships". This will take just a couple of days, I said, gathering supplies of balsa wood, glue, craft-knives, paint, string and card. Four weeks later, the drakkar was finished. There was severe collateral damage to the kitchen table, a clown-suit and an electric kettle.

The ship had a beautiful dragon's head and a spiral tail. It had a sail cut from the stripes of my son's old clown costume. It had a fat, plastic toy Viking at a tiller made from an ice-lolly stick.

The ship was almost complete when we visited a touring Danish exhibition of Viking artefacts (at the Bayeux tapestry museum in Normandy). There were several wonderful models in the exhibition, based on archeological discoveries of Viking ships. Rather crude original designs, I thought. Nothing like as elaborate and sophisticated as ours. So much for the Vikings as great boat builders.

In the meantime, my younger daughter, aged nine, placed herself in charge of a five-child project to present the story of Joan of Arc and the Hundred Years War. You might think that this would be an awkward subject for an Anglo-Irish child in a mainly French class. Grace explained that the English were "mean" 700 years ago but were "normal" today.

We helped her to prepare an information panel about Jeanne d'Arc and a script for five voices, presenting the war from a scrupulously French point of view. Then, at the last moment, a stand-in history teacher cancelled the Hundred Years War on the grounds that it would "take too long".

The Viking ship, meanwhile, made two voyages to school. On the first, my daughter sat down on it in the back of the car and broke off its dragon's head. After the second voyage, the ship was received as a great marvel. It has been placed in the school library. Its picture has been taken for the school magazine.

Clare and her friends received nineteen out of twenty for the drakkar and their accompanying lecture on Viking ships. I thought that was rather a begrudging reward for all their work. Then I was reminded of the scoring system in French schools above the primary level. The best mark available to pupils is eighteen out of twenty. Only teachers can score nineteen out of twenty. Twenty out of twenty is reserved for God.

■ What a Kiss Can Do
JULY 2008

One of the first stories I wrote when I arrived in Paris was about my son, aged six, receiving a kiss from his teacher on his first day in French primary school. Twelve years later, he has just passed his *baccalauréat* with a Très Bien, the highest grade. Just shows you what a kiss can do.

PART FOUR

Food and Wine

We, les Anglais, love to say that French food is not what it is reputed to be; that French wine is poor and over-priced; that French cuisine has lost its way.

Some of this is true. Taken as a whole, it is misleading rubbish. There may now be a handful of high-price restaurants in London which are as good as, or better than, the top restaurants in Paris. I haven't eaten in them but I'm prepared to believe it. At its most rarefied level, French haute cuisine can be fussy and disappointing and unimaginative.

The great difference between the two countries—and between France and almost any other country, except Belgium—is the quality of the general run of medium or low-priced restaurants in towns or villages large or small. In France, with a little care, you can still eat well almost anywhere. That is not true in Britain; and it is not true in Italy or Switzerland or Germany or the US.

Do the French still care about food? Is the detailed French lunch still a national institution?

Times are changing. The street next to my office in Paris, which once had a couple of excellent local brasseries, is now lined with over-priced and poor sandwich bars. On the other hand, my next door neighbours in Normandy—a retired working-class couple—still drive thirty kilometres to buy exactly the right type of mussels.

French wine is a long and complicated and often sad story. At the top level, it is still the yardstick by which the world judges wine. At the mid-market and lower levels, there are wonderful French wines. But the jumble of labels and *appellations*, and the variable quality, have ineluctably delivered supermarket shelves in Britain and elsewhere into the hands of Koala Creek *et al.*

■ Cuisine – Haute or Haughty
MARCH 1997

In my early days as a reporter, I won only one distinction: I held the record at the *Bolton Evening News* for the most rapid consumption of bacon, eggs and chips in the office canteen.

I have retained an attachment to food, good and plain, preferably in generous quantities. But, until this week, I never had much interest in, patience for, or willingness to invest in, *haute cuisine*.

Three things happened in the past few days to modify that. One was the appearance of the 1997 Michelin Guide, which aroused my curiosity about the status of the leading French chefs, who are almost as feted as movie stars. Another was the discovery, from another newspaper, of a French cut-price system for posh meals, modelled on the airline system of economy flights—a kind of culinary bucket shop. But my first gastronomic experience of the week was accidental. After two months cooped up in a Paris apartment, with occasional day trips for good behaviour, the children had been demanding to go to the countryside.

We were recommended a château in Burgundy, which offers cheap weekend breaks. After two hours on the road, in a slow-moving Amazon of cars, we had reached Fontainebleau, forty miles south of Paris. Two hours later we reached the Château de Chailly: a fairy tale castle with pointed turrets and smartly converted stables for guests.

Three things became clear. First, we were the only people staying in the château, or the château stables, that night. Second, the château restaurant, an ambitious, gastronomic establishment, had been kept open exclusively for us, and was about to close. Third, the children, force-fed on the road, had no intention of going to sleep.

The dinner-suited waiters looked crestfallen. Plainly they had hoped for grander visitors. But Gallic pragmatism and rural French friendliness triumphed. Room service was not normally provided but, since we were the only guests, they would bring the restaurant to us. We could hear the trolley bumping over the ancient cobbles of the château courtyard for several minutes before the food arrived.

With Clare screaming that her bedclothes were an inch too far to the right and Charles watching a German version of *Noel's House Party* on television, we ate an extraordinarily beautiful meal: a meal that was delicate and simple, in the way that strings of pearls are simple; a meal that was meant to be eaten slowly by candlelight with great concentration, as if listening to music.

When the 1997 Michelin Guide emerged on Monday, our château was mentioned only as a hotel, not as a restaurant. This implies that there are 4,000 better restaurants in France, which must be an injustice. But what would I know, with my taste buds ruined years ago by steaming mounds of bacon, eggs and chips?

Having caught the bug, I decided to try out the service provided by Degriftour, a French economy-travel company, which offers a kind of Super Apex service of cut-price haute cuisine. With the economic crisis in France thinning their clientele, a score of top French restaurants joined the scheme two months ago. You can book only through Minitel, the online booking and information service operated by France Telecom. All the restaurants available have at least one star in the Michelin Guide.

To eat at such a restaurant usually costs between 1,000 and 1,500 francs (£110 to £170) a head for a full à la carte dinner with wine. Degriftour offers the same thing, but with a set menu, for a maximum of £55 a head. We booked at Montparnasse 25, a Michelin one-star restaurant, where we had six courses for slightly less than £50 a head.

Six courses sounds greedy but they were small, delicate courses—and all magnificent, though to my corrupted taste no more magnificent than those we ate in our child-infested bedroom at the unstarred château.

Food is such an elemental human need that the whole concept of an elite cuisine at refined prices is bound to raise moral problems: how can you justify paying £170 a head for a meal when the same amount might feed a family for a month? In response, functional arguments are deployed: that by striving for the best, the elite chefs keep up standards; that the best chefs are consulted by mass-food producers on how to improve their lines.

But the justification for haute cuisine has to be something

more amorphously cultural. The pleasure of going to a place like Montparnasse 25 is an artistic pleasure. Like the highest art of any kind—great acting, great painting, great writing—the pleasure of great cuisine is the pleasure of performance: witnessing something simple pushed to an evidently higher level, while maintaining, at its best, a kind of simplicity.

The concept of cooking as an art is a French invention and, like many things French at present, feels itself under threat from modernity. *Le Monde* this week bemoaned the fact that "social penury" was threatening French cuisine. "Substitute technologies, the banalisation of tastes, the changing behaviour patterns of the clientele," said the newspaper's food writer, Jean-Claude Ribaut, "favour the invasion of foreign approaches."

For which read McDonald's, which opened 100 restaurants in France last year; while a three-star restaurant went bankrupt for the first time and several one-star establishments closed. "Good food is the identity of a civilisation," M. Ribaut asserted. The Michelin Guide was trying to force back the hordes of barbary, he said, but could, in the end, do no more than "uphold the memory of a golden age."

I think that maybe Jean-Claude protests too much: with 81 starred restaurants operating in Paris alone, the burger-barbarians have not yet laid France waste. I defy him to name anywhere in all twenty *arrondissements*, or all 96 *départements*, where you can get bacon, egg and chips.

■ Fast Wine
OCTOBER 2002

French wine, at the lower price levels, should be more like Australian wine or Coca-Cola, instantly recognisable and always the same. Who says so? The main French wine exporting federation says so (although the Coca-Cola comparison is mine).

As sacrilege goes, this will appear to many French wine-makers and lovers as if the Vatican had questioned the virgin birth of Christ.

According to the official religion of French wine-making, taste grows from the earth. It should not be imposed in factories by men in white coats. It is a mystical fusion of *cépage* (grape variety), centuries of know-how and that untranslatable French word *terroir*, which means, roughly-speaking, the growing conditions generated by soil and the lie of the land.

On the upper slopes of the wine market, that is fine. The best French wines are sometimes matched in quality by wines from elsewhere but no other country approaches their variety. They still sell well, at home and abroad, despite their high prices.

The lower, and even the middle, slopes of the wine market— the four to seven quid bottle of dry white wine from Oddbins—is a different story. French wine is often a source of confusion and disappointment among wine-drinkers who know what they like but don't care about the difference between cépage and terroir, or Burgundy and Bordeaux.

Australian or Chilean wines come with simple grape-variety labels, such as Chardonnay or Cabernet-Sauvignon. You know exactly what you are getting for your money. The contents are as predictable as HP sauce. French wines, even at the lower price levels, come with a bewildering variety of labels, some based on grape variety, some on the wine-trader, some on the region. The quality can vary absurdly, even between bottles with the same label.

As a consequence, French wines at the lower and lower-middle end of the market are in trouble. Their export market share, especially in Britain, has been steadily eroded by the success of New World wines. In France, young people are turning increasingly to beer, alcopops and soft drinks. Only four in 100 say that they are regular wine-drinkers, compared to 24 in 100 in the early 1980s.

There is now a growing surplus (wine-lake) in poorer-quality wine-growing areas of the deep French South which is beginning to spread upwards to the lower reaches of the classier, generic wines from Beaujolais and Burgundy.

The Fédération des Exportateurs des Vins et Spiritueux, which sells eighty per cent of French wine, has proposed a solution. French wines should be divided into two categories. The higher-quality *appellation d'origine contrôlée* (AOC) wines and the best of the *vin de pays* should maintain their mystical-local traditions and identities. The lesser-quality wines, and even some medium-quality wines, should copy the brutal Australians and others and market themselves under new, simple labels as *vins de pays de France*, with a rigorously consistent taste, developed to suit export and domestic markets.

Such wines would be sold on the basis of their grape-variety (i.e. Chardonnay or Pinot Noir) rather than their region. Up to fifteen per cent of other, coarser grape varieties could be mixed in. Supposedly alien foreign practices, like "oaking" the wine to suit foreign taste-buds, would be permitted.

This is not a complete revolution. Some French wines are already marketed by their grape variety. Some are even designed by itinerant Australian wine-makers to appeal to foreign markets. What is startling is the suggestion that this should become official policy for the bulk of French wine.

Traditionalists (and being traditional does not necessarily make them wrong) will argue that France is being asked to dumb down one of its national splendours, to pander to ignorant foreign tastes. The purists regard the New World philosophy of mass-market wine-making—in which taste is homogenised to suit consumer demand, rather than generated by the soil or terroir—as a commercial form of the phylloxera bug which destroyed French vineyards in the 19th century.

If the pest is allowed to invade the lower end of the French industry, they argue, it would soon spread to the production of quality wines. Some celebrated Bordeaux châteaux, heavily dependent on the US market, are already accused of manipulating their wine to suit the American palate. On the other hand, the exporters will argue that all this mystical talk of terroir is sometimes used to conceal downright bad wine-making in France. The thousands of small cooperatives which dominate the lower end of the wine market are not always able to impose sufficient quality control. The whole industry has been producer-led for too long, the exporters say. If the small growers wish to survive, they must grow what French and foreign consumers want to drink, not what the producers have always produced.

The exporters' ideals have been presented formally to a committee set up by the French government to consider the future of the wine industry. They will be discussed with wine producers next month. Corks will fly.

◼ Repas – Ready to Eat
MARCH 2003

American TV networks may be full of disobliging stuff about the unwarlike French but their contempt does not extend to rejection of French military food. At least one of the US networks has been trying for several weeks, I hear, to buy several hundred French army "meals ready to eat" (MREs—the combat rations issued to frontline soldiers).

During the first Gulf war and the Balkan wars, American news correspondents developed an intense loathing for the MREs issued to US troops. They discovered, through swapping with French colleagues, or on assignment with French units, that the French equivalent—"Rations de combat individuelles réchauffables" (individual, re-warmable combat rations or RCIRs) —were exquisite.

With a second Gulf war looming, one of the big three American news networks has been trying to persuade the French military to supply it with a bulk order of RCIRs to feed its correspondents and technicians in the field.

To no avail, it seems. The defence ministry in Paris has declined to supply the meals on the grounds that they might imply—if they fell into Iraqi hands—clandestine support for an American military adventure of which France officially disapproves.

This is rather petty. France has a perfect right to refuse America its political or military support. That is no reason to deny American television its gourmet combat rations.

The French "rations de combat" 1.5 kilo pack—enough to feed one person for a day—consists of three meals. Breakfast is dried bread or "pain de guerre" (war bread) and instant coffee. Lunch and dinner are selected from fourteen different, four-course menus. The hors d'oeuvres could be rillette de saumon or pâté de campagne or a vegetable soup. The main dish could be saumon au riz et légumes or paella or tajine de poulet (a Moroccan dish) or cassoulet or navarin d'agneau (a kind of lamb stew). There is also cheese and dried fruit.

The spokesman in the French defence ministry who gave me these sample menus, is himself an army officer. He had eaten many of them while serving in Bosnia, he said, chuckling at the recollection. "They are indeed delicious and many of our colleagues from other countries were rather jealous."

By contrast, the Pentagon's Defense Feeding Program at the Soldier Systems Center in Natick, Massachusetts, has invented what it calls the "indestructible sandwich"—a barbecued-chicken roll which can be stored for three years at room temperature and dropped out of helicopters.

Small surprise, therefore, to learn that it was this unit which was responsible for the proliferation of spam (tinned boiled ham) during the Second World War.

There is a book to be written on the subject of combat rations. Did you know, for instance, that the Mongol hordes were issued with sharpened straws to suck blood from their horses when other food ran short? Or that potato chips were first devised by chefs serving with Napoleon's Grande Armée as a quick way of feeding soldiers in the field? Or that the reputation of camembert as the prince of French cheeses was first established when the Norman cheese-makers supplied a free example every day to each French soldier in the trenches in the First World War?

To be fair (even if fairness is going out of fashion), the Pentagon claims to have made great strides in the quality of its MREs since the 1991 Gulf war. In those days, a typical meal was "smoky frankfurters", which came to be known as "the four fingers of death".

Gerard Darsch, head of the Defense Feeding Program at Natick, told the magazine *Fortune* recently that he was obliged to improve the menus by abusive letters from ordinary GIs. It was not the four-letter words in the letters that persuaded him, he said, it was the "intriguing combination of four-letter words."

The upgraded American MREs now come in 24 menus which include such delicacies as pasta alfredo and Thai chicken and seafood jambalaya. They are said to be at least as good as airline food.

US TV war correspondents will soon have a chance to find out for themselves. With great shortsightedness, Paris is passing up a wonderful opportunity to "re-warm" the attitudes of American TV journalists towards all things French.

■ Slow Burn Fast Food
MAY 2003

There is a restaurant in our *quartier* of Paris which has served the same main dish, day and night, with no other choices, for 44 years.

It is known all over Paris, and the world, but no-one calls it by its real name. It is not in any of the posh restaurant guides. It has been savagely attacked in one of the most prestigious of them (quite unfairly). The restaurant refuses all reservations but customers—both Parisians and tourists—queue happily for up to an hour for a table.

Let me repeat that. Parisians, the world's rudest, most impatient, most demanding, most queuephobic people, stand in line, without complaining, and await their turn to eat in a restaurant which offers them no choice.

Like Asterix in the cartoon series of the same name, the restaurant seems to have stumbled on a magic formula. In truth, there is no magic formula, except good, simple cooking, reasonable prices, a convivial atmosphere and the sauce. I will come back to the sauce later but I will not be able to tell you very much.

The restaurant is called Le Relais de Venise (The Venice Inn). It was an Italian restaurant until Paul Gineste de Saurs, a struggling wine-grower from the south-west, bought the site, in Porte Maillot, in the 17th *arrondissement* of Paris, in 1959. He saw no reason to change the perfectly good neon name sign, so he hung another one underneath it, saying: "Son entrecôte".

For the last 44 years, all that the Relais de Venise has served, lunch-time and evening, is entrecôte steak and chips and the house sauce. You get a salad starter and a choice of twenty desserts but the only choices of main meal are "saignant, à point et bien cuit" (rare, medium and well-done). The restaurant is known to its customers as L'Entrecôte, or the Entrecôte Porte Maillot, but it should not be confused with a chain of copy-cat restaurants of that name.

M. Gineste de Saurs died in 1966. Since then the Relais de Venise has been run by his daughter, now an elegant, imposing woman in her late sixties, who likes to go by her husband's names—both Christian name and surname—Madame Thierry Godillot.

"My father knew nothing about restaurants or cooking," Mme. Godillot told me. "But he was faced with a situation where he had to do something to save the family vineyard. He had the idea to do something very simple, something that would offer just one dish. Everyone told him that he was crazy and that it could not succeed. This was long before anyone in Paris had heard of fast food or steak restaurants. Anyway, 44 years later, here we still are."

The no reservations rule is, Mme. Godillot insists, part of the restaurant's success. "Personally, I would never queue for anything but here the queue has become part of our legend, part of our character. There are people who have come to me and said we are celebrating our wedding anniversary and we first met in your queue. There are others who were unemployed and found a job by talking to the person next to them."

The queue, Mme. Godillot says, promotes a rapid turnover of tables which allows her to keep her prices down. It costs €20.50 for the steak and starter. For that price, you get something almost unheard of in Paris—generous second helpings.

If you allow reservations, Mme. Godillot says, people always come late or turn up with fewer people than promised. Tables stand empty. In the Relais de Venise, on a standard night, each table is used four or five times. The queue usually takes 20 to 30 minutes but you can wait just as long, even with a reservation, in other Paris restaurants.

The success of the Relais de Venise (271, Boulevard Pereire, opposite the RER station at Porte Maillot) infuriates some members of the French food police. The gourmet guide, the Gault Millau, ran a campaign against the place for many years. *Le Monde* has asked why people "obstinately" queue for such ordinary food.

Haute cuisine it may not be but the meat is succulent and the sauce is delicious. I asked Mme. Godillot what the sauce contained. She waved her hand, like the druid in Asterix being asked for the recipe of the "potion magique". "Oh nothing much," she said. "Just butter and spices and herbs. It is a recipe which my father got from somewhere..."

■ School Meals, French Style
NOVEMBER 2003

My memories of school meals in England are of cold mashed potatoes, served from steel vats, accompanied by grey strips of pork luncheon meat and congealed baked beans.

When we arrived in Paris a few years ago, I was pleased to find that the children's school canteen encouraged parents to come along to sample the food. In France, I was sure, the *petits trésors* would be treated to succulent and nourishing delights. A proper appreciation of food would be part of the national curriculum: part of the business of being trained to be French.

I went along to the school canteen one lunch-time and the food was plain but not bad at all. I was even offered a free glass of red Bordeaux with my steak, chips and salad.

A couple of years later, the school's own kitchens were abolished. The canteen was taken over by a large catering company. The standing invitation to parents to join their children for an occasional school lunch was withdrawn. The price of the meals went up. The kids began to complain, for the first time, about the food: it was cold; it was tasteless; it was always the same; the staff were rude.

Once, when my son complained that there were no starters left, he was told to "ne fais pas le pédé" which translates roughly as "don't act like a queer". Why, in France of all places, you should have your sexual orientation questioned for wanting to eat the whole of your lunch, I'm not sure.

According to the magazine *Marianne*, a ferocious defender of French identity and traditions from a leftist-conservative viewpoint, this is not an isolated case. There is a growing school canteen scandal in France.

Partly because of the weed-like growth of hygiene regulations, and partly to save money, individual school kitchens and even communal education district kitchens, have been closing down in their hundreds. Of the 900,000,000 school meals served in France each year, more than one-third are now pre-cooked by mass catering companies.

The education ministry still declares, pompously, that school canteens have a "mission to educate the taste" of children. In other words, my original assumption was right. French school canteens are supposed to be part of France's basic training in the "art de vivre" of being French.

The reality is rather different. A school meal in France costs €5.50 to €7. Of this, the raw food content is supposed to be worth €1.50 a meal. *Marianne* says that it is often worth half that amount.

Marianne's investigation suggests that the mass catering companies—*sociétés de restauration collective*—ignore the education ministry guidelines calling for a school diet of fresh fruit and vegetables, fish and unprocessed meat. A recent study by dieticians in eighty *communes* across France showed that the typical school meal contained processed foods, such as chicken nuggets or lasagne, rich in salt and saturated fat.

The big catering companies justify their choices by saying that these are the kinds of meals which children like. Do they? The *Marianne* investigation claimed that up to 80 per of meals at some schools were ending up in the bin. This is confirmed, anecdotally, by my own kids, although my son has now gone to another school, with its own kitchens, where he says the food is much better.

All, certainly, is not lost. A little time ago, I ate in a village restaurant in the Alps not far from Grenoble. The entire village school filed in and sat down to lunch. The restaurant was also the school canteen.

Overall, France, which claims to be worried about increasing obesity among young people, is not living up to its own high ambitions and propaganda. French anti-globalist campaigners like José Bové protest against "la malbouffe" (bad grub) invading France from abroad. French school text books mock the American diet. School meals are supposed to be an education in taste. And yet a whole generation of French people is being educated to eat badly.

■ Mancunian Haute Cuisine
MARCH 2005

The smallest restaurant in Paris is run by an Englishman who has never learned (officially) how to cook.

The results are extraordinary. Chris Wright's tiny bistro—Le Timbre (the postage stamp)—is beginning to attract the admiring attention of the French culinary press.

"I had a chef, a young Frenchman, a great lad in many ways, except he didn't like working during meal times, which was a bit awkward for a chef," said Chris, 32, who comes from Whitefield, just north of Manchester. "So I thought, I'll have a go myself."

For a Mancunian to emigrate to Paris and start a successful restaurant offering classics of French cuisine is as unlikely as a French footballer going to Manchester and inspiring United fans to sing "La Marseillaise".

On second thoughts, someone called Eric has already done that. Since Chris Wright is (inexplicably) a Manchester City fan, we will let the comparison drop there.

Le Timbre, which is in the sixth *arrondissement* between Montparnasse and the Luxembourg Gardens, has one small room, with space for 24 customers, a chef and a waitress. Whether that makes it absolutely the smallest restaurant in Paris is a matter of dispute. (Chris says he knows one around the corner with room for just 21 diners.)

This is a part of Paris where you can find wonderfully exotic combinations. The Brazilian all-night samba club across the street has gone bust. Chris's restaurant used to be a Sri Lankan crêpe house.

There is nothing exotic about Le Timbre. It is an understated Parisian bistro, of the kind that is hard to find nowadays. The meals offered by Chris (menu from €22 at lunch, €31 at dinner) are French standards: rognons de veau (calf's kidneys), parmentier de queue de boeuf (oxtail and mash).

The free listings newspaper *A Nous Paris* described the results as "sumptuous", "convincing" and "talented". Their only complaint was that Chris speaks French "like Jane Birkin", with an approximate knowledge of grammar and a complete indifference to which nouns are "le" or "la".

I had the rognons de veau (plural masculine), one of my favourite dishes. It was about the best that I have ever tasted. The Australian foodie couple at the next table raved about their meal: far better, they said, than the €60 plus dishes they had eaten at a posh restaurant off the Champs Elysées the day before.

Chris took a few informal cooking lessons from a friend of his original, wayward chef. Otherwise, he learned by trial and error and by "cooking the dishes that made me want to come to France in the first place. A lot of it is a question of the ingredients," he said. "If you buy only the best possible stuff, there is a limit to how much damage you can do."

Chris was a fine arts graduate who drifted to Paris eight years ago and worked as a waiter and finally a restaurant manager. He started Le Timbre (3, Rue Sainte-Beuve, near Metro Notre-Dame-des-Champs, Tel 01 45 49 10 40) just over three years ago. He is now fully booked every evening and has a steady lunchtime trade.

Contrary to received opinion, Chris says, starting a small business in France is not difficult. The problems come if you want your business to grow. Chris would love to open a bigger restaurant but the high social payments and red tape for hiring staff are daunting. "In Britain, everything is done to encourage a business to get bigger. Here everything seems to encourage you to remain on a small scale, working six days a week, hiring as few staff as possible..."

On the plus side, he says, that preserves traditional ways of doing things, which explains why French cuisine, in middle of the range, is "still the best in the world". On the other hand, at the top level, he says, the cost of hiring staff has discouraged the innovation needed to keep French *haute cuisine* at the cutting edge.

This is a theory which could be applied more widely to the French economy.

In the meantime, the next time you are in Paris, if you want to experience French cooking at its best, at reasonable prices, as practised by a young man from Whitefield, try "Le Timbre".

■ Beaune of Contention
AUGUST 2006

Where would you find a wine list in France without a single bottle of Bordeaux?

Easy. Go to Beaune, capital of the Burgundy wine industry.

In a Beaune restaurant, we were given a list with twenty pages of Burgundy wines and then—as a sop to the obstinate—two pages of "wines from the provinces of France". The sub-list contained bottles from every French region, except Bordeaux.

Small-minded, the Burgundians? No, just proud.

I was in Beaune with two readers of *The Independent*, Chris and Mary Shepherd, who bid successfully in our Christmas charity auction for a day in the Burgundy vineyards. We had a wonderful day, organised by the "bureau interprofessionnel" of Burgundy wine growers and traders, visiting the ripening grapes, tasting the 2005 vintage from barrels (and older wines from bottles) and talking to the people who produce them.

Much noise has been heard from Bordeaux this year, both good and bad; both ecstatic and catastrophic. The great châteaux in that other wine-growing region say—with some justification—that their 2005 vintage will be exceptional. Although not yet bottled, the finest 2005 clarets are already selling at silly prices to wine lovers and speculators.

Meanwhile, smaller producers of lower-quality "generic" Bordeaux are marooned on the rocks of the world glut of wine. They are unable to sell their 2004 generic claret, never mind the 2005, at any price.

Much less, good or bad, has been heard from Burgundy. Why? The Burgundy growers and traders—often the same thing—make three points. First, their 2005 vintage is probably every bit as good as Bordeaux. Burgundians prefer to wait and see, however, before talking of the "vintage of the century". Second, Burgundy does not have the same class distinctions as Bordeaux, segregated between the posh châteaux and the rest. In Burgundy, the *domaines*, or wine-holdings, are small plots scattered over many vineyards, both high quality and lesser quality. Third, Burgundy did not make the same over-planting mistakes as Bordeaux in the 1980s and 1990s.

As a result, the glut of lower-quality wine in the world is a problem for Burgundy but not a disaster.

Two other points emerged strongly. First, Burgundy vineyards are going over in a big way to natural production of wine without chemical fertilisers, pesticides or weed-killers. They prefer not to make a fuss about this on the label. They do not want a kind of "tree-huggers'" wine image. They believe that the quality of natural wine will speak for itself. Second, there is a younger generation of growers and traders taking over in Burgundy. They are aware of the best, and worst, of what has been done in the New World. They are aware that French wine must adjust to the challenge, while avoiding some of the self-defeating short-cuts used in the past (such as placing chemicals in some of the best wine-growing soil in the world).

Vincent Girardin, 45, in Meursault, has built his own twenty-hectare (fifty-acre) domaine in the past 27 years. Typically for Burgundy, this ranges from generic Chardonnay to small sections of two "premier cru" vineyards, Bâtard-Montrachet and Bienvenues-Bâtard-Montrachet. The white wines produced here are among the finest on the planet. Add their neighbour, Montrachet, and you can leave out the among.

"There is still a peasant attitude in Burgundy," said M. Girardin. "We don't have châteaux, like Bordeaux. We have vineyards. We are close to the earth and to the vines. And that's the way we want to keep it."

Grégory Patriat, 31, is the wine-maker at an established Burgundy name, Maison Jean-Claude Boisset in Nuits-Saint-Georges. He has made his way up from field worker. The house owns its vineyards but also buys grapes from famous "grand" and "premier" cru plots to make wines under its own label, choosing only the best grapes available. This is a shift towards the New World way of doing things.

M. Patriat, whose wines are superlative, is frank about some of the mistakes made in Burgundy in the past. Many vineyards—even the finest—were replanted with a variety of Pinot Noir grapes called Pinot Droit, which produces large, succulent grapes—"as big as beetroots," M. Patriat says—but poorer-quality wine. He will buy grapes only from the vineyards which still have the gnarled, smaller Pinot Noir vines (which are being widely reintroduced).

And what of the 2005 vintage? "Down in Bordeaux, every year is the best wine ever," he said. "Here, we don't shout as much. We are quietly confident that the 2005 will be fantastic and that 2006 may be equally good."

I told him about the Beaune restaurant without a single Bordeaux on its list. "Quite right," he said. "Why come to Burgundy and drink inferior wines?"

PART FIVE

Politics

OK, *d'accord*, there is a little on politics. But these articles are about politics on the rebound, or they stumble upon political issues from unusual directions. How, for instance, did the former Prime Minister Jean-Pierre Raffarin come to kill my daughter's cat? Why is Carla Bruni-Sarkozy a cartoon anti-heroine? Why did Sarko take a foul-mouthed stand-up comedian to meet the Pope?

To M. Raffarin, I owe an apology. I find that my only references to him in this selection are slighting or dismissive. He was not a successful prime minister but he is a very likeable and decent man. He once told me off, in a very friendly way, for not wearing a coat on a cold day. Since he left office, he has turned into a kind of Jiminy Cricket, everyman, all-purpose conscience of the French centre-right. Since the French centre-right never had a conscience before, this can only be a good thing.

It is customary to say that Nicolas Sarkozy has woken up French politics and French government and that is, I suppose, partly true. But like many other people I find that I miss Jacques Chirac now that he spends all his time (rather than just half his time) drinking beer and watching sumo-wrestling tapes. Chirac was a monster in many ways but a loveable monster.

Sarkozy, whom I have met only once, is just as you see him on the TV: a vain, hyperactive, brilliant, shallow, determined, erratic man with the attention span, energy and personal charm of a ten-year-old boy. His mission is not to reform France so much as change the way that France thinks about itself and make it less self-regarding and more can-do. He may succeed.

■ On the Front Line
MARCH 1997

The man at the bus stop started talking to me, something almost unheard of in Paris. I had Clare with me and he told me that he had a small daughter of his own. He had also lived abroad, confirming my wife's theory that the French (Parisians anyway) are much friendlier when they have been subjected to foreign influences.

He was a specialist in tax avoidance who had lived in Britain, Africa and Washington. He spoke interestingly and pessimistically about the problems of the French economy. Times were hard but would get worse. Since I had also lived in Washington, I asked whether he had enjoyed being there. "Ah, non, it was much too coloured for me," he said. Seeing my negative facial sign-language, he added: "In any case, it was too coloured for a French person."

The question arises: are the French racist? In the ideological sense of obsession with race and white supremacy, I think not, despite the rise of the Front National. In the broader sense of cultural solipsism, even cultural intolerance, there is a case to answer. The French call it *nombrilisme*—preoccupation with one's own belly-button.

We have come across it ourselves. We have invited school-friends of Charles's to come to the house, sending formal notes to the parents in the approved manner, and received no reply whatsoever. The parents who do respond have some kind of foreign experience or connection. They tell us the reaction of the other parents is typical. They have rigidly structured lives and an approved pattern of friends. They have no interest in making connections with foreigners.

Here is a seeming paradox. On one hand you have the overpowering self-satisfaction and self-confidence of the French. On the other, you have a nation gripped by a great crisis of confidence. The mood into which France has plunged in the past two years is composed of many things, but underlying it is a fear of the modern world, a fear that the French economy and French culture will be swamped in the techno-global world of the 21st century.

The paradox is no paradox but two sides of the same coin. France is more worried than other nations about loss of identity because it thinks it has more to lose. It will have to speak to foreigners; travel abroad. It fears bad culture drives out good. Put more pejoratively, France is anxious about having to measure its superiority against the rest of the world on a daily basis.

At its extreme, as propagated by the Front, this has become a conspiracy theory. France is the victim of a conspiracy by the forces of Anti-France, comprising the Jewish lobbies, freemasons, homosexuals, the Trilateral Commission, the European Commission and Jean-Marie Le Pen's new bugbear, the US. They are plotting to abolish culture and identity and replace it with a lowest-common-denominator world culture.

At some rallies, this view is promoted in Orwellian cadences: *croques monsieur* good, hamburgers bad; Orangina good, Coca-Cola bad; berets good, baseball caps bad. One should not laugh too loudly. This is a new and effective way of extending the FN's message beyond the purely racial to something more amorphously and powerfully cultural. It plays on legitimate anxieties but is based on a lie.

The obsession, and it is not just a FN obsession, with a fragile, and threatened, French cultural purity is a distortion of history and a trap. The kind of stultifying inwardness it implies would be—already is—a bigger threat to French greatness than globalisation or illegal immigration. France has always been strong enough to absorb influences from the world and be for ever French. France has much to offer the new global world. It will, arguably, also benefit from having its doors and windows opened wider and becoming less *nombriliste*.

This week I was in Toulon, a Front National-run town which has long had the reputation of being the most intolerant in France. I was waiting, with some dread, for a Le Pen rally for fanatical *frontiste* pensioners. I went to a café, which had check-clothed tables spilling into the sunshine.

The *patron* and the one waiter were evidently, but not aggressively, homosexual. Other customers included an Arab family who were on first-name terms with the waiter, two old men from a Marcel Pagnol Provençal novel who kept falling asleep over their lunch, a table of yuppies who chatted among themselves and into their mobile phones, and a group of women in their thirties who joked vulgarly with the waiter and pinched his bottom.

The experience, and the food, inoculated me with a sense of well-being before I entered the rally. Despite its cosmopolitan *joie de vivre*, the café was unmistakably and incorruptibly French.

■ A Pont Too Far
MAY 1997

The workmen next door to the office have stopped their ceaseless drilling. The children rarely seem to go to school. Black, the peripatetic school rabbit, has moved in with us for a five-day weekend. There is a luxurious choice of parking places in the street. The newspaper kiosk on the corner is closed. So, tragically, is the patisserie next door. It is, in short, Paris in the month of May.

August is the laziest month in France; but May is the oddest. The month is punctured by official 24-hour holidays—May Day, Ascension Day, Pentecost. It is further cluttered by *ponts*, which are like the Pont d'Avignon, bridges to nowhere: official and unofficial extra days of holiday, which join up the real holidays with the weekends.

Thus this week there were only two days of school. Thursday was a religious holiday (Ascension Day). Friday was a pont. Wednesday was thrown in for good measure. Last week, with May Day falling on Thursday, Friday became a pont and there were three days of school. Next week is normal. The following week, with Pentecost on the Tuesday and a pont on the Monday, school is down to three days again.

Charles cannot believe his luck: three half-term holidays in the same month. The same pattern is repeated throughout the civil service (which invented ponts) and much of business and industry, especially in the capital. The provinces appear to work a little harder.

The ponts, it is maintained, regularise what would otherwise be a chaotic situation. Hundreds of thousands of people would take the bridging days off anyway. The result is that much of the country spends the month in a kind of twilight between work and leisure; barely recovered from one long weekend of traffic jams and relatives before it is time to drive into another.

May is, notoriously, a thankless time to conduct business in France. If your business is with the administration, and anything out of the routine, you might as well forget it until June. It so happens, however, that this particular month of May, the French nation is trying to conduct an important piece of business with itself. In the parliamentary elections on 25 May and 1 June, it must decide whether to continue with one of the least popular governments since polling began; or turn to the left. (Anything familiar there?)

It also so happens that most of the campaign falls in the talk-to-me-later month of May, one of the worst possible times to call an election. Or rather: it does not just so happen. President Jacques Chirac, it is widely believed, picked those dates deliberately. The initial plan was to have the statutory two rounds of polling on 1 June and 8 June. The President chose to have the heart of the campaign carved up by long weekends, which would make it difficult for the opposition parties to build up any momentum, or consistently attract the attention of the French people.

The President is a calculating man but he has a history of electoral miscalculations. In one sense, the campaign is going exactly as he expected: nowhere. All around the country, candidates report that their meetings are poorly attended; volunteers hard to come by. One opinion poll last week reported that 51 per cent of the electorate had little or no interest in the election.

Just down our street, there is a primary school which will be a polling station. It has been fenced around by vast steel temporary notice boards to discourage candidates from fly-posting. At this stage the boards would normally be a colourful jumble of earnest faces and vacuous slogans ("Let's change the future"; "A shared leap forward"). At the last count, there were two posters, one severely ripped.

Apathy and lethargy, Mr Chirac calculated, would be agents of the government. They would freeze the opinion-poll lead of the centre-right and benefit incumbent members of the National Assembly, four-fifths of whom are members of the governing coalition. But three weeks into the election, opinion polls are drifting towards the left. It is the government's campaign which seems most becalmed. A nervousness, approaching panic, is haunting the centre-right.

Mr Chirac, who was supposed to be above the fray this time, joined in the campaign this week, earlier than expected. It was as if a football manager had run on to the pitch in his sheepskin coat and tried to head in a corner.

The time of year is not the only explanation for the lifelessness of the campaign. The French remain in a morose and pessimistic mood. The prime minister, Alain Juppé, is a poor campaigner, and thoroughly disliked. The Socialist leader, Lionel Jospin, is a good campaigner, with a dated and unconvincing programme.

The bridges of May are taking their toll, however. The president called the election, nine months before he needed to, because he said the country needed a new *élan*. As one semi-dissident senior figure in Mr Chirac's camp said this week: "The problem is that to have élan, to take a leap forward, you need a run-up. For a run-up you need a clear runway. Every time we take a run, we fall over all these ponts."

Next week, a full week, without holidays, will be crucial. Afterwards, the nation will plunge into Pentecost, which may be a pont too far.

As *Le Monde* pointed out, this last long weekend ends, for many, on 21 May, four days before the first round. Four days to overcome apathy and boredom.

The president hoped a stop-start campaign would lock in his side's advantage; he may have turned the election into a lottery.

▪ Paranoia Politics
APRIL 2002

Bernard is one of those improbably ugly men that you occasionally find in France. His face appears to have been dismantled and reconstructed in the wrong order.

He is a cheerful, fifty-something paranoiac, who works as a fixer for a TV station, loves the rock group Oasis and has mysterious sources in the French security services. A month ago, Bernard came to me with a hot political tip. Jean-Marie Le Pen, he predicted, would win through to the second round of the French presidential election. I laughed at him, of course. At that time, Le Pen was nowhere in the opinion polls; he was running a vague, low-profile campaign.

I saw Bernard again the other day. I apologised for not having taken him more seriously. He pulled a face (as if he needed to). It was obvious that Le Pen would do well, he said. He was the only French politician who spoke honestly to the people. (He hastened to add that he was not personally a "Lepenniste", though I have my doubts.) All the other politicians—Jacques Chirac, Lionel Jospin—were just crooks and puppets, he said.

Puppets? Yes, they were puppets and prisoners of "les lobbies". The lobbies? What lobbies? *The* lobbies, said Bernard, as if they were also a pop-group. The Jews, the freemasons, international capital, the Americans.

France is an odd country in many respects, well-educated, intellectual, well-informed and, at the same time, superstitious, credulous, cynical to the point of being gullible.

Last year, the town of Abbeville in the Somme was seriously flooded for weeks. The experts blamed the fact that it had rained quite a lot. The local mayor accused Lionel Jospin, the prime minister, of ordering the pumping of water from the overflowing Seine, across 100 miles and several ridges and valleys, to rescue Paris and drown Abbeville. Many people in the town believed him. I had lunch at about that time with two highly educated, intelligent Parisians, one an estate agent, the other an advertising executive.

Both said how disgraceful it was that Lionel Jospin should have opened the flood gates in the Seine to inundate Abbeville.

You get the same kind of irrational cynicism in the United States, a country which resembles France much more than the French imagine. Take Jean-Marie Le Pen for instance. Whenever I have seen him in the (considerable) flesh, I have had the same thought. He pretends to be a French patriot. In fact, he is an American TV preacher, who has taken up French politics. With his vulgar, bombastic eloquence, with his manner of strolling around the political platform, microphone in hand, he is pure Jimmy Swaggart.

The strong vote for Le Pen can be explained in many ways. There is a white under-class in France, which feels excluded from prosperity and power; there is a rise in crime and violence, but nothing so bad as Jacques Chirac, Le Pen and French TV make out.

But, beyond that, France, like America, is a country of small towns and big open spaces, of trivial television and low readership of newspapers. It is a country given to rumour and exaggerated gloom and huge swings of mood and opinion. It is a country which easily falls prey to pessimism and paranoia. (The US sins are optimism and paranoia.)

Le Pen understands and exploits all of this skilfully. Whether he believes his own conspiracy theories, I doubt. My impression has always been that he is an opportunist and political entrepreneur (he has certainly made a fortune from politics).

Some of his chieftains are more sincere delusionaries. Farid Smahi, regional councillor in the Paris area, and one of the few people of North African origin to belong to the National Front, told journalists last week that it was not Osama Bin Laden who attacked the US on 11 September. It was the "murderers of Kennedy". Who were they? "Les lobbies", of course.

■ Letter from America
FEBRUARY 2003

A grateful transatlantic reader writes: "You limey saddo. Who gives a shit about your dreary little island and what you hypocrites think..."

This is, broadly, the tone of several e-messages that I received from the US after I defended France's right to have its own opinion on Iraq. There have also been nastier ones and many intelligent ones, on both sides of the argument.

However, the nastiest blow of all was landed by the far-right American propagandist who wrote a column which dismissed the French as "cheese-eating surrender monkeys". When I read that phrase, I knew that the arguments had gone beyond Iraq or Saddam Hussein or Oil or Terrorism or George W. Bush's re-election. We had entered a transatlantic clash of civilisations and I was on the side of the cheese-eaters.

There are many similarities between France and the United States, which explains why the two countries love to hate each so much. Both are large, empty countries, founded on abstract principles. Both believe that they have universal lessons to teach the world.

However, there are also profound differences between the two countries and these differences are symbolised by cheese.

In its roughly 800 years of existence as a nation, France has generated 176 different kinds of cheese. (Charles de Gaulle put the figure at 258, and said that it was impossible to govern a country with so many; Gérard Poulard, France's foremost cheese-waiter, says that there are well over 1,000, if you count all the varieties of one-farm goat cheeses.)

The United States, in its over 200 years of existence, has developed only 24 kinds of cheese. One of these—the most commonly found—is called "American Cheese" (www.cheese. com reports: "American Cheese is smooth, with light, yellow or orange color. The cheese is usually cut into square slices and it does not separate when melted. It has a mild taste.")

Iraq, as befits a totalitarian country, has only one kind of cheese—
"meira" (www.cheese.com says: "Meira is made of sheep's milk.
The curds are cut into strips and matured in a sheepskin bag for
six up to twelve months.") It sounds as if it should be listed among
Iraq's weapons of mass destruction.

America is a country which believes passionately in freedom,
ingenuity and free-enterprise. It has produced only two dozen
kinds of cheese (some of which are excellent copies of French
and British cheeses). However, if you walk into any American
supermarket, you will see that the United States has produced
over fifty different kinds of peanut-butter. They all taste the same
but they have radically different labels.

France is a country which is over-taxed and over-administered by
a suffocating bureaucracy. It has somehow managed to create 176
(or 258 or 1,000) different kinds of cheese, all of which are subtly
different from one another. A *lait cru* (raw milk) Camembert, eaten
at just the right moment (when there is only a thin crust of dry
cheese in the centre), is one of the great achievements of humanity.
Ditto Roquefort; or Saint-Nectaire; or Cantal; or Chaource and so
on and on (and on).

According to the *Wall Street Journal* book of political and
economic orthodoxy, the American Way produces enterprise,
variety and choice. The French Way produces stultification.
Cheese defies this ideology. No wonder that cheese-eating is a
term of insult for American right-wingers.

If we are being offered a choice between a cheese-eating
civilisation and a peanut-butter eating civilisation, I am with the
cheese-eaters. Post 11 September, American politics, and even
American journalism, seems to be going the way of peanut-butter.
There is room for endless freedom of choice, between labels. The
contents of the ideas are not allowed to vary.

However, America—the real America—is not just a peanut-
butter civilisation. Figures produced by the US Department of
Agriculture point to a subversive, and extremely encouraging,
fact. The number of card-carrying cheese-eaters in the United
States is growing dramatically. Americans now consume
almost 13 kilos of cheese per person per year (half as much
as the French but 50 per cent more than the British). French

cheese consumption is growing gently. Unpatriotic American cheese-eating has doubled in the last 25 years.

■ Stop, a Movement Has Started
JULY 2003

In France, when you hear the word "mouvement", you know that everything is about to stop. A "mouvement social" is the politically correct phrase for a strike. France has been subject to a lot of sudden mouvements—in other words partial paralysis—for the past month.

The other day I had to drive a tiny hire-car all the way from Lake Geneva to Paris because the planes and trains were on strike. After a six-hour drive through violent thunder storms, my sympathy for the present mouvements was somewhat diminished.

Just over a year ago, many French electors refused to vote, or voted for the nasties of the far right, or loonies of the far left, because they said that the mainstream politicians did nothing or, in any case, failed to deliver their promises.

I was asked at the time to write a short commentary on the election for the newspaper *Le Figaro*. Politicians in all countries, I said, lied to their electorate. France was unusual because the electorate also lied to the politicians.

French voters claim that they crave a government which will "move France forward". In truth, I wrote, they don't. If any government tries to change anything, a section of the population stops work and marches in the street to protect the status quo. Much of the rest of the country applauds.

I received a number of pained letters from *Figaro* readers attacking me for being anti-French. (Moi?)

One year later...

The centre-right government, elected with an overwhelming majority last June, is attempting—no doubt imperfectly—to deliver some of its promises. It wants to reform the pensions system before it collapses; to reduce the size of the state in order to make the French economy more dynamic; to transfer some of the power of the central government to the regions and *départements.*

And so...

A section of the population, led by teachers and railwaymen, is intermittently stopping work and marching in the street to protect the status quo. Much of the rest of the country—65 per cent according to recent polls—applauds.

The strikers say that they are defending the "public service" in France, which they believe—or claim to believe—is threatened with the dilapidation which has overcome some public services in Britain. In truth, the strikers seem to equate personal privileges and corporate union privileges with the public good.

Some teachers have been on strike for four weeks, just as their pupils approach the *baccalauréat* and other exams. Others are threatening to set up picket-lines to block their own pupils from taking the "bac" from this week. In other words, to defend some abstract notion of the inviolable essence of "the French school", they are ready to sacrifice the future of individual children in their charge.

What is the cosmic threat to the French way of education? The government suggests that teachers should work a couple of years longer and that school nurses and janitors—not teachers—should be transferred from national to local control. Teachers have a lot of other grievances, some imagined, some real, but an important background issue is maintaining the power of the teaching unions in a centralised school system.

In some ways France in 2003 resembles Britain circa 1977. In Britain Margaret Thatcher arrived to break up corporatist privileges. In doing so, she also smashed up many public services. It does not have to be done that way.

Fine that France should invest in high-speed railways and excellent schools. Fine that France should treat public sector workers with respect. Not necessarily fine for train drivers to work an eleven-hour week and retire on 75 per cent pensions at 50. Not fine for the teaching unions to maintain an unhealthy grip on everything from the kindergarten curriculum to individual teaching appointments.

There are signs that the strike movement is fading (in any case, the teachers will be going on holiday soon). If the government wins, it will be a small enough step forward but—for anyone who wishes France long-term wealth and happiness—an important one.

———

I was stranded beside Lake Geneva because I had been to the G8 summit in Evian, which was even more pointless than these things usually are. Summits do, however, mimic life in telling ways.

The great majority of the world's press (over 2,500 of us) were housed in a temporarily converted sports centre. The air-conditioning could not cope and we stifled in temperatures of over 30°C. The travelling White House press corps were given their own hardboard tent with air-conditioning set at arctic levels, just like American offices, cinemas and restaurants in the summer.

President George Bush departed half way through the three-day summit; so did the White House press corps. The hardboard tent remained for another 36 hours with the air-conditioning still roaring away and all the press desks empty.

A few dishevelled, heat-struck journalists, including me, tried to enter. We were chased away, as if we were Mexicans trying to cross the Rio Grande.

▪ Streets of Name
JULY 2003

The Quai François Mitterrand will be one of the grandest addresses in Paris but no-one will live there, except a handful of pigeons and down-and-outs.

The city of Paris—amid some controversy—has decided to rename the right bank of the Seine alongside the southern wing of the Palais du Louvre after the late Socialist president. Until now, that stretch has been called the Quai du Louvre and, for a short distance, the Quai des Tuileries.

To one side of the thoroughfare is the river. To the other side stands the world's largest and most imposing museum. Some would say that this was the perfect place to name after François

Mitterrand—an exalted street with no residents. Mitterrand was a stunning orator, a great and sinuous politician, but an aloof and patrician personality, who led a secret second life for all fourteen years of his presidency.

The controversy about the re-naming was stirred partly by right-wing politicians on the Paris city council, who thought that this was a good opportunity to tease the Socialist mayor, Bertrand Delanoë. M. Delanoë was elected two years ago as a Mr Clean who would scrub away the scandals associated with the two previous mayors (including Jacques Chirac).

Why, the right-wing councillors shrieked, was M. Delanoë honouring a man like Mitterrand, who had been immersed in financial scandals, doubtful friends and political manoeuvres? Even the Greens—allied to M. Delanoë—joined in. Why honour a man like Mitterrand who approved an act of anti-ecological state terrorism, the attack on the *Rainbow Warrior* in Auckland harbour in 1985?

A second front against the Quai Mitterrand was mounted by traditionalists and some residents of the 1st *arrondissement*, who argued that it was wrong to change historic street titles. The Quai des Tuileries has had its name since 1731, the Quai du Louvre since 1804.

Mayor Delanoë gave the same response to both groups: it is a tradition in Paris—and France as a whole—to rename streets after great statesmen and national figures. Mitterrand deserved to be remembered, if for nothing else, for his "grands travaux" (great works) in Paris, including the glass pyramid which surmounts the new underground access to the Louvre. The Louvre quays were the perfect memorial to a man who had done much for Paris and for the arts.

In truth, this is a somewhat lame argument. It used to be traditional to rename streets after French, and international, public figures but it is a tradition no longer. There are many Parisian streets named after 19th-century and early 20th-century French leaders (but no Avenue or Boulevard Napoleon). There are four Parisian streets named after American presidents (Washington, Wilson, Franklin Roosevelt and Kennedy); one named after a British prime minister (Winston Churchill) and one after a British king

(George V). There are also Parisian streets for artists and writers, from Bizet to Balzac and Gershwin to George Bernard Shaw.

However, the only French politician of the Fifth Republic (post 1958) to have a street or square named after him in Paris—against his own strict instructions—is Charles de Gaulle. Even now, 23 years later, no Parisian calls the Place Charles de Gaulle by its official title. It remains the Etoile.

There is no street for the late President Georges Pompidou (although he does have the modern arts centre, always known as Beaubourg). There is nothing for ex-President Valéry Giscard d'Estaing, but perhaps he has to wait until he is dead.

Mayor Delanoë's greatest ally in the battle for the Quai Mitterrand was his long-time political enemy—and Mitterrand's long-time political enemy—President Jacques Chirac. The Elysée Palace gave instructions to the president's centre-right supporters on the Paris town council that they must abstain, rather than vote against the name change.

President Chirac, 71 this year, has an obvious vested interest in reviving the tradition of political street names. Which part of the capital's real estate does he fancy for his own posterity, one wonders?

I would, respectfully, suggest the Rue Vaugirard on the Left Bank, the longest street in Paris. It goes on forever; it is full of twists and turns; and finally it leads nowhere in particular.

■ Death of a Cat
AUGUST 2003

Jean-Pierre Raffarin has killed my daughter's cat.

She was a half-wild cat, very thin and very old, which used vaguely to belong to our hopeless, and now departed, farming neighbour in Normandy, Jean-Michel. When he disappeared, the animal was looked after by our neighbour Madeleine and my daughter, aged nine.

Because she loves cats and cannot have a pet of her own in our flat in Paris, Clare doted on Minette, her weekend cat in Normandy.

A few days ago, Minette disappeared. Clare came back to the house after a fruitless search for the cat and declared, in tears, with a nine-year-old's conviction: "It's Monsieur Raffarin's fault. It's all M. Raffarin's fault that my cat is dead."

Clare barely knows who Jean-Pierre Raffarin is, or what he looks like, but she knows that he is the prime minister. Like many people in France, she assumes that the prime minister is responsible for anything bad that happens and, on extremely rare occasions, for good things that happen.

In this instance, influenced by Madeleine who has become a surrogate granny, Clare had a specific trail of clues which traced Minette's disappearance, or death, back to the Palais Matignon, residence of the prime minister.

Earlier this year, Madeleine was authorised by her doctor and her employer to retire early on health grounds from her job as caretaker of several blocks of flats near Caen. She was therefore able to live full-time at her house, next door to ours, twenty miles away in the Norman hills. She was able to offer a virtually permanent home to Minette and several other semi-feral cats which haunt the village.

A month ago, Madeleine's employer retired and the business was taken over by his brisk and business-like son, who challenged her right to retire early. Despite her worsening health, an independent medical report concluded that, under the present rules, Madeleine must go back to work for another three years or lose part of her pension rights.

Madeleine connects this decision directly to the prime minister's efforts to reform the French pension system. "M. Raffarin says I cannot retire," she says. "M. Raffarin says that I must work, even though I am sick."

Because she can no longer live in the country, except at week-ends, Madeleine cannot offer a permanent home to the village cats. As a result, she believes Minette wandered away or died of hunger. (In truth, she was a very old cat and might well have died of natural causes.)

To Madeleine and Clare, however, the chain of evidence is clear and complete. The prime minister killed Clare's cat.

Under the present French constitution, the prime minister plays an almost medieval or pre-democratic role. Like a sort of Lord Chamberlain or Grand Vizier, he is the man held responsible for great and petty evils. The President of the Republic, the prime minister's boss, normally enjoys a kind of royal privilege, not only a legal immunity but an indulgence in the hearts of the people, who vaguely assume that—unlike the prime minister—he understands their problems and would help them if he could. Usually President Jacques Chirac plays this—ultimately hypocritical—part brilliantly.

Thus the recent searing heat-wave, which may have killed 10,000 mostly elderly French people, was self-evidently M. Raffarin's responsibility, if not M. Raffarin's fault. It was M. Raffarin who was obliged to interrupt his holidays and declare a medical emergency, by which time the heat-wave was already over.

President Chirac remained on holiday under the cooling showers of Quebec, where the worst thing that happened to him was that his wife's pet dog, Sumo, was attacked by three savage strays and had to be rescued by the presidential bodyguards.

M. Chirac said nothing about the heat-wave back home; he did not cut short his Canadian idyll. He did not want to be associated with the bungled reaction of the government. (In fact, the fundamental cause of so many deaths, apart from the devastating heat, was the insistence of the French nation, and its medical system, on virtually closing down in August.)

On this occasion, however, M. Chirac seems to have overdone the royal aloofness. He returned to a barrage of public and media complaints. Over 10,000 of his fellow citizens had died and M. Chirac had said nothing.

A few months ago, both M. Chirac and M. Raffarin were at record levels in the opinion polls. Their fund of popularity is drying up as rapidly as the nation's rivers and corn crops. They cannot afford to lose another stray cat.

■ Chirac, the American
NOVEMBER 2003

Tony Blair spoke in French on the French TV news last week after his summit with Jacques Chirac. Several people told me how startled and delighted that they were to hear a British leader speaking their language.

Mr Blair's French—learned when he worked as a waiter in Paris as a young man—is good but it is no better than Jacques Chirac's English. Curiously, M. Chirac also gained his linguistic skills while working as a waiter, or rather a "soda-jerk" in a Howard Johnson's in Boston in the early 1950s.

Unlike Mr Blair, M. Chirac refuses to do interviews or speak publicly in English. He can certainly still speak the language. A couple of years ago, I watched an unedited TV tape of M. Chirac showing the actor Paul Newman around a French children's home. For forty minutes, he chattered away in excellent English, with an American accent. The President of the Republic told the actor that he still has a certificate, signed by the original Howard Johnson, declaring that "Mr Jack Chirac made a first-class soda jerk".

■ The Sarko Show
DECEMBER 2007

The republican monarchy invented by Charles de Gaulle—aloof, discreet, solemn, haughty—vanished last week somewhere between Cinderella's castle and Space Mountain.

Nicolas Sarkozy wants to reinvent France for the 21st century. He has started by reinventing the French presidency for the Age of Celebrity. The President of the Republic has become the host of a permanent chat show; the only contestant in a Big Brother house called the Elysée Palace; the star of a soap opera, which—as *Le Monde* pointed out—started off as "Desperate Housewives" and now threatens to become the "Bold and the Beautiful".

The centre-left newspaper, *Libération*, describes M. Sarkozy as a "bling-bling president", a non-stop blur of microphones, photo-opportunities, millionaires' yachts, Rolex watches, dark glasses, mobile phones, jogging shorts and, now, trophy girlfriends.

Nicolas Sarkozy, divorced two months ago, took the beautiful model-turned-singer Carla Bruni to Euro Disney last weekend and made sure that the happy news would appear in newspapers and magazines all over the world.

The home-loving, slipper-wearing Charles de Gaulle would never, in any circumstances, have dated a beautiful Franco-Italian pop star and ex-model. The elegant, Machiavellian François Mitterrand might have done so, in secret, but he would never have mingled with the crowds at Euro Disney. Jacques Chirac doubtless dated scores of Italian pop-singers but never encouraged the paparazzi to take their picture.

At the end of the week, the twice-divorced president flew off to visit Pope Benedict XVI. The president greeted the pope cheerfully like an old friend then, as his official delegation was introduced to His Holiness, rudely checked his mobile phone. The Sarkozy entourage included Jean-Marie Bigard, a devout Catholic and France's most popular, and most foul-mouthed, stand-up comedian. The presidential party also included Carla Bruni's mother, Maris Bruni-Tedeschi. M. Sarkozy had apparently wanted to take Carla to Rome as the official "First Girlfriend" but the Vatican thought that this was going too far.

In a speech after accepting an honorary canonship, M. Sarkozy, the bling-bling president who hardly ever attends mass, said: "In this world, obsessed with material comforts, France needs devout Catholics who are not afraid to say what they are and what they believe."

He also insisted that France's roots were "essentially Christian". At one level, it was a thoughtful and brave speech, which argued that Christian and secular values need not conflict. On another level, M. Sarkozy shattered the convention that French presidents, as high representatives of a secular French republic, should not defend or promote one religion above others. The French left was incandescent. The president knew that they would be.

All of this is classical Sarko. Everything is done with confidence;

everything is done rapidly; everything is performed with mirror, or compact video camera, metaphorically in hand. Genres are confused; values muddled; conventions trampled.

The French film director, and occasional political commentator, Claude Chabrol, says that he sees nothing wrong, in principle, with a change of presidential style. The old Mitterrand-Chirac act—I'm-all-powerful-but-not-responsible—was wearing thin. But where, he asks, is Sarkozy going? The much trumpeted, mold-breaking economic reforms have been rather modest so far. "Perhaps there is a plan but it seems to be all thought up on the hoof," M. Chabrol said. "(Sarkozy) is an intelligent man but he does not think very deeply."

Both *Le Monde* and *Libération* have resorted to using the snobbish "V" word, "vulgarité", to describe M. Sarkozy's behaviour.

There *is* something rather vulgar about M. Sarkozy but his vulgarity and his energy are inseparable. He is not part of the traditional French ruling class: effortlessly superior, understated, fundamentally unenterprising, sustained by "old money" or the administrative certainties of the "grandes écoles". He represents a New France of media and advertising and money: brash, self-promoting and full of energy and ideas, not always good ones.

It remains to be seen whether Sarkonomics or the Sarko reform programme amount to much. The Sarko style presages the emergence—for good or ill—of a France which is rather unFrench: less subtle but less hypocritical; vain but not so arrogant; in-your-face but less bound by tradition.

This is proving to be a brutal culture shock, not just on the left, but for many people who would naturally vote on the right and support a centre-right president.

France may never be quite the same again but that is, after all, what Nicolas Sarkozy promised.

■ The Dreaded Banlieues
JUNE 2008

My fourteen-year-old daughter goes every Friday evening to an athletics class at a stadium just outside the Paris city boundary. To her fellow runners—male and female, black, brown and white, big and small—she is known as "la petite Parisienne" (the little Parisian girl).

Clare is actually quite big and not really a Parisian. All the same, to the children in her running club, aged ten to fifteen, she speaks with an impossibly posh French accent and she comes from a strange and alien place, the city of Paris.

They, too, can speak received French when they want to. They prefer to speak—deliberately exaggerating to tease her—the rich, complex slang of the Paris suburbs, a mixture of Arabic, English and African languages with French grammar and French words spoken backwards or clipped in half.

The athletics stadium where her (excellent) running class is held is 100 metres from the Boulevard Périphérique and the boundary of the city of Paris proper. It is, nonetheless, in the "banlieues" (suburbs) and—although not in a troubled or dangerous suburb—part of a very different world.

The urban motorway which hugs the boundary of Paris proper is a sort of ten-lane medieval city wall. Inside the Périphérique is the beautiful city beloved of tourists and the home, for the most part, of the white and the well-off. Outside the Périphérique are the banlieues, a few of them leafy, wealthy and white; some of them poor and abandoned and dangerous.

President Nicolas Sarkozy took last week a bold, and somewhat puzzling, initiative to break down the barriers between Paris and its banlieues. He selected ten teams, each including architects, sociologists, philosophers, geographers, engineers, ecologists and transport specialists, to think up bold schemes and visions for a "Greater Paris". (Philosophers? Yes, philosophers.)

The teams, one of which will be led by the British architect Sir Richard Rogers, will report back in the first half of next year.

The idea is sensible and long overdue. The city of Paris needs to be re-connected to the dynamism of its banlieues. The banlieues need, economically and psychologically, to be re-connected to the French capital.

President Sarkozy's initiative has, nonetheless, puzzled and alarmed many people. Instead of starting with proposals for some kind of greater-Paris political framework, like Greater London, the Elysée Palace has jumped straight to the grandiose building stage. The Socialist leadership of the Paris town hall and the greater Paris area, the Ile de France, have been kept at arm's length.

Critics fear that M. Sarkozy has no real interest in breaking down the invisible wall between Paris and its banlieues. Instead, they say, his plan is a pretentious smoke-screen behind which property developers will be encouraged to create vast new satellite cities of offices. Already, plans are going ahead for three new tower blocks as tall as the Eiffel Tower at La Défense, just west of the city.

This ambitious project was launched four years ago by the former head of the council in the wealthy Hauts de Seine *département*. His name was Nicolas Sarkozy.

▮ The 99th Département
OCTOBER 2008

My son has made a startling discovery which will confirm the deepest fears of the leader writers of *The Sun*.

Britain, according to French officialdom, is part of the 99th *département* of France. So is the United States. So are China, Russia, Gabon, Lithuania and Kazakhstan. In fact, the whole of the rest of the world, save Monaco, is merely the 99th département.

This discovery explains many things. It explains why Nicolas Sarkozy thinks that he rules the world, even if he no longer reigns supreme in the heart of his ex-wife. It explains why President Sarkozy decided this week to save the planet by building fewer motorways in France. It explains why France was devastated not to win its own Rugby World Cup. (Technically, however, France did win. South Africa is also part of the 99th département of France.)

My son is sitting his *baccalauréat*, the French equivalent of A Levels, next June. He recently had to sign his official examination entry form: the "confirmation d'inscription au baccalauréat general". He was born in Washington DC and has Irish, British and American nationality but has been living in France for eleven years.

None of these complications troubled the French educational bureaucracy. His form was filled in as follows. Name: Lichfield, Charles. Nationality: Foreigner. Born: Washington. Département: 099. Country: United States.

Département 099? What is département 099?

There are 95 départements in Metropolitan France, numbered from 01 (Ain, near Lyon) to 95 (Val d'Oise, north of Paris). Their numbers can be found on all French car number plates.

There is no département 96. That space is perhaps reserved for Wallonia, when Belgium finally splits in two. All the overseas départements—Martinique, Guadeloupe and Guyane in the Americas and Réunion in the Indian Ocean—count as département number 97. Monaco, supposedly a sovereign nation, counts as département number 98. Has anyone told His Serene Highness, Prince Albert Alexandre Louis Pierre, Prince of Monaco and Marquis des Baux, that he is, in fact, the ruler of "département 98"?

The whole of the rest of the world, my son explained to me, is département number 99.

Surely this could not be so, I thought. Not even French officialdom would so sweepingly reject the claims to separate identity of other peoples? Was France so similar after all to the British and the Americans, to whom the rest of the world is merely a source of anger or amusement?

I was reminded of the celebrated *New Yorker* magazine front cover which showed the world, as viewed by the typical inhabitant of Manhattan. New Jersey took up seventy per cent of the globe.

Could the whole of the rest of the world, in the French official mind, consist of one département of France?

A little investigative journalism (one phone call and a trawl of the internet) proved that my son was entirely correct. For the education ministry, all foreigners who take the baccalauréat have been born in département 99. According to the interior ministry, the votes of all French citizens who live abroad are cast in département 99. According to the social affairs ministry, all foreigners who use the French state health and pension system, the Sécurité Sociale, started life in département 99.

Much now becomes clear. Consider.

This had been a Black October for President Sarkozy. He had staked much on France winning the rugby World Cup, even announcing in advance that the France coach, Bernard Laporte, would enter his government. When France lost to England in the semi-final, the president was apparently incandescent. "Bang goes one per cent of GDP," he complained.

The president's wife, Cecilia, finally won the divorce that she had been seeking for several months. In two interviews she said, in effect, that she no longer loved her husband. She was not prepared to live a public lie as someone defined as merely the "wife of" a powerful husband who she no longer loved. Maybe that makes Cecilia Sarkozy into a feminist icon, of sorts.

The former prime minister Dominique de Villepin—supposedly Sarkozy's ally; actually a kind of one-man opposition—says privately that "a man cannot govern France if he cannot hold onto his wife." Ninety per cent of the French people tell pollsters that they disagree. In truth, judging by the remarks of my neighbours in Normandy and Paris, they perhaps do not entirely disagree.

Meanwhile, President Sarkozy is dealing with the first big challenge to his plans to make France work harder. A second transport strike looms unless he can persuade the railway unions that steam locomotives have (sadly) vanished and there is no longer any justification for engine drivers to retire at fifty.

The provisional signs are that M. Sarkozy and the more moderate unions are cooking up a deal which will blunt the strikes—and the reforms. The results will then be declared a "rupture" with the fudged reform agenda of the past.

After his environmental conference this week, President Sarkozy promised to save the planet by insulating French homes properly and sending more goods by rail and canal. Much that was agreed at the conference makes sense. However, a couple of months ago, the French state railways announced that they were winding down part of their freight operation. More goods will have to travel by road. No-one seems to have told M. Sarkozy.

France has a way of doing things differently from the rest of the world. Small wonder. It now turns out that France believes, at the heart of its being, in its deepest national sub-conscious, that it *is* the rest of the world.

What happens elsewhere does not matter too much. President Sarkozy's confidence in his own divine right to succeed rapidly recovered from the economic growth-threatening defeat of the France rugby team. Challenged on the stuttering outlook for the French economy last week, he said: "France will have the highest level of growth in the world. France will have the lowest level of unemployment. I have been elected. I will succeed."

This may seem an empty boast, mere bravado. Not necessarily. If the whole world is really France, it becomes a statement of the obvious.

What of poor Cecilia, meanwhile? She divorced the president to avoid the public eye. She has since been on the front cover of every French magazine, serious and non-serious. The king of the French paparazzi has predicted that she will become the new Princess Diana.

Cecilia is said to be considering fleeing into exile. But exile where? Wherever she goes, she will still be in département number 99.

■ Carla, the Cartoon
NOVEMBER 2008

And now, Carla Bruni the cartoon heroine. Or rather the cartoon villainess—a strange blend of Cruella de Vil and Snow White, with a mission to take over the world and remould it according to her own champagne-socialist tastes and ambitions.

France has been giggling, and staring aghast, at a retelling of the story of the political romance of the century in a strange new medium: an investigative comic-book. *Carla & Carlito* (12 Bis Fayard, €12) is the rollicking narrative of how a right-wing, authoritarian, lonely president came to meet, and marry, a left-wing, beautiful, man-eating pop singer, human rights activist and former top model.

The 62-page cartoon book, researched by one of France's best-known investigative journalists, manages to add new details to this familiar story (backed up by two pages of scholarly footnotes). The book reveals, for instance, that President Nicolas Sarkozy is known to his own staff at the Elysée Palace as "Carlito"—or little Carla—because he has fallen so deeply under the influence of his wife.

The facts are mingled with unashamed fantasy and told through inspired imagery, such as a sequence of Disney-like frames showing Carla Bruni hypnotising the president with cat-like eyes and a front-cover image showing a tall, confident Carla carrying a tiny president in a baby sling. The book also includes a passage from an article about Carla Bruni from *The Independent* last March, which is reproduced in a bubble coming from the mouth of a reader. According to the book's cartoonist, Riss, the archetypical reader of this newspaper wears a bowler hat and looks uncannily like the late prime minister, Harold Macmillan.

Fantasy is one thing; politics is another. The authors, the investigative journalist Philippe Cohen and storyline writer Richard Malka, have attempted in satirical comic-book form to make a contribution to a growing political debate in France. Who on earth is Carla Bruni? And what does she want?

The nation's first impressions, that the Italian-born Mme. Bruni-Sarkozy was an air-head and adventuress in quest of public attention and new experiences, are beginning to fade. They are being replaced by another image of Mme. Bruni-Sarkozy as a clever, manipulative—and perhaps, given the country of her birth—Machiavellian woman with a personal and political agenda of her own. *Carla & Carlito* comes down on the Machiavellian side of the argument. The final pages—"purely imaginary, but so true to life," according to the authors—foresee the possibility that Carla might one day emerge as the "French Hillary" and run for the Elysée herself.

The book is the sequel to two previous bestselling illustrated books by the same authors on President Sarkozy's rise. The new book—far better than its predecessors—coincides with another, more traditional investigative book which reveals a fascinating, but disturbing, new side of Carla Bruni-Sarkozy.

The French satirical newspaper, *Le Canard Enchaîné*, broadly equivalent to *Private Eye*, has for several months been publishing a front page spoof diary called "Le Journal de Carla B". In this diary, "Carla" peddles a simplistic left-wing agenda while both mocking and adulating her "little" husband and seeking all means to project herself in glossy magazines. It was revealed in April that Mme. Bruni-Sarkozy loved this diary and had invited its author to lunch. A critical book on *Le Canard Enchaîné* published last week suggests that the "Carla B" diary may not be entirely a spoof after all. The book, *La Face cachée du Canard Enchaîné*, says that Mme. Bruni-Sarkozy feeds tit-bits and storylines for the Carla B journal to the newspaper in order "to send out the right messages". It remains unclear whether she is doing this with, or without, the approval of her husband.

Both books cast new light on the endlessly discussed but never explained relationship between President Sarkozy and Mme. Bruni. On the one hand, there is a right-wing president with repressive and authoritarian social instincts, and political and economic views of variable geometry. On the other hand there is a wealthy woman whose personal instincts, and friends, belong to the libertarian-artistic left.

Mme. Bruni-Sarkozy is already said to have influenced her husband to make a humanitarian U-turn on two high-profile issues: the threatened extradition of a sick, former left-wing terrorist to Italy and the planned organisation, jointly with Britain, of charter flights to dump Afghan refugees back in their home country.

Members of President Sarkozy's centre-right party, the Union pour un Mouvement Populaire (UMP), are becoming increasingly puzzled by Mme. Bruni-Sarkozy's role. "She has become a kind of tagged-on left-wing conscience for the president," one UMP deputy said. "If that is part of a strategy by the president to occupy all the political ground and neutralise the left, that's maybe acceptable. We sometimes wonder, however, how much this is the president's idea and how much it is Mme. Bruni-Sarkozy's."

In *Carla & Carlito*, President Sarkozy emerges as an aggressive, feckless, driven man, motivated by a constant desire to humiliate his enemies and show off to his friends. It is Carla who emerges as a calm, calculating, media strategist, pushing President Sarkozy subtly—and not so subtly—away from his apparent instincts as a right-wing hard-liner and towards her own aristocratic-bohemian view of the world.

Philippe Cohen, one of the authors, told me: "Sarkozy is a man who has always been influenced by women, who has always needed the presence of a strong woman. Contrary to what some people say, he is not a man of strongly held opinions. He can be influenced and he is being influenced by Carla on some issues: not maybe on the financial crisis or Afghanistan but certainly on social and humanitarian issues. Where all that will lead? I don't know but it is clear that we have not heard the last of Carla's influence, as long as she remains amused by life in the Elysée."

In one cheeky frame—not backed up by a footnote, to denote authenticity—Carla is shown leaning over the president's shoulder trying to persuade him to smoke a marijuana joint. On the table in front of him is a dossier entitled "repression of drug-users".

■ Bring Back Jacques
APRIL 2009

A bizarre phenomenon is sweeping France: Chirac nostalgia. As President Nicolas Sarkozy blusters his way through the economic crisis, attitudes to the previous president—immobile but lovable, devious but calmly presidential—have become tinged with a warm glow of selective memory.

Will the rest of the world, will even the Americans, become so exasperated with Sarkozy that we also learn retrospectively to love Jacques Chirac?

President Barack Obama is said to have been deeply irritated by President Sarkozy's look-at-me antics before and during the G-20 summit last week. To threaten to walk out of a summit in which the bulk of the final statement had been agreed days in advance was the height of bad manners. To queue-jump the summit chairman,

Gordon Brown, by racing into a press conference, claiming credit for the G-20 success, while patronisingly praising "mon ami, Gordon" and others, was crassly selfish.

Was M. Sarkozy ever likely to wreck a summit whose most important achievement was going to be a show of unity between west and east, north and south? No, he wasn't.

To American commentators, who had convinced themselves that Sarko was "one of us", his behaviour was disconcerting. To observers in France, and Europe, this was vintage Sarko: a little moralising drama; some common-sense; a touch of exaggeration; a hint of self-contradiction. As ever with President Sarkozy, it was difficult to separate the good from the bad; the pragmatic, can-do, plain-spoken leader that he claims to be from the self-dramatising, directionless politician that he often becomes.

France and Germany did influence the final communiqué, probably for the better, but that work was mostly wrapped up days before the summit began. Gordon Brown did not get his big, new stimulus package, which the French can't afford and the Germans don't want. Paris and Berlin got a useful form of words on tax havens and international supervision of financial markets.

If real history was made at the G-20, it was through the presence of China, India and the others and the refreshingly collegiate approach of President Obama. So why all the fuss from President Sarkozy?

Partly because the Nato summit followed so closely upon G-20. Having made the sensible decision to end France's semi-detached relationship with the Atlantic Alliance, the French president wanted to show that he was no Anglo-Saxon poodle. He also wanted, in the eyes of French domestic opinion, to distance himself from the disgraced, post-Reagan-Thatcher, markets-rule fundamentalism that he had (sometimes) praised in his own rise to power.

Two years after his election, Sarkozy finds himself in a curious double-bind. He is presented in street demonstrations as a heartless French Thatcher, inspired by an "ultra-liberal" agenda which has proved morally and intellectually bankrupt. He is accused by the far-left, the moderate-left, the soft-centre and part of his own centre-right of imposing a series of draconian, Anglo-Saxon-inspired reforms on the French social and economic model.

In truth, Sarkozy has done no such thing. He is being excoriated for his rhetoric, not his achievements. As a new book by two senior French economists points out, Sarkozy has done little more than continue the shuffling three-steps-forward and two-steps-back pattern of previous governments. Pierre Cahuc and André Zylberberg (*Les Réformes ratées du Président Sarkozy*, Flammarion) have minutely analysed the proclaimed advances on the 35-hour week, taxation, pensions, trade union and university reform. They conclude: "There is a huge gulf between what he says and what he does. He claims greater transparency and organises greater opacity. The Sarkozy Method consists of launching lots of reforms at the same time and then conceding new special advantages to each sector to prevent blockages... Those things which he claims to have reformed have been made worse."

Thus, President Sarkozy, the Chirac acolyte turned anti-Chirac, is more Chirac-like than he seems. Minus the charm and minus the calm.

It was always simplistic to see Sarkozy as a Gallic Reagan or Thatcher. From the beginning, there was a statist and protectionist strand to Sarkonomics. Fortunately, when it comes to protectionism, the President also talks the talk more than he walks the walk. Much of his allegedly unfair support for the French car industry in recent weeks has also proved to be posturing and bluster.

In fairness, one should also point to two or three important Sarko achievements. His presidency of the EU last year was a model of what can be achieved by bringing energy and enthusiasm in the European game. He is the first French leader to promote politicians from racial minorities. His decision to end the oddity of France's half-in, half-out relationship with Nato was sensible and courageous. So was his recent decision to end decades of official hypocrisy and shift the weight of agricultural subsidies in France away from rich, large farmers to smaller, poor ones.

In these and other areas, President Sarkozy's chief aim seems to have been to change the way that France thinks about itself: to break down cosy illusions; to remove actual and imagined barriers to enterprise and creativity. There has been a flash flood of small business start-ups, with some government help, since the start of the year. Maybe Sarkozy is having some impact after all.

On the other hand, the recession is only just beginning to bite deeply in France. President Sarkozy has himself spoken privately of his fears of a 1968-style street revolt this spring. The bursting of the global financial bubble has vindicated simplistic arguments on the French left against all forms of enterprise and capitalism.

With the 2012 presidential election in mind, President Sarkozy would like to reposition himself as a kind of Tony Blair in reverse, a statist "reformer of capitalism", rather than a pro-capitalist reformer of the state. That was the intended message of his pre G-20 antics.

His chances of getting away with it depend on the severity of the French recession and the continuing absence of any serious alternative on the French left. For that reason alone, the London summit of April 2009, may come back to haunt Sarkozy.

One of the accidental winners at G-20 was the head of the International Monetary Fund, the former French Socialist finance minister, Dominique Strauss Kahn. As the global "trillion dollar man", he will have a vastly increased profile in the next three years. What better platform to launch a French presidential bid in 2012?

■ Jamais on a Sunday
JULY 2009

France is country of rigid rules, apart from all the exceptions. Looked at another way, it is a country where the exception is the rule. Since that is the rule there are, of course, many exceptions.

Pity, then, President Nicolas Sarkozy as he tilts, Don Quixote-like, against the French ban on Sunday trading which has existed since 1906.

Ban? What ban?

If you enter any small French town or large village on a Sunday morning, there will be at least one bakery and at least one butcher's shop open (something unthinkable in small-town Britain). French cities and large towns have dozens of such shops to choose from.

This is, after all, France. No-one can be expected to eat day-old bread; or pâté; or lamb chops. Food shops and markets have a complete exception from the Sunday trading ban, except for large supermarkets, except in some areas where (as an exception to the exception), they are allowed to open (but not usually in the winter, spring and autumn).

If you go to the inner suburbs of Paris or Lille or Marseille on a Sunday (but not to Lyon) you will find many large stores and malls open which are covered by local exceptions, which may or may not be entirely legal. These exceptions apply mostly to "leisure activities", which include, for some reason, buying furniture. There are also exceptions for "tourist areas", which means that some parts of Paris—the Marais area, for instance—are a hive of commercial activity on a Sunday and others are not.

President Sarkozy likes to complain that the Sunday shopping ban applies to the southern side of the Avenue des Champs Elysées but not to the northern side. This is, unfortunately, a myth. The ban applies to both sides of the most beautiful avenue in the world (apart from those shops which have been granted exceptions, which happen mostly to be on the northern side).

Today, the French National Assembly, the lower house of parliament, will almost certainly approve a new draft law which seeks to give clarity and common-sense to this jumble of Sunday trading rules and exceptions.

Clarity? What clarity? In order to gain the support of rebellious members of his own party, the UMP, M. Sarkozy's new law has been peppered with exceptions of its own. At the same time, it has been attacked as a heartless assault on the very essence of the French way of life by a curious coalition of those who usually agree about nothing: Catholics and Protestants; right-wing traditionalists and most politicians on the left.

The law to be voted today is a much-tattered relic of President Sarkozy's original campaign promise to "legalise Sunday working for everyone willing to work". This was part of a broader pledge, or threat, to make France "work harder and earn more".

A first, ambitious version of the law was wrecked by M. Sarkozy's own parliamentary troops last year. The new version declares Sunday to be sacrosanct and then lists the exceptions and the exceptions to the exceptions. If passed, it will open the way for all shopping malls and big stores to open every Sunday in large conurbations, such as the suburbs of Paris, Lille and Marseille. The greater Lyon area, where M. Sarkozy's supporters dug in their heels, has been declared an exception because it is not an "area traditionally characterised by end of week shopping".

The law would also allow all shops to open on Sundays in "areas much frequented by tourists", unless those tourist areas happen to be in Alsace and Lorraine, which are exempted. The centre-right members for Alsace and Lorraine were happy to "abolish Sunday" in the rest of France but not in their own regions.

There was an interesting argument in the four-day parliamentary debate last week about what constituted a "tourist area". With 70,000,000 visitors a year, almost the whole of France could claim to be a tourist area. There are already two competing definitions under French law, one narrow and one broad. It was decided to apply the narrower definition, applying, in theory, to only 500 French communes, out of 36,000.

There is one huge anomaly in the draft law. Workers in large shops in the Paris, Lille and Marseille areas can refuse to work on Sundays. If they do work, they will be able to claim double wages, plus a day off. Workers in smaller shops in tourist areas can be ordered to work on Sundays, on normal pay.

If passed today, the law still has to go to the upper house, Le Sénat, which is likely to introduce even more exceptions. The much amended draft has become so untidily self-contradictory that it may, in any case, be shot down by France's version of the US Supreme Court, the Conseil Constitutionnel.

Why, then, such stridency and talk of an end to the French way of life? The Catholic Church complains that the law will destroy the sanctity of Sunday (even though only one in ten French Catholics attends mass). The left complains that the law will push France down the slippery slope to US-type, shopaholic dereliction of family values (although France is already one of the EU countries which work most on Sundays).

The three small shopkeepers' federations are against the new law because they fear that it will suck the life out of town centres into shopping malls (and they may have a point). The eight main trade union federations are against the law because they say that their big store members will be bullied into working on Sundays. According to opinion polls, just over half of French people are against the law for a mixture of all the above.

Hyperbole exists on both sides of the argument. President Sarkozy claims that more Sunday shopping will help to end the recession. Even the main employers' federation says that it could only help a tiny bit. M. Sarkozy says that France has become a laughing stock among European nations. He points out that he had to make a personal appeal to boutiques on the Paris Left Bank to allow Michelle Obama and her daughters to go shopping on the Sunday after D-Day. In truth, Mrs Obama could easily have gone shopping elsewhere in Paris on Sunday 7 June. She was given shops to herself mostly for security reasons.

In any case, there are several other EU countries—Germany, Austria, even Belgium—where Sunday closing laws are stricter than in France. Only the Czechs, Swedes and Romanians have no limits on Sunday opening.

No matter. Both sides prefer to argue about myths rather than face up to the messy realities.

This is mostly President Sarkozy's fault. Rather than say that he is making a marginal change in a legal muddle (as some of his ministers admit) he has declared the battle over Sunday to be the battering ram which will create a New France. "For me, it is emblematic," he told doubtful members of his own party in December. "If we drop this, I will be like all the other presidents who have given up reforms after their first two years. If we give way on Sunday working, it will be symbolic."

If the law survives, what will it actually change? In practical terms, not a great deal. Large stores and supermarket chains which have been using loopholes or defying the law to open on Sundays in three large conurbations will be given a kind of amnesty. Many more stores could open in these areas, including supermarkets now closed.

The existing exceptions for tourist areas will be codified rather than changed. There is, however, huge potential for grievance and dispute in the right to higher Sunday wages awarded to some shop workers and not others.

M. Sarkozy's closest supporters argue that the psychological effect of the law could be greater than its practical impact. It should be seen, they say, as part of the president's drive to mess with the French mind: to make the French more entrepreneurial and less consumed by tradition.

To this extent, President Sarkozy is right. The Sunday trading law is emblematic of his two years in power. A marginal reform is proclaimed to be radical in the hope that it will somehow alter the way that the French think about themselves.

PART SIX

Living with *Les Français* and Others

When I was a correspondent in the United States, I managed to travel to all fifty states. Since I arrived in France, I have been keeping a tally of the *départements* I have visited. I am up to 86 of the 94 départements in mainland France. Those that I am missing (train spotting instincts die hard) are mostly in the great, rolling steppes of eastern France where nothing much ever seems to happen. What on earth does go on in Doubs or Haute-Saone?

These articles range from Alsace to Brittany, from the not-so-grim north to the lovely hills of Provence. They also take in such universal French questions as when you should say *tu* or *vous*; how the French celebrate Christmas; and why you can legally drive a car in France without a licence. There is also a peep inside an obsessively secretive part of France, thanks to my son who managed to rise in a decade from being an immigrant child to crashing (by invitation) a couple of French high society balls.

There are also glances at a couple of French icons: the Citroën 2CV and the Tour de France. I once rode in the Tour, albeit in the back of a truck, taking nothing more stimulating than Coca-Cola.

My other claim to immortal celebrity in France is that a puppet called John, bearing a strange resemblance to me and purporting to be the "correspondent of a British newspaper", once appeared on the French political puppet show, *Les Guignols de L'Info*.

■ The Town I Loved So Well
MARCH 1997

Irony is one of those journalistic words which becomes as worn as a piece of soap in a cheap hotel. This week, for the first time in ten years, I went to Strasbourg, one of my favourite cities (a city in which I have often had recourse to worn pieces of soap in cheap hotels).

I experienced something with so many layers of crude irony, that it might have been scripted for a television movie.

In a town which has been fought over by the French and Germans for several centuries, I saw young French men and women and young Germans fighting side by side. To be precise, they were, in the spirit of anarchic European unity, smashing up kerbstones and hurling them at the CRS, the French riot police. They were doing so (supposedly) to protest against the semi-submerged racism and antisemitism of Jean-Marie Le Pen's Front National.

The battlefield they chose—without thinking about it or, as far as I could see, about anything other than their evening's entertainment—was next to the Synagogue of Peace on the Avenue of Peace. The battle was all over in less than five minutes. The fashionably black-clad young French and German anarchists scattered at the first baton and tear gas charge by the CRS—themselves fetchingly attired in a new design of felt-lined, smoke-blue helmets.

I was triply annoyed with the Benetton and Gap anarchists. They had broken with the spirit of an otherwise peaceful demonstration against the FN's national congress. They had given the odious Le Pen—a malevolent clown—something to bray about the next day. And, if I am honest with myself, I was most disappointed that, after I had stumbled on the scene at just the right moment, they did not provide me with a better punch-up and a better story.

It would happen in Strasbourg. Brussels is a famously surreal city, appropriately the home of René Magritte. But Strasbourg, the other Euro-capital, is also given to the surreal. It is an oddly attractive Franco-German mongrel: a mixture of German jolliness and French wit. Strasbourg food, more importantly, has French quality and German quantity.

I first went there in 1980 to cover the European Parliament and went back often over the next seven years. The Parliament, with all its pretensions and barminess, was an intriguing place. The different nationalities of the EU were tipped out of the isolation of their comfortable Brussels homes and offices and pitched together for a week at a time.

Strasbourg, as I knew it, was a place of weird political alliances, impossible cross-cultural friendships and ill-advised affairs. It was epitomised by "Bang the Bells", a bar and restaurant in the gloomy backstreets near the station, patronised by French stage-criminal types.

It was run, with a tongue of iron, by a rotund middle-aged lady in an eyesight-threatening nylon dress. I have forgotten her name. I have forgotten the real name of Bang the Bells, if I ever knew it. It had been colonised by Irish Euro MPs and, up to a point, British Labour members, then in the full rage of socialist Euro-scepticism. Mostly the cross-cultural relationship in Bang the Bells was Franco-Irish. It was called Bang the Bells because you had to ring to get in after a certain hour. Karaoke was perpetrated in Bang the Bells long before the word entered the English language. One night John Hume, the leader of the SDLP, was obliged to sing, in a fine quavering baritone, "The Town I Loved So Well".

Another night Frank Cluskey, Dick Spring's predecessor as the leader of the Irish Labour Party, a sweet bear of a man, was approached by an Irish visitor. "Mr Cluskey," she said, "is this how socialists eat?" Frank looked down at what was a perfectly normal gargantuan Strasbourg meal. "Yes, missus," he said. "Through my gob like everyone else."

After the riot *manqué* on the Avenue of Peace, I walked into the city centre. Its narrow old streets had been wholly occupied by roving gangs of French and German kids from that day's demonstration. They were smashing the occasional window, lighting bonfires, playing tom-toms, juggling with clubs, rolling joints. It was like being in a medieval city which had just been stormed by a foreign army.

The Strasbourgeois were nowhere to be seen on the streets

but were, mysteriously, occupying their normal places in all the restaurants. I joined them happily for a while.

Afterwards, I was drawn by migratory instinct towards Bang the Bells. I knew it would not be there. Madame of the lurid dresses did a runner years ago. Some misunderstanding about tax, apparently. I found what I believed to be the historic site. It is now occupied by a perfectly ordinary-looking formica and aluminium bar. Ah, the town I loved so well.

■ Les Vacances de Monsieur L
SEPTEMBER 1997

In the profound darkness of a wooded ridge, high above the gorges of the Dordogne River, angry Gallic cries disturbed a languid, storm-threatened evening. "We are the Earth team. Earth leader where are you?"

"Go away. I can't help, I am the Fire leader and I've lost my team." Since I was part of the Air team, and as far as I could tell, our entire group was hopelessly lost, I couldn't help much either.

Fifty grown people, and one seven-year-old boy, were stumbling about in the gloom and heat, trying to locate three simple games— darts, Trivial Pursuit and a memory contest—hidden somewhere in the seventy acres of grounds of a small château with pointed, fairytale turrets.

It was Charles's fault. I had seen quite enough of holiday entertainment, French-style, at the karaoke evening the night before. (In French karaoke, quavering renditions of Edith Piaf replace tuneless versions of Frank Sinatra; "La Vie en rose" and "Je ne regrette rien" stand in for "My Way".) But Charles, aged seven, is a devotee of entertainment of any kind, from opera to *Noel's House Party*. He insisted on taking part in the fun and games every night.

Our task was, on a modest scale, like *Jeux sans frontières* meets orienteering. The teams had to locate and complete all the hidden challenges and get back to the converted barn which was Fun HQ. The sadistic twist was that no team could attempt a challenge until every member of the group was present: hence the anxious wailing for friends lost in the dark.

This was not Butlin's, nor even Club Med. It was a charmingly disorganised family-run *colonie de vacances*: a three-star hotel, with three other categories of accommodation—bungalows, chalets and campsites—scattered in the surrounding forest. We were in one of the chalets and the only non-French family around.

There was a record number of foreign tourists in France this summer but we were in Corrèze, President Jacques Chirac's home *département*, which is pretty but unspectacular and not near the sea. The tourists were further south or further west.

The atmosphere was informal and relaxed: entertainment of the dottiest kind was provided but there was no enforced jollity. There were scores of rules and rigid timetables: but none was ever applied. No-one rose before 10 a.m. The *pièces de résistance* were the 19th-century château and its elegant, but grubby, Thirties swimming pool, overlooking ridge upon ridge of west-central France. It was as if there had been another French revolution: the bourgeoisie had been disposed of; and the château turned over to cheap holidays for the workers.

Holidays of this kind, in the green depths of France, away from the crowds, away from the foreigners, are becoming increasingly popular with French people, who, like everyone else, like to go on holiday in France. But our fellow holiday-makers showed no sign of resenting our interloping presence; amusement yes; resentment no.

One of our chalet neighbours was a muscular young Parisian policeman, with two neat, long-healed bullet wounds in his side. Aristide was on holiday with his wife (Francine), his mother-in-law (Francine) and two tough little boys, Mathieu and Thomas.

At first, he would roar with laughter whenever he saw us, as if the concept of foreigners was irresistibly funny. Maybe it was my blue canvas shoes and black socks. Black socks, usually worn with sandals, are said by the French to be the certain sign of an Englishman on holiday.

There was also a strange little girl, aged four or five, who would come to stare at us, but refuse to say anything. Clare, three, found the way to deal with her. She covered her from head to toe in pieces of grass: the little girl still refused to move or say a word. But Charles and Clare played *boules* with all the other children; and Charles rode his bike with them into the woods. By the end of the week, even Aristide could almost talk to us with a straight face.

I was, however, cruelly discriminated against on the night of the manoeuvres in the dark. Our team leader was an earnest young man who had missed the whole point and thought the idea of the game was to come first. When we finally located the Trivial Pursuit (in the campsite showers), I came to his rescue. I knew what the capital of Ireland was.

None the less, when we found the darts, in a tumble-down hut, our leader brushed me aside. I may be useless at boules; Clare regularly defeats me. But as an Englishman, trained in the pubs of Staffordshire and Lancashire, I thought I had a national right to throw the darts. The leader insisted on doing it himself. He missed all the targets and we scored *nul points*. To Charles's disgust, our team came last.

■ The French – At Play and Work
OCTOBER 1999

We begin in a small playground in the 16th *arrondissement*. This part of town used to be the most bourgeois-fashionable place to live in Paris. It is now somewhat out of favour (too many rich foreigners) but is still the heartland of the conservative, the connected, the well-heeled and the self-important.

The mothers and nannies sit on the benches round the edges of the playground, reading gossip magazines or intellectual news magazines. They pay no attention to the beautifully dressed children who are, as usual, kicking one another, stealing one another's sand toys and trying to push the smaller ones off the ladder to the slide. (The national aversion to queuing starts early in France.)

One three-year-old boy takes exception to another three-year-old boy and bites him savagely on the arm. The victim howls. The biting child's *maman* does not even glance up from her magazine. The bitten child complains to his own mother. She refuses, at first, to have anything to do with him. When she finally looks up, she shrieks, not at the aggressor, but at her own son, for failing to defend himself. The only sensible course of action, she suggests, was to bite back. Then she returns to *L'Express*.

This is a fairly typical Parisian playground incident. Do not be fooled by the sight of French children sitting in restaurants immaculately dressed, unnaturally silent and unshifting for hours. In my experience, French children—or at least Parisian children—have two behavioural gears: saintly catatonic under the eyes of their parents or teachers; savagely hyperactive at any other time.

My Irish wife, who has spent two-and-a-half nerve-racking years observing French playgrounds, has drawn an even more sweeping conclusion: French children, especially *haut-bourgeois* children, do not know how to play with other children; they are not encouraged to be civilised with other children; they are encouraged to be assertive and rudely independent, except in the home.

Provincial French children are much better behaved than Parisian children. Some Parisian children are delightful, but my wife's observation seems to be broadly accurate: our own small children have the scratches and teeth-marks to prove it.

The scene now shifts to Nato HQ in Brussels. During the Kosovo war, a friend who is a diplomat for a Nato country was temporarily drafted into that strange building. He was working closely with officials from all the Nato nationalities. A Francophile (as am I), he was surprised to find that the French officials in Nato were universally distrusted and even feared.

At a macro-political level this is understandable. France, as a semi-detached member of Nato, does not always work for what the other countries believe to be the alliance's overall interest. During the Kosovo war, however, this was not an immediate or serious problem. France, as a nation or government, defended its point of view tenaciously but behaved, on the whole, impeccably.

French officials in Nato were distrusted—even by other French officials—for other reasons. They were sneaky and underhand; they would seek ways of tripping up colleagues to make themselves look good; they would put their own immediate comfort and interests before those of the team; they would never be helpful unless there was an obvious gain for themselves or their departments.

At the end of my friend's time there, a French official, also on temporary attachment, approached him and said that he had been "ashamed" to see how all nationalities had worked as a team except the French ones. The French hadn't even worked constructively with one another. He, too, had the scratches and teeth-marks to prove it.

Beware, of course, of generalisations. In my own work in France, I have often come across people who have gone out of their way to help, when there was no possible gain to themselves. (I think, for example, of a shepherd's daughter who led me in her car fifty miles along obscure Alpine roads so that I could interview her father, and of a gendarmerie sergeant who drove me home across the byroads of Normandy when I had stupidly lost my car key.)

Such people, admittedly, are almost always in the provinces; or they are provincial people who happen to be living in Paris. You would never expect such kindnesses from the French "officer classes", the narrow, self-perpetuating and self-regarding elite which staffs the upper slopes of French bureaucracy, politics and, until recently, business.

From the age of two they are trained in self-advancement, self-assertion and extreme competitiveness. The *grandes écoles*, the elite colleges which spawn such people, and to which they aspire to send their children, publicly list their graduating students in intellectual rank order (*le classement*).

An acquaintance who worked at the Ecole Nationale d'Administration, or elite civil service college, was startled to find that students thought it quite proper—part of the education—to devise dirty tricks to reduce someone else's final rank and boost their own.

The scenes I have described are part of a Great French Paradox which infuriates, and fascinates, foreigners. Here is a country that believes fiercely in fraternity, solidarity, and often seems to champion the rights of the state above the individual; yet it is also one in which anti-social behaviour and everyday rudeness abounds, from driving through red traffic lights to allowing dogs to foul pavements.

André Midol, a Parisian campaigner for more civic attitudes who also advises companies and local governments on French group behaviour, believes the paradox may be no paradox: it is precisely because France is a rather authoritarian, possessive society—at the level of state, school, church and family—that people accept less responsibility for their behaviour. There is an attitude of "look after yourself, and your close clan, the state is there to look after the rest."

M. Midol agrees that French children are often bad at playing with other children. They are taught, he says, to try to stand out, to compete, to denigrate, rather than value, others. It makes French people less able to cope with the demands of the post-modern, wired world: a non-hierarchical world, a world that values openness and cooperation and teamwork.

But how do you explain that to a three-year-old in a designer dress who has just bitten your howling child?

■ My Wife's Affair
JUNE 2001

My wife is having an affair.

Not a romantic or sexual affair, but a musical affair.

Two years ago, Margaret took up the piano after a break of twenty years. Her teacher was a kind, young, not fully qualified music student, who lived in one room in the attics of our apartment building in Paris.

A few weeks ago, a French acquaintance who had also resumed the piano after many years, invited Margaret to share another "brilliant" but expensive teacher whom he had discovered. They began to have joint lessons. Margaret also continued the lessons with her original teacher, who had become a friend.

The new teacher was a bald Polish-German in his sixties who wore a rumpled, tweed jacket, faded jeans and a homburg hat. He had previously taught, she heard, in one of the big, Parisian musical academies. We will call him "The Professor". He addressed Margaret only as "Madame". He ordered her to cut her long nails.

"Madame, you cannot possibly play the piano with long nails." He was both flattering and critical of her playing. "Madame, I could tell from the moment that you started playing that you were educated in a convent," he said. (He was right: she was.) He suggested that, though technically good, she was too inhibited to play in the way that he expected, with the swaying, trance-like body and head movements of concert pianists. ("Inhibited" is not a word that Margaret's friends would normally consider a good description of her.)

He was also rude about her French co-pupil. "But of course the French can't play the piano," he said. "Only the Poles, Germans and Russians can truly play the piano."

It was Margaret who said that she felt like she was having an affair. Her first teacher—flattering, competent but undemanding, like a husband—did not know of the existence of her second teacher—who was as tempestuous and *exigeant* as a lover.

The double lessons did not go well. Her French fellow student would stride around looking bored while Margaret played. She wanted to work on pieces that he did not like.

It was agreed that they would have alternate, separate lessons every two weeks. There was a misunderstanding. The Professor turned up at our address when he was supposed to go to the other one. He left a calling card of a kind which—so I thought—disappeared in the 19th century. It carried only his name, no address or telephone number. "A strange person called for you," our concierge said, giving the card to Margaret. Our concierge is a Bosnian Serb Jehovah's Witness. If she finds someone strange then you can be sure that they are strange.

Some mystery, by now, surrounded the exact identity of The Professor.

The other week, Margaret learned that he was conducting a choir. She went along, with a friend, to one of the best-known Parisian ecclesiastical landmarks. There was The Professor, no longer in faded jeans but in black tails and white bow tie, before a capacity audience, conducting, rather brilliantly, a prestigious French amateur choir.

The Professor has now emigrated for the summer season to the south of France, where he conducts choirs and orchestras to entertain the higher-brow tourists. It emerges that he is an almost celebrated, just-below-the-top-rank professional conductor and concert pianist.

Margaret was taken aback. It as if she was a Sunday morning footballer who found that she was being coached by Eric Cantona or Arsène Wenger.

■ The Grand Tour
JULY 2001

This is the way the Tour de France should be. A small town of ageing stones occupies a narrow, wooded valley. A château with pointed turrets stands on the hill. People, young and old, line the streets, harvesting the plastic and teeth-rotting largesse, thrown from a high-speed carnival of absurdly decorated sponsors' cars. We are close to the dead centre of France and it is hot enough to melt a bicycle tyre.

An hour distant, and heading down our way, are 150 of the fittest young men in the world. Some of them—Lance Armstrong, Laurent Jalabert—are already legends of the two-wheeled world: names to place (almost) alongside those of Merckx and Anquetil and Poulidor.

Three gendarmerie cars, orange lights flashing, screech around the bend. "That's no good," says one woman. "They don't give you anything but summonses." *Au contraire*, says an older Tour hand. They give away pens and pencils. Sure enough, everyone dives in the road for a gendarmerie pencil. (The secret is to stand at the back of the crowd and pounce on the over-throws.)

Despite repeated drugs scandals, despite the drugs trial of senior cyclists and trainers in Lille last autumn, despite rumours about new drugs, all seemed normal as the 88th Tour de France made its way northward this week towards Paris and tomorrow's sprint finish on the Champs Elysées.

And yet all is not quite the same. The Tour organisers deny it. So do the police and gendarmerie. Reliable, independent figures are impossible to come by. But it seems to me—watching the TV since the Tour began in Dunkirk, and watching the race live this week—that the crowds are not so big as they were; not so joyous and not so reverent.

Officially, the Tour attracts ten million spectators—some say fifteen million—as it pedals around France, making it the most watched live sporting event in the world. When I rode in the Tour four years ago (drinking Coca-Cola in the back of a Roads Ministry truck), the crowds were stunning. They lined the entire 130-mile stage, up to ten rows deep in the villages and towns, across lower Normandy and Brittany.

This week in Creuse—admittedly an under-populated part of France—I parked my car easily within fifty yards of the Tour route, only an hour before the race arrived. Nowhere—except close to the finish line—were the crowds more than two rows deep.

Bernard Carraz, sixty, from Savoie, was on holiday nearby and had come to watch the parade. "I've seen many Tours over the years," he said. "And quite honestly, I don't think the crowds are what they were. You used to have to wait all day to be sure of a view like this." (We were standing virtually alone at the end of a long, dipping straight.) "Partly, I think people like to watch the race on TV. Partly, it's all the talk of drugs. People don't have the same veneration for the Tour that we had when we were young. Most of these people have come for the gifts from the publicity caravan. Me, too, if I'm honest."

A couple of minutes earlier he had scrambled in the gutter for a miniature Camembert.

Further up the road, Robert Micard, 69, disagreed with every word. "The Tour last passed through this town nine years ago, when there was no media obsession with drugs, as there is now. I'd say the crowds are bigger, much bigger, today than they were then. The truth is people don't listen to all that drugs stuff any more. They don't care. Drugs have always been in cycling. They always will be. These are young men. They have a right to risk their bodies. Why always blame them? No-one wants the race to go slower, not the organisers, not the sponsors and not the fans either."

This has, officially, been the cleanest Tour for years. However, eight professional cyclists have tested positive for the red-blood-cell-boosting drug EPO since new tests were agreed in April. There has been a controversy in this year's race over the allegedly excessive and abusive use of corticoid painkillers (which are tolerated in small quantities).

Martial Gayant, briefly a wearer of the leader's yellow jersey in 1987, before leaving pro-cycling to become a trainer of amateurs, is back with the Tour this year for the first time in a decade. M. Gayant, a trainer of the Française des Jeux team, told the sports newspaper *L'Equipe* on Thursday: "I have been bitterly disappointed, since mixing with the pro cyclists again, to hear all this talk of new 'products'."

The diehard cycling fans may not care. They still come from Belgium and Holland and Germany and Italy and all parts of France to follow the race in their camper vans. The magic of the Tour also continues to charm the people of a small town like this one. Two minutes of a great international sporting event are brought to a few yards from their front rooms (to say nothing of the free t-shirts and key-fobs and boiled sweets and little plastic flags).

But does the Tour still have the same grip on the imagination of the wider French population? "The Tour used to be one of the things that held France together. It was part of our identity, a celebration of France, of its diversity," said Marcel, a prosperous-looking, late middle-aged cycle fan (wearing a give-away Michelin baseball hat). "I don't know whether the crowds are bigger or smaller. I'd say they were smaller. But, more important, look who's *not* here. Where are all the teenagers and young people in their twenties? They don't care about the Tour like we did. It's football, football, football for them."

The last of the advertising caravan finally passes. The Tour is a superhuman test of endurance for the riders: a marathon almost every day for three weeks. But not just for the riders. Imagine having to dance inside a giant rubber croissant on the back of a truck, all the way from Dunkirk to Paris, by way of the Alps and the Pyrenees?

The crowd has gone quiet. A helicopter appears over the valley. "Voilà. Ils arrivent. Ils arrivent."

A gendarmerie motorbike with a blinding, blue, front light screams past, followed by three TV motorbikes. In between, fragile and almost invisible, are four cyclists, trying to make a break for the finish line, twenty miles away. A minute later comes the pelloton, a multi-coloured wasp's swarm of impossibly slender young men on impossibly slender bicycles.

It is all over. "But where's the Tour de France?" says a child. "That was it," says her granny. "You can tell your friends that you saw the Tour de France."

What a great sport; what a great race. What a pity.

■ Enfants Terrible
SEPTEMBER 2001

British visitors to France often get the wrong idea about French children. They see them sitting angelically in restaurants, dressed like adults, with serious expressions on their faces. They assume that is how French children always behave.

That is how the Jean-Christophes and Aurélies perform when they are taken to restaurants by their parents (under threat of death for misbehaviour) or when in class wading through the French school curriculum. At other times, half of them behave like champagne corks released from shaken bottles.

My wife has just returned, mentally exhausted, from a three-day trip to a scientific theme park—with 120, mostly French, eleven-year-olds. Staying at the same hostel on the site were two British school parties, from comprehensive schools in Yorkshire and Lancashire.

Many of the French children were rude, quarrelsome, noisy and demanding; their teachers often found it necessary to scream at them. On the first evening, as the French children fought over their dinner, one British school party filed silently into the dining room, took up their places without a word and ate with perfect table manners. The French teachers looked on astounded.

So did the French children, for a few moments. Then they started sniggering at the dress sense of "les Anglais": all purple trousers, orange T-shirts and garish football tops. The British teachers sat complacently with their charges, in perfect control without having to raise their voices. My wife, too, was impressed, but suspected that this was a pre-arranged performance to put one over on the French.

The next morning, Margaret asked a young French teacher how he had slept. "Miserably," he said. His room was next to a dormitory occupied by those "vulgar" English children. Once closed up in their dormitories and released from patriotic duty, the British kids had spent the night subjecting one another to unspeakable tortures.

"And where were the English teachers?" he asked rhetorically. "Drinking beer and wine downstairs."

■ Hero of the Nation
OCTOBER 2001

As the father of three children, I travel half price on the Paris Metro. I have a thirty per cent discount on the French railways and (if the children are with me) on internal air travel. I pay substantially less tax and qualify for generous family allowances, whatever my income.

To be the father or mother of three children or more in France is to be a privileged person: an official hero of the state; the parent of a *famille nombreuse* (numerous family). For 150 years, France has been troubled by its shortage of children, in comparison with its faster-breeding neighbours (especially, in the 19th century, the Germans and the British). There has been, in the words of one demographic expert, "une préoccupation du désert"—an obsession with emptiness.

Now, abruptly, for the first time in two centuries, France finds to its surprise and joy that it leads Western Europe in the production of babies.

It may be just a statistical blip. The lead is small: 1.89 babies for every woman in France, compared with 1.88 in Ireland and only 1.68 in Britain. But the incentives for procreation given by the French state seem finally to be paying off. Although French women are having their first babies later and later, they are increasingly likely to go on and have a second. According to a report published this week by the French Demographic Institute, 779,000 babies were born in France last year, a five per cent increase on 1999. They have been pouring out at the same rate during 2001, producing France's biggest baby boom for twenty years. The relative collapse of birth rates elsewhere—especially in southern Europe and Ireland—has left France as "championne d'Europe des bébés", in the triumphant words of one newspaper.

To grasp the psychological importance of this, you have to go back two centuries.

Every other European country had a population explosion in the late 18th and early 19th centuries. Advances in medicine and diet meant fewer people died young but, for several decades, the birth rate remained as high as ever. As a consequence, the European population soared.

Not in France. French people also stopped dying young but they also stopped having so many children. Long before family planning happened in other countries, the French began to practise birth control, mostly though coitus interruptus, since condoms were not yet widely available.

Why they did this remains a mystery: some historians put forward economic or legal explanations, to do with French inheritance laws. Others suggest that it was something to do with Jean-Jacques Rousseau and the cult of the child. Families, even poor families, wanted to cherish a small number of children rather than neglect them in large numbers.

For whatever reason, the French birth rate collapsed long before it did elsewhere. France, which for centuries had been the most populous country in Europe—and one of the most thickly populated—saw other nations catch up and even go ahead. At the turn of the 18th and 19th centuries, there were 27.6 million people in France and about 10.5 million in Britain. Both countries now have about 60 million.

In other words if France, which is geographically twice the size of Britain, had grown as rapidly as we did in the first half of the 19th century, there would be 150 million French citizens today. France would be the overwhelmingly dominant country in Western Europe; it would rival the United States as a power on the planet.

The French authorities grasped the significance of the baby shortage in the mid-19th century. Subsidies to families have existed since the early 20th century. The Vichy government from 1940 to 1944 enormously increased them, partly for Catholic fundamentalist reasons. The policy is still pursued vigorously.

Until recently, there were doubts whether this huge investment in procreation had any effect. Some experts continue to have their doubts.

None the less, the subsidies—especially the tax breaks—are offered by some demographers as one reason young French people are having more babies. (There has also been a mini-boom in teenage pregnancies, which had not previously been much of a problem in France).

Other stubborn demographers point out that—European baby champion or not—the birth-rate in France remains below the score needed to maintain the population at its present level. They forecast that the French population will peak at about 64.5 million in forty years' time and then begin to decline.

The same fate, or worse, awaits other European Union countries (Italy 1.19 babies per woman; Spain 1.20; Austria 1.32). Here is the demographic lesson. Babies are strategically important. France, the dominant power in the 18th century, lost its place in the 19th and 20th not because of the Revolution or the Napoleonic wars or through the loss of Quebec, but because it stopped having babies thirty or forty years before other countries. It is time for a Common European baby policy.

■ French Friends
MAY 2002

After five years in France, we have started to make French friends. That may sound slow but the status of "friend" is something which is never awarded lightly in France.

One of my wife's new friends is a doctor. Margaret consulted her about a minor problem and found herself being screamed at when she announced that she had paid the receptionist in advance. "You are a friend. You don't pay," she was told, as if she had committed a serious *faux pas*. She was instructed to claim her money back as she left. A further consultation was arranged with her friend's husband, also a doctor. Once again, there was no question of paying.

When I lived in France twenty years ago, I had the same experience. Surface friendliness is not valued by the French; friendship is hugely important. When you make a French friend, you enter a whole circle of friends. You join a club, with privileges but also commitments and responsibilities. If you try to make social arrangements outside the group, you are treated as if you are unfaithful, even treacherous.

Sophie, another French friend of Margaret's, almost spits in the street when reminded of Barbara, an American woman whom she befriended a few years ago. Their children were also friends. Since Barbara returned to the United States, there has been not a letter, not a phone call, not a postcard, not an e-mail. "In France, we do not behave like that," Sophie says. "Friendship is important."

If you meet a couple at a Parisian dinner party and you decide to invite them to your home, you must also invite the people who introduced you. If you fail to do so, you are assumed to be trying to steal their friends. By inviting both couples, you are offering to connect their circle with yours.

This is part of what makes this country so impenetrable to outsiders, and also so wary of the world outside. France operates through overlapping networks of friends, or cronies, or clients, who have known each other for years and take their relationships seriously. In Britain, or the United States, everyone is pally with everyone else. Friends, though they exist, are not so vital.

To fail to make lasting friends can be dangerous in France. President Jacques Chirac is famously a man with a large number of friends, many of whom have just been appointed to the new French government. This is part of the secret of his survival. Of Lionel Jospin, it was always said that he had few friends in politics. That may be part of the explanation of his failure.

Anglo-Saxon attitudes to friendship vary enormously on the two sides of the Atlantic, however. Before I set out for the United States in 1988, I consulted a senior America-hand and former editor of

The Spectator. His summary of the difference between the US and Britain was: "In America, even your enemies sneakingly want you to succeed. In Britain, even your best friends secretly hope that you will fail."

■ In the Swim
JUNE 2002

Despite their recent disappointment in Korea, the French are a great sporting nation. While we have been busy destroying playgrounds, France has been building them by the hundreds. Every large village, it seems, has a football field and a tennis court which would be the pride of a medium-size town in Britain.

Swimming, however, is another story. Paris is short of swimming pools and the French, in my experience, do not understand swimming. Swimming, as a physical exercise, should be about pain and boredom. Parisians refuse to accept this. They think of swimming pools as small, urban beaches, where they can show off their new costumes, pick one another up and have fun.

In America, where I used occasionally to swim, they know all about swimming. There were strict disciplines on lane directions and speeds, enforced humourlessly by the swimmers themselves. My wife was berated for swimming too fast in the slow lane in the Washington YMCA pool, when she was seven months pregnant.

In the Parisian swimming pool where I go most Monday evenings with my twelve-year-old son, there is no discipline, no sense of direction and very little swimming. At any one time, two-thirds of the swimmers are standing about in the shallow end, chatting one another up. If you insist on doing complete lengths, you have the strange sensation of swimming through a cocktail party.

The other great hazard of Parisian swimming pools is perfume. The French are among the heaviest users of perfume in the world. The other day I hit a perfume slick in the water so thick that I began to choke. If it happens again, I will float on my back until the Ligue pour la Protection des Oiseaux comes to scrub me with detergent and feed me raw fish.

■ Ah, les Anglais
JUNE 2002

Tomorrow is the annual Queen's Birthday Party reception at the British ambassador's residence in Paris.

Known to the initial-loving representatives of HMG (Her Majesty's Government) and the FCO (Foreign and Commonwealth Office) as the "QBP", the reception is one of the hottest diplomatic tickets in town.

Acceptances from the French great and good and from British expats have poured in even more rapidly than usual in this jubilee year. The QBP is to be graced by an HRH—the Duke of York. The French, despite their regicidal activities two centuries ago, cannot resist a touch of royalty.

Most diplomatic receptions are paralysingly dull but I have to admit that the QBP is usually chatty and good fun. A group of grim-suited French guests remarked on this fact when I was talking to them at the QBP last year. It was all "très British," they said.

We stopped talking to watch the military band parade in complex patterns up and down the embassy lawn for a while. We agreed that this was, indeed, "très, très British". Afterwards, they were astonished to find that the soldiers from the band had been invited to drink and eat with the posh guests. That, they said, was "très, très, très British". It would never happen in France, they said, half-admiringly.

It can sometimes be difficult to explain why the French bothered to have a revolution.

■ De-Constructing the Maison Secondaire
OCTOBER 2002

There are now 2,000,000 weekend homes or "maisons secondaires" in the French countryside and fewer than 700,000 farms. I imagine that the imbalance in Britain is even greater.

It seems to me that most of Britain, or England at least, has become one large suburb, punctuated by the occasional farm. Hence the anger and confusions of the recent Countryside March through London. What is the countryside now anyway?

As the proud owner of one of those 2,000,000 French maisons secondaires (there are 3,000,000 if you include the ones in coastal towns), I had a smug belief that France was different. There is "real countryside" still in France, I said; you can walk for miles around our little house in the Norman hills without seeing a car or another person; we, at least, live a proper country life while in Normandy, growing our own leeks and spying on the neighbours. Etc, etc.

A French structuralist anthropologist, who specialises in studying the tribal patterns of French life, has shattered my illusions. Professor Jean-Didier Urbain is, amongst other things, responsible for the best three-word definition of the French that I have come across. He says that the French are "individualists en masse". In other words, they like to do things on their own, so long as everyone else is doing the same.

M. Urbain's latest book, *Paradis verts* (Green Paradises, Payot, €19.95), is an attempt to puncture some of the myths about the French urban dwellers' attachment to "la France profonde", to the rural way of life, to "the provinces". Contrary to what most French weekenders claim, the vast majority do not migrate, like salmon, each weekend to the village of their ancestors. They buy houses where their friends buy houses in fashionable, or cheap, parts of the countryside, within easy striking distance of Paris or Lyon or another big city.

When in the countryside, they like to grow their own flowers and vegetables (one-quarter of all vegetables eaten in France are now home-grown, according to one study). They like to promote local "crafts" and bemoan the replacement of "traditional" farming with ugly and smelly new (but profitable) forms of agriculture, such as vast fields of cereals and intensive pig and poultry units. They like to think that they are on good terms with the permanent country-dwellers, but they are secretly detested.

M. Urbain says that this is part of a Robinson Crusoe syndrome. Weekenders do not flee into the countryside to reconnect with anything but to disconnect, briefly, from the modern world.

They play at being hermits, while assembling as many urban conveniences as possible in their dinky, restored cottages.

Ouch. Stop it. It's all so true that it hurts.

I have a vegetable garden; I took the side of my feckless but picturesque, ex-farming neighbour Jean-Michel, when the real country people hated him. I deplore the fact that Jean-Michel's former fields, with their tumble-down fences and wandering, headstrong horses and pretty cows, have been turned into a neat cereals ranch by a young, successful farmer from the next village.

We seem to be on good terms with our neighbours, except the grumpy, deputy mayor of the commune next door but no-one gets on very well with him. Our other next-door neighbours have virtually adopted our middle child, Clare, as a surrogate grand-daughter. But they—though country people originally—are also weekenders, working and living in Caen twenty miles away during the week.

In fact, our little hamlet has become, depressingly, a perfect example of what M. Urbain is writing about. When we bought our cottage four years ago, there were two small working farms in the village. Both have now gone.

Of the seven habitable dwellings, two belong to retired farmers; four are weekend or holiday homes; and one is rented by a family whose breadwinner works in a factory in Caen.

M. Urbain's point is not to complain about all this. He suggests that it is inevitable, even desirable in its way. His main point is that France is fooling itself about the true nature of the French countryside. France, like England, is becoming a giant suburb. "City residents, by going into the country, are not becoming country folk," he says. "It is the countryside which is becoming residential."

■ Vous, Not Tu, You Brute
NOVEMBER 2002

Advanced French lesson, number one. Should an ape say "tu" or "vous"?

The two French forms of "you"—the familiar and the formal—provide endless trouble to the people who write French subtitles for English language movies. My friend, Brigitte, is engaged in subtitling DVDs for the 1970s American TV series version of *The Planet of the Apes*.

Should the apes say tu or vous? After much discussion with her colleagues, it was decided that the apes should say tu to humans, because they are the inferior species. The humans should say vous to the apes, as a sign of respect.

Another recent task was Billy Wilder's movie *Sunset Boulevard* (1950). Should the fated young protagonist (William Holden) say tu to the ageing movie star (Gloria Swanson) or vous? Brigitte decided that it was clear from one point (although not made explicit) that the young man was going to bed with the old woman. From that scene onwards, she followed the tradition in French movies (and French life) and had them say tu.

■ Rude? Nous?
JULY 2003

The legendary rudeness of the French is a misleading national stereotype, just like the alleged stupidity of the Belgians or the efficiency of the Germans or "le fair-play" of the British. Isn't it?

Not entirely. Every so often, you do come across monstrous, or heroic, acts of French rudeness which could not easily arise elsewhere (except in New York).

Incident no 1: I was sitting with my son on the terrace of a café on the Champs Elysées. Normally, of course, I do not visit such places. We were waiting for a movie to begin. It was a movie about

French gangsters trying to stage a robbery in Chicago. Like all French movies for the last twenty years, it had Gérard Depardieu in it.

A group of German tourists came in out of the rain and sat down at two uncleared tables. The waiter told them curtly that they must wait to be offered a table. They began to speak to him in German and then in English. "This is France. I speak in French," he said. They waited and waited. He refused to serve them. Eventually, when the rain had stopped, they left. As they did so, one of the Germans, a middle-aged woman, leaned over to the waiter and said loudly into his ear: "merde" (shit). He gave her a delighted smile and said: "You see, madame, you *do* speak French."

Incident no 2: I was invited, with other British journalists, to a posh lunch at the National Assembly. A moderately well-known French politician wanted to tell us that Franco-British friendship would survive the Iraq war. We had a good lunch in a gilt-infested room which had paintings with vaguely disturbing, sexual themes on the walls.

One of the guests, a forty-something politics professor at a celebrated Paris institution, arrived when lunch was almost over. He grunted an apology, sat down and said to the waiter: "cheese". He smoked a cigarette while eating his cheese. He made no attempt to contribute to the conversation until our host suggested that he might like to say something. He stated that the considered view of most of his students, left and right, was that American behaviour towards France over Iraq was "extremely rude". He went back to his cheese and his cigarette.

I should also point out, however, that an old friend and colleague made a flying visit to Paris from London the other day to conduct impromptu street interviews on an obscure and facetious subject. He expected the Parisians whom he accosted, Ancient Mariner-like, to insult him. Without exception, they replied to his questions with bewildered courtesy.

Strange as it may seem, the French consider themselves to be a well-mannered nation. Much attention is given to teaching French children the accepted social codes. When my son Charles stayed with a French family for a weekend, he was severely told off for propping his elbows on the table. "In France, only married women are allowed to put their elbows on the table," he was told. "That way they can show off their rings." This may have been a joke.

Rudeness in other nations is often synonymous with ignorance. When the French are rude, they know that they are being rude. The French use manners as a weapon and a shield and an identity badge.

France operates on family, tribal and commercial allegiances or, at least familiarity. If you are outside the tribe, if you are a new customer, French or foreign, especially one unlikely to turn up again, you may well be treated rudely. Come back to the same place three times and you will be treated like a family friend. If you ask abruptly in English on the street for directions, you will be treated abruptly. If you enquire politely whether the person happens to speaks English, you will probably be treated politely.

What social codes should apply to professors of politics at celebrated Paris educational institutions, I have no idea.

■ Tu or Vous 2
DECEMBER 2003

To tu or not to tu, that is the question. It is a question which defeats many outsiders' attempts to penetrate the complexity of social relations in France. After seven years, I still get it wrong.

To whom am I supposed to say "tu" or "toi", the familar form of the second person, equivalent to the old English "thou"? When should I use the more formal "vous"?

There are supposed to be Tu-Vous rules but the rules are complex, perverse and always shifting. The small, harmless-seeming tu is a little grenade of a word, which can explode with vivid and contradictory meanings. It can be a term of endearment; it can be a deliberate insult; it can be a way of suggesting that you are socially or racially superior to another person; it can be a way of claiming membership of an elite.

If a Parisian motorist questions your driving skills (as inexplicably happened to me driving around the Etoile the other day), he makes an intricate French arm gesture and suggest that tu art a cretin/

filthy animal/pederast. Whatever insulting noun he selects, it is the tu that carries the real sting. You are supposed to say vous to someone you don't know, unless they are under the age of, say, sixteen.

But "vous" can also get you into trouble. I recently infuriated my thirteen-year-old son by calling one of his school-friends vous. "Thanks dad, now she thinks that you are a weirdo," he said. It was as if an English parent had insisted on calling his son's friend "Miss Smith".

The Empress Josephine once wrote to a neglectful Emperor Napoleon, addressing him glacially as vous. He wrote back a two word note: "Vous toi-même" (You thyself).

At the simplest level, the rule is that you say vous to adult strangers and tu to near relations, close friends and children. Children are inculcated in tu-vous protocol at school. They can call their teacher tu, until they are six or seven. From the age of eleven—later in some schools—both teachers and pupils are expected to "vouvoyer" (use the vous form).

But there are confusing clauses and sub-sections in the rules, according to generation, tribe and social class. People of the same profession—lawyers, doctors, journalists, footballers—call each other tu, even if they are complete strangers. People who have been to one of the exclusive finishing schools for the French elite (the *grandes écoles*) call each other tu (an example of the familiar form being used as a form of snobbery, to assert membership of a clan).

Some people from posh old families—for instance, Bernadette Chirac—never say tu to anyone, not even to their husbands, not even to their children. The charming, very correct old lady who lives next door to us in Paris told me the other day that she had been addressing her two sisters-in-law as vous for 52 years. "I think 'tu' is used more easily in the lower social orders," she said. "For the old families, especially in northern France, 'vous' is the only correct form, except for a very few intimate relations, and sometimes not even then."

Our friend, Martine—one of the few French people whom I address as tu—says that she believes there is a generational shift. "Young people today, people in their twenties, call themselves 'tu' at the first meeting," she said. "I have no real objection but it sounds wrong to me. I have never felt it right, for instance, to call my mother-in-law 'tu'."

Martine also pointed out another small point of tu-vous lore which had escaped me. When she goes to the market, it pains her to hear customers addressing street traders of Arab origin as tu. It is their way of asserting a racial or master-servant superiority, she said.

Is the tu form gradually taking over, as some people suggest? I doubt it. Every generation seems to shift or challenge the rules but the institution survives.

Tu-vous is ingrained into the French way of life, not just the way of speaking. The easy familiarity and first name terms of the British and Americans are, to the French mind, a meaningless chumminess. In France, formality is respectful; familiarity is earned and means something.

■ The French Way of Christmas
DECEMBER 2003

Search where you like, you will not find a Parisian wearing a Santa Claus hat with red flashing lights.

A sweet and dour German woman complained to me the other day: "The French have no sense of fun. They are too southern. They don't understand Christmas. Have you ever seen a pretty, French Christmas tree?"

There is a great deal to be said for the quietness, and tastefulness, of Christmas in France: no holly-borders; no infestations of cheeky robins; no illuminating Santa hats; no reindeer-antler bonce-bouncers.

Christmas in France is a private, family affair which starts on the evening of the 24th and is all over by the 26th. Excessive consumption of food is encouraged; excessive consumption of drink is not. A recent survey discovered that the average French family spends €400 on Christmas, less than half the average spent in Britain.

However, my German friend does have a point. Sometimes you wish that the French were more seasonally-adjusted.

In the square near our flat, there is a municipal Christmas tree, which has three tatty, blue balls. The Champs Elysées has been using the same Christmas decorations every year for as long as I can remember. White lights, scattered permanently in the trees, are switched on some time in early December. The effect is charming but tired, like an elegant old lady wearing a cheap necklace.

Our local flower market offers magnificent tall Christmas trees but most Parisian families go for trees about as big, and decorative, as loo brushes. At over €300 each for the taller examples of the needle-holding varieties, they can perhaps be forgiven. Our own large, but cheap, needle-shedding tree, with its collection of tasteful ornaments, bought by my wife in America, always attracts astonished comment from French friends.

In an attempt to find a pretty, French, Christmas tree, I turned to the tenth annual Paris show of "designer Christmas trees"— trees conceived by 120 of the world's leading fashion designers and auctioned for a children's charity. Surely Karl Lagerfeld, Tom Ford, Giorgio Armani and others would know how to decorate a tree? The show, which lasts until 3 January at the Artcurial auction house, 7 Rond-point des Champs Elysées, is fun but is more about the designers than it is about Christmas or trees.

Karl Lagerfeld's "tree" is a white woman's jacket on a silver coat-stand, draped with tinsel and baubles. Tom Ford's tree is a collection of photographs of babies' faces, arranged in a fir tree shape on piano wires inside a golden frame. Giorgio Armani's tree is red and made of styrofoam. Gaspard Yurkievich, the Argentinian menswear designer, has sent a small television on a yellow pedestal (presumably a statement about the electronic substitute for Christmas trees in many homes). Only the Christian Dior fashion house sent anything which resembled a fir tree: a fake tree with a white plaster woman's head at the peak.

There is, however, one traditional form of Christmas decoration at which the French excel. The large department stores in Paris compete with each other to have the most original, or witty, or artistic window displays. They even provide little platforms to allow toddlers to press their noses to the glass without being held up by *maman* or *papa*.

This year Galeries Lafayette on Boulevard Haussmann has an ambitious sequence of animated displays showing the problems that Santa Claus encounters delivering presents to, amongst other places, Count Dracula's castle and a haunted Scottish mansion.

Printemps next door has moving tableaux made from dolls and soft toys on strings. An orchestra of frogs (the creatures not the people) boogies to a jazz number. A crowd of over-sexed teddy bears in liquorice-all-sorts stripes attempts endlessly to seduce a crowd of dolls in pink skirts.

This might be a satire on the typical French office Christmas party—if office Christmas parties existed in France.

■ French Letters
SEPTEMBER 2004

France is in the midst of the "rentrée littéraire", or literary "return to work".

Book-reading France, the phrase implies, takes a break from reading each summer to play beach volleyball or lounge in deckchairs. When the bronzed bookworm returns in September, he or she is confronted by an Eiffel Tower of new books: 672 works of non-fiction and 661 novels this year, all published in the space of a month.

The September literary explosion is bizarre, driven by the publishing industry's craving for a large injection of cash from advance sales to bookshops and the fact that most literary prizes are announced in the late autumn.

In theory, the tradition is good for writers and, especially, new writers. Of the novels appearing in France this month, 121 were written by previously unpublished authors. Over a hundred new novelists published in one month? Who says that France has lost its creativity?

In truth, many scores of these new titles will be refused by all bookshops, which have no room to display them and cannot afford to pay the publishers up front for them. Other books will sell a few copies, to friends and aunts of the author, and disappear without trace.

As the newspaper *Le Monde* pointed out, French book publishing is as rational as throwing bottles into the sea. Young writers can find themselves published relatively easily. Afterwards, it is sink or swim. Mostly sink.

François Busnel, editor of *Lire* magazine, says that the September avalanches of new books—and similar avalanches in January and March—are "uniquely French, driven party by cynical motives in the publishing industry but, on the other hand, they do have a positive side."

There are no literary agents in France. Aspiring writers have to make the rounds of the publishing houses. The fact that publishers need to stuff lists for the September rentrée gives young writers a chance, which some of them deserve, says M. Busnel. Press comment and word of mouth can occasionally turn an unknown into a winner.

Such an unknown went on to become one of the great, book-shifting phenomena of French fiction writing in the 1990s: Amélie Nothomb.

Mme. Nothomb, 36, is like so many celebrated French people, a Belgian. She was rejected by dozens of publishers before her first novel *Hygiène de l'assassin* became an unexpected runaway success in September 1992.

French novels are usually advertised by pictures of their authors, looking rumpled and truculent and smoking a cigarette. Mme. Nothomb's books are advertised by her well-scrubbed, elfin good looks and her Mona Lisa smile. Every year she produces a short novel for the rentrée littéraire. Year after year, her book shoots to the top of the fiction bestsellers' charts. Year after year, she is overlooked for the biggest literary prizes, such as the Goncourt, the Femina and the Medici. She did win the less sought after Académie Française award in 1999. (The prestigious prizes are widely assumed to be fixed to allow the publishing houses, and their favourite writers, to take turns. The prizes remain prestigious.)

Mme. Nothomb's father is a senior Belgian diplomat and her books—beautifully written in a poised, rather old-fashioned

French—are based on her experiences as an anorexic-bulimic, observant, rootless young woman, who spent her childhood and teenage years in a string of exotic locations, from Tokyo to New York. Her twelve novels are starting to attract attention abroad. A couple of them were published in English earlier this year.

Amélie Nothomb's latest book is called *Biographie de la faim* (Biography of hunger). It is a monologue by an anorexic-bulimic, observant, rootless Belgian woman called Amélie whose father is a diplomat etc., etc. There are no characters, dialogue or plot. In other words, it is not really a novel at all but a tedious autobiographical essay and nowhere near as good as her earlier books.

Biographie de la faim has nonetheless been published as a "novel". It has shot to the top of the French "fiction" charts and has been included on the first "long list" for the Goncourt "fiction" prize.

"Ah, ha," I said to a literary acquaintance, "It is plainly Madame Northomb's 'turn' to win the Goncourt at last." "Not the slightest chance," I was told. Her publishers, Albin Michel, won last year. It is another publisher's turn. Furthermore, Amélie Nothomb is popular. The Goncourt always goes to a writer who is much too important to be popular. Ah, ha.

■ Driving Legally, Without a Licence
NOVEMBER 2004

Anyone who has driven in rural France will recognise the following maddening experience.

As you spin along (within the speed limit, of course) you come behind a tiny, square, grey car which sounds like a sewing-machine and looks like an old fashioned television on wheels. The car is travelling at 45 kilometres an hour in a ninety kph zone. It seems unable, or unwilling, to progress beyond second gear. Behind the wheel is an implausibly large woman in a flowery cotton-print dress.

Here is an alarming fact: over 200,000 people are believed to be driving illegally without licences in France. Here is another fact, which may sound even more alarming: there are another 100,000 people driving without licences in France perfectly legally. Some of them are as young as sixteen. The normal solo driving age in France is eighteen.

The car described above is known to the French as a "voiturette" or a "voiture sans permis". Although it has four wheels—and increasingly all the other usual motor car features, such as CD players and air conditioning and centrally adjustable wing mirrors—it can be driven without a licence.

Through a strange loophole in the motoring regulations in France, and several other EU countries, lightweight voiturettes, weighing less than 350 kilogrammes (55 stone), powered by tiny diesel scooter engines, are counted as low-powered "motorcycles with four wheels".

They are turned out of the factory with the legal maximum speed of 45 kph (just under thirty mph). They are frequently and illegally souped up by unscrupulous garages in France to a dizzy sixty kph (just under forty mph).

Voiturettes used to be the epitome of rural frumpiness: the Gallic equivalent of the British three-wheeled Reliant (which went out of business three years ago). They have, in the last two or three years, achieved a bizarre new status as the height of cool amongst wealthy Parisian teenagers and some adults. You would rarely see them in Paris a few years ago. Now they are everywhere.

A new generation of voiturettes looks trendier and has top of the range radio/CD players and even leather seats. They sell in France for around €11,000, which is not much cheaper than the smallest real cars. They are, however, extremely cheap to run.

Under French law, there is nothing to stop adults, or even late teenagers, from piloting a two-seater voiturette without any kind of formal training. From this year, sixteen-year-olds have been required merely to pass a five-hour course in basic driving techniques and the highway code.

The French "voiturette", in a more powerful form capable of reaching 70 mph, is also starting to appear in Britain, as a replacement for the defunct Reliant. Under British law, however, you can only drive one if you have, at least, a B1 motorcycle licence.

Microcar, maker of the MC-1, the snazziest of the new range of voiturettes, denies that its car is becoming urban and cool. The company, based near Nantes, says that sales in cities have crept up a little in recent years but there is no urban "voiturette boom".

Garages specialising in voiturettes in Paris beg to differ. "Our sales have been booming for two or three years now," said Philippe, a salesman at a showroom in the 15th *arrondissement.* "For sixteen- and seventeen-year-olds from rich families, they are replacing the scooter, which is cheaper but much more dangerous. Because the little cars look much better than they did, it's become trendy to own one, no longer a kind of social disgrace."

I suspect that the ten voiturette manufacturers in France (which dominates the world market) are wary of being seen as a purveyor of cars to sixteen-year-olds. They insist that their "typical customer" is still a "rural woman over sixty". If the typical customer comes to be seen as an unlicensed teenager, there is likely to be pressure for a change in the law.

As things stand, there is no statistical evidence that voiturettes are dangerous. Taking teenagers off scooters and small motorbikes may, arguably, be a good thing.

The combination of voiturettes and urban lifestyles is, however, an experiment in progress. Oddities are starting to arise. A celebrated French ballet dancer, Patrick Dupond, 45, has been convicted twice this year of being over the alcohol limit at the wheel of a voiturette. *Quelle honte!*

■ Tree Hugging
DECEMBER 2004

For the last seven Christmases, I have bought the family tree from the celebrated flower market in the Place des Ternes near the Arc de Triomphe. Each year, I knew that I was being ripped off. One winter, in a moment of madness, I spent €240 on a tall, perfectly formed tree which was guaranteed to hold its needles. By the twelfth day of Christmas, we had spent a euro for every remaining needle.

Driving along in Normandy the other day, I saw a sign advertising "sapins" (Christmas trees). A farmer stood in a roadside plantation carrying a chain saw. Choose your own tree, he said. There was a choice between sapins which looked like Valéry Giscard d'Estaing, tall and cadaverous, and those which looked like the prime minister, Jean-Pierrre Raffarin, as broad as they were tall with no obvious point. I chose a "Raffarin", two metres high and two metres across.

How much would this tree be, I asked nervously? "Ten euros," the farmer said.

We have a decorated hedge rather than a tree this year but, at ten euros, it is a very fine hedge.

■ Conga Dancing for European Unity
MARCH 2005

The other day sixty French and German fifteen-year-olds danced the conga through our apartment. There is still life and energy in the European Dream. Ask our downstairs neighbours.

A class of thirty teenagers from Cologne was on a week's exchange visit to my son's school. In an absent-minded moment, we invited them, and all Charles's classmates, to a pizza party and "boom" (ie disco) in our flat.

The kids were, without exception, charming.

The German teenagers had a tendency to stamp and jump a lot. They kept sneaking German rock music—which sounded like heavy metal performed on tubas and kettle drums—onto the stereo. The German boys were, on the whole, taller, than the French boys. The German girls were, on the whole, more pneumatic than the French girls.

Otherwise, in terms of dress and attitude, it was difficult to distinguish between them. They, and we, all got on very well. A French girl and a German girl, both small, blonde and bespectacled, arrived together. They might have been twins.

The conga was my son's idea. We also had a brief France v Germany limbo-dancing contest.

I have been reading a great deal recently about the First World War. To see so many young French and German people flocking together without a backwards or hostile thought was rather touching.

Earlier on the same day, I had been at a conference in the British embassy on Franco-British relations, Europe and the proposed new constitution for the European Union. It was an excellent conference, bringing together journalists from both countries. I left the embassy much better informed and rather depressed.

The views of the British journalists, and one historian, ranged from the predictably and arrogantly Euro-sceptic to the cautiously hopeful that the British public might be persuaded next year to vote for a modest and mostly technical, new EU treaty.

What depressed me (although it should have been no great surprise) were the eloquently gloomy contributions of the French speakers, including some of the best known figures in French newspapers and television. They complained that French politicians, from President Jacques Chirac downwards, had abandoned all sense of purpose about Europe. They complained that many French people—especially the left wing and the 50 per cent of French workers employed by the state—now saw Europe as a threat, rather than an opportunity. One veteran French TV commentator complained that young French and young Germans had no passion for the EU. To the post-war and post-wall continental generations, he said, Europe was about easy travel and cross-border shopping.

I'm not a European federalist. I never thought that a European super-state was a) a good idea or b) ever likely to happen. When I first went to cover Brussels in the "money back" early 1980s, I was vaguely anti-European. I came to believe that the tedious, imperfect EU does much—and much that only it could do—to promote important national interests (such as peace, prosperity and happiness) for all Europeans, even the ungrateful British.

This pragmatic argument has never sold well in pragmatic Britain. We all love cheap, European air-fares but how often do we remember that we owe them to Brussels?

On the continent, the EU was originally sold—maybe oversold—as a noble and spiritual cause. Now a less ambitious and high-flown European project is distrusted by some and regarded by others as part of the political wallpaper. In Britain, the EU is menaced by relentless, ideological propaganda; on the continent by apathy.

That night my modest and rational (I believe) European faith was restored by the sight and sound of 60 French and German teenagers doing the conga through my front room.

However, in the interests of balanced reporting (as invariably observed in the British Euro-sceptic press) I have to admit to two things. The language that our young French and German guests spoke amongst themselves was English. "No-one's interested in learning French. What's the point?" one extremely large German boy said. Later in the week, French teachers in Charles' school threw a wobbly—as only French teachers can—with the whole German group. Lessons had been prepared for them, in German, on French history and Franco-German relations. The German kids preferred to gossip about the best and cheapest shops in Paris.

■ Three Men on a Walk
APRIL 2005

There was a Frenchman, an American and an Englishman...

For a day—a marvellous day—we walked through the Lubéron hills of Provence, passing farmhouses the colour of old cheese, clumps of wild rosemary and thyme, and ancient villages clinging precariously to sheer hill-sides.

The American, Mark, and the Frenchman, Hervé, were on a week's walking tour. They were plotting their own route from restaurant to restaurant, and guest house to guest house, using one of France's least discussed cultural treasures, its dense tangle of public footpaths.

I had, jealously, heard Mark and Hervé—fifty-something fathers like me—planning their tour as we stood outside our daughters' Paris school. Since I was going to the French deep south to attend a wine producers' riot, they let me join them for a day.

Mark is a doctor from Maryland, taking a career break in Paris with his wife and daughter. Hervé is a globe-trotting businessman in the specialist paper industry.

They are teasingly quarrelsome friends. "It's like having a child," Mark said. "I'm his mother. I just left him alone for a minute to go into a store in a village and he wandered off. I didn't see him for an hour." "Yes," said Hervé, "And do you know what I found him doing? He was sitting outside a café, in the most beautiful village in France, drinking a Coca-Cola."

Mark and Hervé's five-day tour of the Lubéron (Peter Mayle country) was based on the methods advocated by a wonderful book, *France on Foot*, written by an American chef, Bruce LeFavour (Attis Press, $24.95). The book does not lay down bossy itineraries for French walking holidays. It tells you how to create your own. Since France's network of footpaths is so immense, Mr LeFavour argues, anyone able to hold a map the right way up, while reading a selection of restaurant and guest-house guides, can plan their own tent-free route. Join up the dots between one excellent meal and comfortable bed and the next.

France has 112,000 miles of footpaths. This is the offical figure. There are far more. There are 38,000 miles of Sentiers de Grande Randonnée (GRs) or long-distance footpaths. There are 25,000 miles of regional paths—Grandes Randonées du Pays or GRPs. There are officially 49,000 miles but in fact probably more like 100,000 miles of local paths or Petites Randonnées (PRs).

The tracks are, in theory, marked by blazes of paint on trees or rocks, with elaborate runes to indicate turns or dead ends. The long-distance paths or GRs are marked in red and white; the regional paths in red and yellow; and the local paths in yellow, orange or blue.

This is the theory. In reality, there are stretches where every tree tells you how to behave and then, abruptly, nothing: no runes, no rules, no signs, no clues. In other words, French footpaths are a microcosm of France.

We got mildly lost a couple of times but we rapidly stumbled onto another path. Hervé accused us of chattering too much and not paying attention to the signs or the beauties (stunning, admittedly) of the Lubéron.

We were discussing, for instance, Anglo-Saxon and French attitudes to friendship. "In America," Mark said, a friend is someone you've met." "In France," Hervé said, "you are only allowed five friends but they are your friends for life." Only if a friend dies, I suggested, does a Frenchman have a vacancy for another one. "Exactly," said Hervé.

Whoops, missed the path again.

We were also listening to Mark's compelling and gruesome tales of his time as a senior doctor in Maryland's principal trauma unit. "You would think," Hervé said, "that walking with a doctor would give you a sense of security. No. You have to listen to Mark's stories of the most terrible things that can happen to the human body."

"Motorcycle and scooter accidents were the worst," Mark continued. "I once had to treat this teenage girl who was riding behind her boyfriend when they left the road at eighty mph, entered a field and hit a tree stump. She shot seventy feet through the air and broke her hip. I asked her how it felt to fly through the air like that. She replied: 'actually, it was kind of neat'."

Walking with Mark and Hervé was also kind of neat. I left them quarrelling happily over who had the hotel key and who had the right to the room with a shower.

■ Right Track? Or Left?

MAY 2005

I recently visited La Cité du Train, the new French railway museum in Mulhouse in Alsace. The museum is excellent—highly recommended for all unreconstructed train spotters (like me) who happen to be in eastern France this summer.

Whilst there, I discovered an oddity, which shows how much France (never mind Europe) is still not one country.

French trains, like British trains, have always taken the left-hand of two tracks. German trains have always travelled on the right.

The railways in Alsace were built while the province was part of Germany (1870–1919). To this day, trains in Alsace take the right hand track. When SNCF trains arrive from the rest of France, 86 years after Alsace became French, they cross over from left to the right.

Isn't that fascinating?

■ Armani Man
MAY 2005

Foreigners can be a terrible nuisance. The other day I was walking innocently down the Avenue de Friedland near the Etoile, when a car stopped and the driver beckoned me over, pointing to a map.

I went over to his battered little car. "I am an Italian," the man said in French. "I am in the fashion business." He turned over the lapel of his white jacket, as if to prove his point.

He pointed to a large plastic bag,

"I have here a Giorgio Armani suit, which I am supposed to take back to Italy. I don't want to do it. You are a fashionable young man. You can have it. For free."

Smelling a rat, and rapidly calculating that no Giorgio Armani suit ever made would be likely to fit me, I turned down his generous offer. He swore at me in Italian and drove away.

I told my story to my wife. She agreed about the suit. She also reminded me that something uncannily similar had happened to her in almost the same spot two years ago. An Italian in a battered car had called her over, holding a map. When she leaned into his window, he drove away.

Was it the same man? No. Mine was thin and thirtyish. Hers was fat and fiftyish.

Can anyone explain what is going on?

———

The younger generation can also be a terrible nuisance. Charlotte, eleven, a friend of one of my daughters, lost her tortoise a month ago while visiting her family's house in Provence. It is difficult to imagine a tortoise running away but that is apparently what happened.

Four weeks later, the tortoise had still not progressed beyond the next door neighbour's garden. It was discovered there last week. The neighbours rang Charlotte in Paris with the good news.

"Could you send it to me in the post?" she asked. Silence at the other end of the line.

■ Armani Man 2
JUNE 2005

I have stumbled on a mystery "sans frontières". I have uncovered a bizarre and unsettling pattern of pan-European crime (quite apart from the unforgiveable French and Dutch "no" votes in the euro-referenda).

In my last column, I described an incident in which I was approached in Paris by an Italian in a car who wanted to give me an Armani suit. When I refused the gift, he swore and drove off at high-speed.

I, and *The Independent*, have since been inundated with e-mails and letters describing similar puzzling encounters.

Paul Wheeler sent me the following message from London. "I was walking towards Cromwell Road when a car screeched to a halt and the driver called out. I assumed he wanted directions until he asked if I spoke Italian. When I said I didn't, he carried on rapidly in fractured English, and from the little I understood, was saying he had to get to Heathrow quickly, but first needed to get rid of some men's Italian clothes lying on his back seat. 'I have Armani, Versace, everything. You want them? Is free. Here, come, look.' He was well built, in his forties and seemed overwrought. When I walked on, he yelled something I took to be less than polite, then made a tyre-burning five point turn and sped off."

David Roberts had the same experience in Brighton last month. "I was approached by a man in a car and I was expecting him to ask for street directions. He told me he was an Italian and made a point of showing me his EU Italian passport and air tickets... He pointed to a plastic bag on the car seat beside him and told me he had a jacket in it which I could have as a present... I declined and he drove off. Throughout the encounter he was polite."

Other letters or anecdotes tell of sightings of Armani Man at locations across Europe from Verona to Paris. He has also appeared in Bristol, in Norfolk, in a Sainsbury's car park in Derby and at the Birch Service Station (westbound) on the M62 near Manchester.

What is going on?

The first deduction that we can make is that, like Santa Claus and the Loch Ness Monster, there cannot be just one Armani Man. There must be legions of Armani Men, all using the same pitch or script. He is variously reported as being young, old, middle-aged, short, tall, thin and well-built, rude and polite.

What is his game? I consulted the Metropolitan Police press office and the Préfecture de Police in Paris.

Scotland Yard, just like in the Sherlock Holmes stories, showed the intellectual curiosity of a truncheon. A bored-sounding woman in the press office refused to even pass on the details of this authentic "three-pipe problem" (Sherlock Holmes' phrase, as quoted by Mr Wheeler).

The Préfecture de Police in Paris was very interested indeed. They asked me to send them a long, written account of my assembled evidence. They rang back to say that the Armani Man "phenomenon" was "unknown to the Paris police".

It turned out that the police head of communications was being fired that day. I do not think that he treated this important investigation with the care that it deserved.

Searches on the internet reveal that Armani Man is also active in the US—more fruitfully than in Europe, it seems. There are several plaintive messages from Americans who have handed over sums as large as $400 to distressed Italians in cars wanting to get rid of "free" Armani suits or jackets.

It appears that Armani Man is just a vulgar con-man. The suits are bait to hook the gullible. They lead into a complex sob story about robbery or personal bereavement. How disappointing.

P.S. I also said last time that no Armani suit would be small enough to fit me. As a result, I received an e-mail from Messrs Norton and Townsend, a tailoring company in London which measures you in your home or office.

Thank you, gentlemen, but I think I will stick with my present tailors, the shipyards of Les Chantiers de L'Atlantique in Saint-Nazaire.

■ Crossing Borders
APRIL 2006

I joined the Munich to Paris express train at Ulm in western Bavaria. I had the—for me—delightful prospect of a seven-and-a-half-hour train journey across Europe. There was even a restaurant car: a throw-back to the lost civilisation of Agatha Christie, Hercule Poirot, Wagons Lits and the Orient Express.

The ticket inspector was a jolly and jokey man, confounding the stereotype of German officialdom. He looked at my ticket and beamed. He seemed astonished to discover that a passenger on the direct Paris express should be travelling to Paris. He went into a Benny Hill-routine of naughty, French-sounding noises: "Ah Pareee, ooh, ooh, ooh, lah, lah, lah, hah, hah, hah."

The train was full until Karlsruhe. When it crossed the Rhine at Strasbourg it was empty. It then filled up again and, after Nancy, there was not an empty seat.

In other words, the direct Munich-Paris express was not one train but two: a German train to the Rhine valley; a French train from Strasbourg to Paris. There are probably several explanations: cheap air fares; the time of year. All the same, the train seemed to be a symbol of Franco-German relations or lack of relations. Sixty-one years after the war, after half a century of official friendship, the continental giants are living back-to-back lives.

Today (Mon, 8 May) is a bank holiday in France to commemorate the "French" victory over Germany in May 1945. None of the other leading allies in the Second World War still celebrates this date.

The official alliance between Paris and Berlin is at perhaps its lowest ebb in half a century. Chancellor Angela Merkel sees no point in cultivating a soon-to-vanish President Jacques Chirac. Privately, she says that she sees no point in the old Franco-German axis now that the fulcrum of the European Union has shifted to the east.

And yet the determined, wilful post-1945 Franco-German friendship—a friendship imposed from the top, a twinning of elites—is far from dead. The two countries have just introduced a common history book for the equivalent of sixth form students, rewritten by a committee of French and German historians. This book—the first attempt anywhere in the world to write history across borders—covers the period post-1945. The historians had few problems squaring national views of the Cold War and the creation of the European Union.

The next volume covers the Napoleonic and Franco-Prussian wars, 1914–18 and 1939–45. The historians' efforts to harmonise Franco-German prejudices and memories of a century and a half of mutual destruction are eagerly awaited.

This week, an influential pressure group, Le Monde Bilingue, run by an octogenarian French resistance hero, Jean-Marie Bressand, will issue a manifesto urging the people of France and Germany to make renewed and intensive efforts to learn one another's language. M. Bressand, who narrowly escaped execution by the Germans in 1943, is depressed by the collapse of interest in German in French schools and French in German schools. He blames an "unhealthy and undesirable" worldwide obsession with learning English (shades of President Chirac's linguistic protest at the Brussels summit in March). "Our young people have become fixated with the US and Britain. They are not interested in Germany," M. Bressand told me. "The English language, unfortunately, is now obliterating all interest in German, which should be the European language par excellence..."

M Bressand is a born resistance fighter. This time he is fighting a lost cause.

Even the French *haute bourgeoisie* has become obsessed by the need to make their offspring fluent speakers of English if they are to remain the elite of the next generation. German remains a fetish in academically pushy schools: a badge of distinction, fostered by a social and political elite. In French state schools in poorer or middle-class areas, German teaching hardly exists.

On the last leg of my train journey, I treated myself to a meal in the restaurant car. Unfortunately, it was a German-run car. The food was miserable: microwaved motorway meals, which would have appalled Agatha Christie and gummed up Hercule Poirot's "little grey cells". As the train approached Paris, the German waiters offered a free meal to the French ticket inspector. He ate with a sorrowful expression.The head steward—a German woman in her forties, large enough to sing in a Wagner opera—sat down to chat with him. This was her first visit to Paris, she explained. Normally she was stuck on the Hamburg run. Unfortunately, she had to leave again early the next day.

"Could you not organise a strike?" she asked the ticket inspector. "You, the French railways, you are always on strike. Could you not have a little strike tomorrow so that I could see Paris? Maybe a little, two day strike?" The ticket inspector said, unsmiling, that he would see what he could do.

They were, of course, speaking in English.

■ Painful Memories
MAY 2006

In France, the past is rarely another country. History is buried in shallow graves.

In rural France, for instance, you often find that local clans divide according to family allegiances of 1940–44: pro-Vichy or anti-Vichy; pro-Resistance or anti-Resistance.

This is a different, more solitary kind of story—the story of Monsieur P, seventy, my neighbour in Normandy.

Monsieur P loves animals and lives, the year around, in a rented, battered caravan. He is a retired postman and a gentle, timid man. He came into my garden the other day, wanting company and a chat. We sat down and had a beer.

After a few minutes of conversation, about vegetables and flowers and rain, Monsieur P. told me that he was an ex-terrorist. In the early 1960s, he had been an active member of the Organisation Armée Secrète (OAS), the movement against Algerian independence which killed 2,700 people, including 2,400 Algerians, between May 1961 and September 1962.

The OAS specialised in random, drive-by mass shootings of Arabs in Algeria and the bombing of pro-independence French politicians and Algerian activists in France. They made two unsuccessful attempts to assassinate President Charles de Gaulle—

events loosely described in the novel and movie, *The Day of the Jackal.*

Monsieur P said that he was not ashamed of what he had done. All the same, I had the impression that he was deeply ashamed of many of the things that the OAS had done. He said that this was the first time that he had talked about his terrorist career for many years.

Monsieur P looks younger than his age. He has a flat in town but prefers to live in the caravan, with his two dogs. He told me that he was a "foot soldier" in the OAS while working as a junior official in La Poste in Paris in 1961–2. "Within France, we tried to avoid killing innocent people. In fact, we tried to avoid killing as much as possible. In Algeria, I know that things were different..."

He declined to go further into details but said that, as a "post office man", he had been "well placed" to help the OAS "plastiquer" (blow up with plastic explosives) their targets in France. "People don't understand," he said. "People today don't understand. For me, it was a question of honour."

"In June 1944, I saw de Gaulle come ashore at Courseulles (a small port and seaside town on one of the Normandy landing beaches). I was eight years old. I was as close to him as you are to me now. I revered the de Gaulle of 1944, of Free France, but I had nothing but hatred for the other de Gaulle, the de Gaulle who betrayed us after 1958."

"Until 1961 I was a professional soldier—a sergeant—fighting with the French army in Algeria. I knew that Algérie Française was doomed. The idea that Algeria was just another part of France was crazy. The Arabs were not stupid... But de Gaulle double-crossed us and negotiated, not with the moderate Arabs but with the extremists. He left the Algerians who fought on our side—the Harkis—to be murdered. To me that was a betrayal of French honour, a betrayal of the French army. I joined the OAS, not to preserve French Algeria, but to fight de Gaulle, the man I had revered as an eight-year-old."

France's failure to heal the scars of history can be explained in many ways but it is often linked to the patrician, top-down nature of French politics. There is a national obsession with betrayal-from-the-top, which is sometimes justified, sometimes not.

In 1968, President de Gaulle gave an amnesty to all those who had worked for the OAS, except for one or two senior members who were involved in the assassination plots against him. Monsieur P has nothing to fear from his past. All the same, he keeps the past mostly secret, festering, unresolved.

Most of those nostalgic for French Algeria and the OAS—and there are many—are supporters of the far-right Front National. Not Monsieur P. He says that since the early 1960s he has despaired of all French politics. "Nothing that I have seen since then—Mitterrand, Chirac, this Clearstream (smear) scandal, which no-one can understand—has made me think any differently."

He made as if to spit on my lawn. "All our politicians are the same. Treacherous, selfish, mendacious..."

He went back to his dogs and his caravan.

■ A Miracle Play
JULY 2006

Menaced by the irresistible advance of a brainless, alien culture, there is one French village which has sworn never to surrender.

That may sound like the start of an Asterix story but we are talking of the present, not of Roman times. The community in question is not a Gaulish hamlet but a pretty village of warm stones with a moated château and a medieval church.

Janvry could be anywhere in deep, rural France. It is, in fact, twenty miles south of central Paris. Creeping forward on all sides are the motorways, superstores, bungalows, tyre franchises, fast food restaurants and furniture showrooms which have turned the outer suburbs of greater Paris into America-sur-Seine.

Janvry has found a magic potion to resist submission to commuter-land nonentity, blandness and selfishness. Every two years or so, the village becomes a kind of suburban Oberammergau, staging an epic, elaborate musical play in which the majority of the 636 people in the village play some part.

I went along two years ago, expecting to be underwhelmed, and was astonished by the extravagance and professionalism of the show. I went again to see the new show this year: *Les Secrets de la licorne* (the secrets of the unicorn).

If anything, the spectacle is even more ambitious. It has an original script, written as usual, by the mayor, Christian Schoettl. It has several original songs which would not disgrace a West End musical. It has a burning village. It has 62 actors, aged between 79 and ten months, all but one of whom (guess which) speak or sing. It has a mysterious, green fog from which a live unicorn emerges, to die on stage and then be resurrected. It has three horses, two cows, a baby llama, a municipal camel called Victor and two donkeys descended from animals which used to belong to Ingrid Bergman.

Most of the animals belong to the village. They have been collected by the mayor over the years to add interest to the show. In between bi-annual performances, they form a petting zoo and are loaned out to villagers to mow their lawns.

The hero of the story is, as usual, the village of Janvry itself, in medieval times. With the help of its magic unicorn, the village remains a sanctuary of modest community values, resisting the casual ignorance and violence of the world outside.

Any British amateur dramatic epic would be played mostly for laughs. There are plenty of laughs in the Janvry show, usually at the expense of neighbouring villages. "I haven't seen one of those before," says a villager when the camel appears. "It must come from Fontenay."

There is also, however, a rather subtle message about identity and rejection of outsiders and the preservation of values on a human scale. A troupe of Arabs (accompanied by the camel, Victor) is told to camp elsewhere. In revenge, they reveal the secret of the unicorn to a pair of hunters who shoot the animal for its horn (presumably not realising that it is made of wobbly plastic).

The theme is applicable more widely to a France anxious to maintain its identity in a global sea of sameness. Putting up crude barriers, and rejecting outsiders, is not necessarily the way to preserve what you hold most dear.

The mayor of Janvry, M. Schoettl, 51, is the show's writer, director and impresario-in-chief and a very creative and effective politician. He recently won a campaign to have a bus stop—or bus pull-in—erected on the nearby A10 motorway to allow local commuters to leave their cars at home. This is the first motorway bus stop in Europe.

M. Schoettl says: "There is an Asterix side to what we are doing, struggling to preserve our identity, except that Asterix is always fighting and hurting people. We want to entertain people, to amuse people, to persuade people that, look, it doesn't all have to be anonymous housing estates and offices and shopping malls. There can be islands of beauty and community."

On the night that I went to the show with my wife and daughters, there was a sell-out audience of 500 people. At exactly the same time, the France football team was playing a crucial match in Germany.

Score: Janvry 1 World Cup 0.

■ French Letters 2
FEBRUARY 2007

At the start of every year, France conducts a kind of literary lottery. Over 600 new novels are tipped onto the shelves of French bookshops. One or two sell. Most vanish without trace.

A debate is raging this year about the future of the novel in France. Why are so many of them unreadable beyond the 11th page?

A series of essays suggests that the problem is that too many French writers write about their favourite subject—themselves. They have given up on plots and characters. Instead, they write in adoring detail about their own lives. This genre is called "auto-fiction", a kind of interminable blogging in print.

There is also, however, a thriving thriller genre, known in France as "polars" or "livre noirs". They have characters. They have plots. Daringly, the story is sometimes set outside the literary ghettos of central Paris.

Since I had to travel to Brest, at the far western end of Brittany, I looked around for material on a town that I scarcely knew. I stumbled on a short thriller, published a couple of weeks ago: "Last Exit to Brest" by Claude Bathany (Métailié, €7).

This is a gripping, dark—and funny—story of murder, theft, rock music and provincial life. The narrator-anti-hero, Alban Le Gall, is a placid, gay, 40-something nightclub bouncer, built like a fridge-freezer. He becomes the manager of a middle-aged rock group, called Last Exit to Brest. He is determined to look after them like a mother, even when their drum kit becomes, literally, tangled up in local banditry and revenge killings.

As in all good thrillers, there is an overwhelming sense of place. Brest, a once-beautiful and mythical naval port flattened by Allied bombing and shelling in 1944, is a character—maybe the principal character—in the book. The town was hastily rebuilt in the late 1940s in what M. Bathany calls "neo-soviet" style. He describes Brest, once his home town, as a "sombre gouache" painting, a study in monochromes, brightened by "the grey wings of seagulls".

Unusually for a French novel, this is also a funny book. The depressive guitarist of the group learns five chords on his guitar. "Hearing of the punk rock movement in 1976, he realised that... he had learned two too many". In its heavy metal period, the group "wins critical acclaim in the engine-oil-soaked back yards of the north Breton coast."

Much of the story is told through "articles" in the local daily newspaper, *Le Télégramme de Brest*. M. Bathany exaggerates to absurdity the wandering, would-be lyrical style of some French regional newspapers. (In fairness, I should say that *Le Télégramme de Brest* is actually a rather good and brisk newspaper, which does not write in that way.)

I spoke to Claude Bathany on the telephone. He is 44. This is his first book. He used to maintain cash machines (a trade which plays a small role in his thriller). He is now a "house-husband" in Rennes, looking after two small children while his wife works. This may, or may not, be an ideal job for a writer. "You should think of Brest as a kind of French Liverpool," he told me. "It is a town with a dark sense of humour, which I try to reflect in the book. It is also a town with a thriving rock music scene, although it has yet to produce the French answer to The Beatles. To me, Brest and rock music go together."

Brest is also a lively, gutsy town which exercises a mournful but irresistible spell over its inhabitants. A local journalist and lecturer, Mikael Cabon, told me: "Brest is ugly. Let's face it. But it is easy to love a beautiful town and much harder to love an ugly one. If you love Brest—and we do—it is genuine love."

M. Bathany's hero, towards the bloody end of the book, has a chance of escaping with three million francs (£300,000) or facing up to his certain death at the hands of local gangsters. He considers fleeing but "only for a few seconds, because, thinking about it, I realised that I would have to leave Brest. You have to admit that that was inconceivable."

M. Bathany left Brest. He now lives in Rennes. Worse, his next book will be set in Paris.

■ Rotten Weather
JULY 2007

Gazing at the emerald hills of Calvados, you might be in Ireland or in west Wales. Normandy is always green. This summer it is a shining, translucent green.

Small wonder. Rain has been falling since early May.

There have been few pauses in the rain but there are ugly, brown gaps in the greenery. Three weeks ago my potato patch was a tropical forest of dark, green leaves. The crop seemed certain to be my best in eight years. Two weeks ago, I noticed a few small brown patches on the leaves. Within a week, the foliage was reduced to a slimy tangle of grey-brown sludge. My outdoor tomatoes began to wither from the base. The leaves shrivelled and turned brown. The small, green tomatoes rotted and fell to the ground.

Potatoes and tomatoes are closely related but they react to *Phytophtora infestans*—potato blight—in different ways. Tomatoes are usually the more resistant. Not this year.

Normans call blight "la maladie"—the sickness. We have had mild outbreaks of la maladie before but nothing like this. My neighbours, Michel and Madeleine, even keener gardeners than I am, have watched in distress as their beloved crops have been devastated.

Michel was born in the village 63 years ago, in the midst of the battle of Normandy. He spent the first weeks of his life hiding with his family in the iron ore mines (now closed) in the valley. He cannot remember a summer like this. "They say Normandy is wet but we have never had constant rain for weeks and weeks before," Michel said. "And it is not just the rain. It is the cold. It has been like autumn. We still have the heating on in mid July. That has never happened before."

The rain threatens to ruin crops far more valuable than mine or Michel's. Potato blight is a form of mildew, a fungal infection which blows in the wind or lurks in the soil and spreads rapidly in wet weather.

Biblical rains have swept the whole of western and central France for the last ten weeks. (Yes, I know Britain has not been dry either.) As a result, another form of mildew—vine mildew—is ravaging the vineyards of Bordeaux and, to a lesser extent, the Rhône and Loire valleys. Some growers have already lost all their grapes. Serious damage to this year's vintage is inevitable unless drier weather comes soon.

Vegetable and cereals growers in France are also complaining that the cold, wet weather will reduce the quantity, and quality, of this year's harvest. My one-eyed farming neighbour, Pierre, had hoped to cut his wheat and barley in the first week in July. He is still waiting. Every day that it rains, flattening the crops, dampening the grain, reduces his yield.

Food prices are already rising in Europe, partly because of increased demand from China, India and elsewhere. This year's wet weather—following a run of hot, dry summers—may be just an aberration. On the other hand, it might be a further warning that cheap food is about to become a thing of the past.

All our familiar arguments about farm subsidies and food surpluses could vanish in the next few years. A permanently disturbed weather pattern through climate change could reduce farm yields, just as the demand for food is rising.

At least one damp straw was blowing in the wind last week. Michel Barnier, the French agriculture minister, suggested to Brussels that the policy of "set-aside"—paying farmers not to grow cereals crops—should itself be set aside. The increasing demand and poor weather made subsidising fallow fields pointless, he said.

All this may be good new for the EU budget but bad news for those who advocate a less intensive, less polluting pattern of farming.

The European Commission is currently threatening to fine Paris millions of euros a day for its failure to prevent artificial fertilisers and pig slurry from contaminating rivers and beaches in Brittany. As food prices rise, intensive production will doubtless come back into fashion. Blast the rivers, the hedgerows and the wildlife.

How was the weather in Normandy this weekend? Warmer but still wet.

■ Far From Elementary
JANUARY 2008

Did Sherlock Holmes bungle his most famous case? Was Hercule Poirot a murderer? Did that celebrated serial killer, Hamlet, Prince of Denmark, also murder his dad? Did Oedipus, the celebrated dad-killer, *not* kill his dad?

The French literary critic and psychoanalyst, Pierre Bayard, is attempting to invent a new literary genre. He calls himself a "critical detective". He reinvestigates the plots of famous books, correcting the errors of their authors and reversing literary injustices. All authors are unreliable narrators, M. Bayard argues. Just because a writer wrote a book, it doesn't mean that he or she understood the story.

M. Bayard, 54, has recently achieved great success in the United States with a book called *How to Talk about Books You Haven't Read*. This work has just been published in Britain (Granta, £12) to glowing reviews.

Much less known in the English-speaking world (sadly) is M. Bayard's series of books explaining how celebrated writers—from William Shakespeare to Agatha Christie—got their own stories wrong.

His most recent work, just published in France, is a re-examination of the criminal evidence in Sir Arthur Conan Doyle's *The Hound of the Baskervilles*. M. Bayard proves (to his satisfaction and mine) that the dog and its master were innocent. Another murderer was at large in the book. Thanks to the incompetence of the world's greatest detective, he or she is still at large to this day.

M. Bayard has asked me not to finger the real killer. His books are, on one level, literary "whodunits". He would not like the suspense to be spoiled for his potential readers. Suffice it to say that the "real" crime on Dartmoor is a fiendishly clever double act of revenge.

The incompetence of Holmes, clearly proved by the book, is also a kind of subconscious revenge, M. Bayard suggests. Conan Doyle had grown to detest his detective and had tried to kill him off. Holmes refused to die. The *Hound* was his come-back book. Author and detective were so engaged in their own personal life-and-death struggle that they missed the real murderer and the real murder.

L'Affaire du Chien des Baskerville (Editions de Minuit, €14.50) completes an "English trilogy" which M. Bayard began in 1998. The first book reopened Hercule Poirot's first case, *The Murder of Roger Ackroyd*, one of the most celebrated detective novels of all time. M. Bayard wittily proved that the evidence has been unfairly stacked against the charming village doctor, who is both narrator and murderer. Agatha Christie and Hercule Poirot framed an innocent man.

M. Bayard, a practising psychoanalyst, literature professor, writer and father, then turned his angle-poise lamp onto Shakespeare. His *Enquête sur Hamlet* tries to clear poor Uncle Claudius of all wrong-doing and suggests—not quite convincingly—that Hamlet killed his own father.

M. Bayard's books make, with great wit and deadpan humour, a point about the nature of writing (and reading). All books contain dozens of other possible books. Each book is different, according to the identity of the reader. Even the greatest works include the elements of quite different stories, which the writers do not consciously comprehend. Far from making the works incoherent, this is what gives them their depth and resonance.

"My central argument is that nothing is fixed in a work of literature. Everything is unstable," M. Bayard told me. "I would even argue that the presence of other, incomplete, works in a book is one of the signs of greatness in a writer. Writing is partly a conscious act, partly an act in which the writer loses control of his creation."

M. Bayard's next work may attempt to correct an injustice which is 2,400 years old. He is convinced that, whatever the ancient Greek dramatist Sophocles may say, Oedipus did not kill his father. He also has a shrewd idea of the identity of the real culprit...

M. Bayard inscribed his Baskerville book to me with the following words: "To John Lichfield, a man with a deep sense of justice". M. Bayard's opinion of me is as "unstable" as he believes literature to be. When I last visited him in 2002, he inscribed his Agatha Christie book: "To John Lichfield, whose innocence in the death of Roger Ackroyd remains to be proved."

■ The Melting of the Frozen North
FEBRUARY 2008

C'est grim 'oop north. Or as they say in France, "Eee bah gum, ch'est mekand kes les ch'timis."

There is a land in the far, far north where red-brick terraces cluster for warmth around the lower slopes of slag heaps; where incest, drunkenness and unemployment are taught in primary school; where the people have empty pockets, loose morals, brutal accents and warm hearts.

This land begins not north of Watford, but south-east of Folkestone.

To the English, the Nord-Pas de Calais is a garden of tropical delights. It is the gateway to the continent. It is the home of supermarkets full of cheap booze. It is the destination for exotic weekends in Lille or Berck-Plage or Boulogne-sur-Mer.

To the French, who seldom go there, the most northerly region of France is a frozen, post-industrial wasteland. It is a part of Belgium which is, unaccountably, part of France. It is a place where unemployed miners speak a dialect which sounds like a blend of Polish and Portuguese. It only rains three times a year but each shower lasts for four months.

As the endless North v South argument flares in England, France has been chortling over its own regional prejudices. The most successful French movie of the moment is a knockabout, somewhat repetitive and harmless farce which mocks the national stereotypes about the Nord-Pas de Calais.

The movie, *Bienvenue chez les Ch'tis*, opened a week early in its home region to huge, appreciative audiences. For the first time, here was a film, made in the local language by a local comic hero, which presented the French north as the joyous and beautiful place that it is (or can be).

Most films about the Lille-Calais area, taking their cue from Emile Zola's *Germinal*, dwell on unemployment, coal mines, suicide, rain, alcoholism and incest. In France, comedy and *joie de vivre* are products of the sun-soaked south. Here, for the first time, is a life-affirming comedy about the north.

The movie opened last week in Paris and more southerly cities to long queues and to gales of laughter (despite the lack of subtitles). The film—a kind of extended TV sketch with one joke—already looks likely to be one of the biggest box office successes in the French cinema since *Amélie Poulain* in 2001.

Its writer and director and co-star is a stand-up comedian-turned actor, Dany Boon, who was born in the town of Armentières on the French-Belgian border. His co-star is an Algerian-born comedian turned actor, Kad Merad. Merad plays a post office manager from Provence who is punished for minor trickery by being exiled in a small town in the north called Bergues. He sets out in anorak and moon boots (in mid-summer) to discover—to his surprise—that the Pas de Calais is a welcoming, beautiful place with a distinctive local cuisine, served with large helpings of chips and mayonnaise from a mobile van.

He dare not tell his miserable wife, back in Provence, the truth. She has fallen in love with him again because he has taken his cruel exile so heroically. All is well until she decides to visit the north herself...

In several amusing scenes, Merad's ebullient-depressive character is given lessons in how to speak the regional language—*Ch'ti* or *Ch'timi*, from which the locals also take their name. The language is a survival of the Picard dialect of early French, with some additions from Flemish. Its most characteristic differences from mainstream French are that the sound "s" becomes "ch" and the sound "ch" becomes "qu" or "k". "Moi" becomes "mi" and "toi" becomes "ti". Hence Ch'timi.

Thus "chien", which usually means dog in French, means "sien" or "his" in Ch'timi. (A dog is a *kien* or *quien*.) One long scene in the movie is based entirely on the confusing possibilities created by mistaking "his" for "dogs".

Pity the "pauvre biloute" (poor bloke) who has to subtitle all of that into English...

■ Secret Society
MARCH 2008

My son Charles arrived in Paris eleven years ago as an immigrant, aged six, without a word of French. He has finally broken through into French high society. He has been invited to a "rallye"—or rather two rallyes on the same night.

Rallyes have nothing to do with cars. They are exclusive social clubs for the teenage sons and daughters—and especially the daughters—of the haute bourgeoisie and nobility. They are part of the means by which the French "gratin" (upper crust) hands down its superiority, and power, from generation to generation, more than two centuries after France declared itself to be devoted to Fraternité and Egalité.

The French upper and upper-middle classes are a secretive people. Two French sociologists, who specialise in anthropological study of Paris high society, Michel Pinçon and Monique Pinçon-Charlot, once said that the wealthy classes living in the western *arrondissements* of the capital (the 8th, 16th and part of the 17th) were "as difficult to penetrate as pygmies hidden in the depths of the equatorial jungles".

In an age when you can "google" your way to instant expertise on almost anything, there is noticeably little information available on the rallye system. Even the French language version of Wikipedia has only a short entry.

There are a dozen rallyes in Paris, each with its own "code" name: Rallye Carouge, Rallye Vasco da Gama etc. From the ages of ten to twelve, children from wealthy or well-connected families are invited in small groups to dance classes and cultural outings.

Not everyone can join. Wealth is not enough. You have to be recommended and vetted. You have to prove that you are "one of us".

As the children grow older, the sub-groups join together for more formal soirées, where they—without even realising it—are taught the social codes and mores of their class. When they reach the dangerous age of sixteen-eighteen, they are invited to a series of glittering balls in prestigious locations, with food provided by the most expensive "traiteurs" in Paris and music by celebrity DJs.

Each mother of a teenage daughter is expected to host at least one large rallye ball of this kind. Since they can cost €30,000 a shot, it is normal these days for five or six girls to share a single ball. Up to 2,000 teenagers might be invited: boys and girls from your own rallye and from other rallyes, as well as a few approved friends, especially boys, from outside the system.

Note that only families with teenage girls are expected to pay for a ball.

The system of rallyes began in the early 1950s, when aristocratic and high bourgeois families finally accepted that they could no longer arrange the marriages of their offspring. Rallyes are, at one level, dating and marriage agencies, to ensure that Marie-Clémentine marries Xavier or Apollinaire, rather than some boy from the *banlieues*, encountered at a discotheque. At another level, they are a way of chaperoning the sexual life of teenagers and restricting access to drink and drugs.

Charles has been invited to two rallye balls next month by fellow-pupils in the final year of a Paris lycée. The fact that he, as a mere foreigner, can receive an invitation suggests that the system is less rigid and exclusive than it once was.

His invitations are elaborate, glossy, folding cards, more than a foot long. Each contains a smaller card stamped with an individual, anti-crasher, code number. One of the cards has a James Bond theme. Its coded entry ticket is in the shape of an 007 revolver.

Does the system still work? As a marriage agency, it works

pretty well, according to the information discreetly gathered by my son. Even though young French people are getting married much later nowadays, it is still normal for BCBG (bon chic, bon genre) youngsters to marry within the tribe to someone that they first met at a rallye when they were twelve or thirteen.

As for restricting access to drink, forget it. Many of the kids get tanked up before the rallye ball even starts. Somehow, that is almost reassuring.

■ Painful Memories 2
APRIL 2008

A decade ago, when I was new to France, I met a frail, former wartime Resistance leader in the Auvergne. What he said about the war shocked me, although it should probably not have done. "We knew the people who were on our side, or we thought that we did. We knew who the active collaborators were. They were our enemy and we respected them, even if we regarded them as traitors. The people who really scared us were all the rest, maybe nine people out of ten. At any given moment, you could never be certain which side they were on."

France is one of its periodical flusters about the 1939–45 war. After 63 years, the subject of who did what under the Nazi occupation is still capable of throwing the country into a fit of anger, posturing and recrimination. One man is principally to blame for France's apparent difficulty in looking its wartime self in the face: the greatest Frenchman of the 20th century, Charles de Gaulle.

By an act of supreme personal will and realpolitik, de Gaulle created in 1945 the myth of a martyred, unbending France, betrayed by a minority of traitors. The truth, as he knew better than anyone, was much more opaque and much more human.

In the last few days, two attempts to face up to the complex, myth-defying realities of the Occupation have stirred enormous controversy in the supposedly brash, new, forward-looking France of President Nicolas Sarkozy.

A docu-drama shown on French television last week revisited

the sinuous war record of the late President François Mitterrand. An exhibition in Paris has revealed to the general public a host of almost unknown, unique colour photographs of the French capital under German rule between June 1940 and August 1944.

President Mitterrand, as a book revealed, or recalled, while he was still in office in 1994, worked as a senior official in the collaborationist Vichy administration before becoming a daring and hunted leader of the anti-Nazi resistance. Until deep into his Socialist presidency, he maintained personal friendships with Vichy figures, including the police chief, René Bousquet, who was responsible for the eager rounding up of tens of thousands of French and "foreign" Jews.

The photo exhibition at the Paris town hall history library shows more than 200 colour shots taken in the streets of the occupied capital by a collaborationist photographer, André Zucca. Far from showing Paris agonising under the Nazi heel, they portray a remarkably familiar city: calm, chic and pleasure-loving, getting on with life as best as it can.

The assistant mayor of Paris for cultural affairs, Christopher Girard, has been campaigning to have the exhibition—due to run until 1 July—cut short. The mayor of Paris, Bertrand Delanoë, has, to his credit, refused to do so.

M. Girard says that the photographs are selective and misleading. Why no pictures of food queues? Why no pictures of round-ups of Jews? In truth, the exhibition shocks precisely because it reveals an inconvenient, but very human, truth. Nine-tenths of Parisians, including Edith Piaf, including Jean-Paul Sartre, spent the war being Parisians. Their principal act of resistance was to laugh at the Germans behind their backs and make jokes about their smelly, synthetic uniforms. Is this really so shocking?

The TV docu-drama gave a rather fair and sympathetic portrait of Mitterrand's wartime vacillations. His support for Vichy was, after all, shared by most French people in 1940–2. Relatively few defected to the Resistance in 1942–4 as he did. (The programme was nonetheless attacked in advance by his widow, Danièle Mitterrand.)

Much more disturbing was the discussion programme which followed. It included large extracts from an interview given by

President Mitterrand in 1994 after the Vichy "revelations". Why, the president was asked, did he maintain a life-long friendship with Bousquet, the Vichy Jew-hunter, who had been assassinated the year before? Mitterrand shrugged: "He was a very interesting man," he said.

Until the end of his life, Mitterrand clung to the de Gaulle version of France's war as a domestic affair in which the Holocaust—to use Jean-Marie Le Pen's odious word—was just a "detail". To his great credit, President Jacques Chirac made a speech soon after he replaced Mitterrand in 1995 apologising, for the first time, for the role of the French State in rounding up Jews. It should also be recalled, however, that thanks to the courage of a minority of French people, proportionally more Jews survived the war in France than in many other occupied countries.

President Sarkozy, who is himself one-quarter Jewish, has let it be known that he believes that Chirac's 1995 speech was a mistake. Since taking office, he has tried to revive a kind of Hollywoodised and sanctified version of modern French history.

Why? And why all the fuss about the photo exhibition? My impression, as an outsider, is that younger generations of French people have long ago accepted the muddy, honourable–dishonourable, truth about 1940–44. They are ready to move on.

■ Sarko Invades Normandy
JUNE 2008

President Nicolas Sarkozy is about to invade Normandy, weather permitting.

The Elysée Palace will announce officially today that the celebration of France's victory over Germany in 1945 (with some American, British and Canadian help) will not take place at the Arc de Triomphe in Paris on 8 May, as tradition demands. Instead, on Thursday, President Sarkozy will preside over an elaborate and expensive ceremony at the small seaside town of Ouistreham, just north of Caen.

Almost the entire French government, the ambassadors of allied nations and hundreds of war veterans will be moved the 130 miles to lower Normandy in a fleet of planes and a special train. Viewing platforms and a staircase have been constructed. The beach has been swept for mines, just in case any of the 2,000,000 explosive devices installed by General Erwin Rommel 64 years ago might have eluded generations of holidaymakers.

Why choose Ouistreham? The small town is the easternmost part of the D-Day landing beaches. On 6 June 1944, it was part of Sword Beach, where 28,845 British soldiers came ashore. They were part of an allied force of 156,000 which landed in France that day.

President Sarkozy will pay eloquent tribute to the sacrifices of American, British and Canadian troops. He will later attend a ceremony at a Canadian military cemetery with the governor-general of Canada, Michaelle Jean.

None of that explains why Ouistreham was chosen for the first official, French 8 May celebration outside the capital. Why not go to the bloodiest beach, Omaha? Or to Courseulles, where General Charles de Gaulle landed on 14 June?

The explanation is that, of the 156,000 soldiers who landed on D-Day, 177—or 0.11 per cent—were French. They came ashore at Ouistreham.

A small force of French commandos, led by Commandant Philippe Kieffer, successfully stormed a German strongpoint in the Ouistreham casino. They helped to clear the way for the British troops to move inland and relieve the glider-borne soldiers holding Pegasus Bridge a few miles to the south.

The bravery of the "Kieffer Commando" is worth recalling. By the end of the battle of Normandy in August, all but 33 of them had been killed or wounded. Many other French soldiers came ashore later in June and July 1944 to take part in the defeat of Nazism. It may seem strange, all the same, for President Sarkozy to commandeer the D-Day beaches, where so many thousands of allied soldiers fought, to pay such an elaborate and ostentatious tribute to a relatively small French unit.

Moving the ceremony out of Paris is part of President Sarkozy's drive to abandon tradition for tradition's sake and do things differently from his predecessors. Fair enough. His speech at Ouistreham beach, close to a steel flame which marks the exploits of the 177 French troops, will announce that a new unit of marines is to be named the "Kieffer Commando". Fair enough.

By drawing attention to a small but heroic French action, which is sometimes overlooked, President Sarkozy is pursuing another part of his agenda. M. Sarkozy wants not just to reform French government but to reform the French collective mind. He wants to sweep away defeatism and introspection and make France a proud and can-do nation once again. This may also seem fair enough but M. Sarkozy's approach comes close at times to reviving the heroic myths of wartime France deliberately fostered by de Gaulle, with often unfortunate results.

In any case, heroism has its limits, it appears. If the weather forecast for Thursday is poor, the whole beach ceremony is to be abandoned and moved back to the Arc de Triomphe. The forecast is for fine weather with a light breeze.

■ A Country Wedding
AUGUST 2008

Few things are more joyous, or prolonged, than a French country wedding. I recently attended a marriage on the island of Groix, off the coast of Brittany.

After the ceremony, we sang French folk songs as we were transported in two buses to a sandy cove. Full champagne glasses had been lined up on the rocks. We walked, happily, across the island to the house of the Young Married Couple. A detailed lunch was served in the garden, followed not by speeches, but by poems and songs written by the guests.

There were two bands. The first was a pair of young women from the Auvergne who played an accordion and the Auvergnat bagpipes. The second was a Serb folk and rock band, who had, several months earlier, been rescued by the Young Married Couple when their van broke down on an autoroute.

The two bands combined at one point to produce a new form of

World Music: Serb-Auvergnat electric folk, with bagpipes. All the guests formed a conga line and danced through the garden and into the house, the first dancers emerging from the living room before the last had entered the kitchen.

The Young Married Couple, Martine and Olivier, are in their fifties and have already been married for over twenty years. They are among our dearest friends in Paris. They also have a house in Groix.

Their first marriage was in a town hall. Two decades, and three grown sons, later they decided to get married in church.

Marriage is a declining institution among young people in France, who prefer to live together and see what comes along. Late second marriages by long-married couples are booming—a triumph of experience over hoping for the best.

■ Celebrating the 2CV
SEPTEMBER 2008

Sixty years ago this year, a strange little vehicle appeared at the Paris car show. It looked like an upside-down pram with a corrugated bonnet and a canvas roof. It had no starter motor and one headlight. Its windscreen wipers were operated by the forward motion of the wheels. Its seats looked like cheap canvas deckchairs. The wheels were as thin as saucepan lids. The car—for it was a car—was available in any colour that you wanted, so long as it was dull grey.

Thus was born the "Toute Petite Voiture" ("really little car") or Citroën Deux Chevaux, a car that suffered mockery throughout its 42 years of production but has come to be regarded as an automotive icon. To generations of foreign visitors, the "2CV" pottering along an empty rural road epitomised France just as much as berets, baguettes, yellow cigarettes or farm buildings painted with Martini signs. Sadly, all save the baguettes are now defunct or very scarce.

The 2CV may be scarce but it is not forgotten. The life and times of the Toute Petite Voiture are recalled in an excellent small exhibition which begins this week at the Cité des Sciences et de l'Industrie in Paris. Peugeot-Citroën, and 2CV lovers, are planning other commemorative events later in the year.

The exhibition includes one of the five remaining examples of an abandoned early production run from 1939. The outbreak of war forced Citroën to stop work on its project. The 250 prototypes were hidden away, and in some cases even buried, to prevent them from falling into the hands of the Nazis. (There is no telling what difference a couple of armoured divisions of 2CVs might have made to the outcome of the war.)

The 2CV was the mid-1930s brainchild of the head of Citroën, Pierre-Jules Boulanger, who also inspired another Citroën icon, the slope-backed DS saloon of 1955. Long before the Volkswagen was heard of, M. Boulanger decided that there was a market for a cheap, easily maintained, basic car to replace the horse and cart on French rural roads and even on the fields.

His specification was for an "umbrella on wheels", a car that could carry fifty kilogrammes and four people at up to sixty kilometres per hour and cross a ploughed field carrying a basket of eggs. Since the seats were removable to allow animals to be carried, this has sometimes been elaborated to "a car capable of driving across a ploughed field with a sheep in the back and a pile of eggs on the front seat, without breaking the eggs (or the sheep)."

The car which finally appeared at the 1948 Paris motor show—the 2CV Type A—was an advance on the original design. It could go up to eighty kph (fifty miles per hour) and had an air-cooled engine which could travel for 100 kilometres (sixty miles) on a gallon of petrol. Although the car was immediately mocked by the French motoring press, it was, in several ways, a revolutionary design.

There was independent suspension on each wheel, but with front and back wheels linked to give a kind of gentle wave movement if the car hit a bump (of which there were plenty on French roads in 1948). The 2CV also had a light, easily-serviceable, almost indestructible air-cooled engine. This was loosely based on motorcycle engines and was held in place by just four bolts. The car had, in fact, a capacity of eight "chevaux" or eight horse power.

The "deux chevaux" refers to the notional, low, French taxation category into which it was cleverly designed to fall.

From its commercial launch in 1949, the car was a triumph—a triumph that even Citroën had not expected. Far too few 2CVs were made at the Citroën plant at Levallois-Perret on the north-western boundary of Paris. There was a waiting list of between three and five years for a 2CV in the first half of the 1950s.

Everyone of a certain age has a favourite memory of a 2CV. When I was fourteen, in 1964, I spent the summer with my godmother in Brussels, who had a 2CV which she called "Caritas" (Charity). By that time, Citroën's colour restrictions had been considerably relaxed. Her car was a pale fawn. The updated 2CVs also had the luxury of two headlights and an electric starter and electric windscreen wipers. Otherwise, little had changed.

We drove the length and breadth of the Benelux in "Caritas". With my godmother at the wheel of a 2CV, the Benelux loomed as large as Canada. She refused to accept that she could drive faster than forty mph.

At that time, 2CVs had three forward gears and then a gear mysteriously marked "S". This, I now understand, stood for "surmultipliée" or "overdrive". The original Citroën specification demanded three gears and this was the engineers' way of providing a fourth gear without alarming their rural customers. In any event, I don't think that my godmother ever risked the "S" gear. It also took me most of the summer, and several crushed fingers, to work out how the maddening, folding rather than winding, side-windows worked.

Efforts were made to expand the 2CV's international horizons beyond Belgium. There was, briefly, a factory making the 2CV in Slough. Citroën produced a pick-up and a van version of the 2CV. From the mid-1960s, the company splashed out on properly upholstered seats.

From 1967 onwards, there was a more modern-looking variant called the Dyane. There were also all-terrain, and souped-up roofless versions and a bright yellow "James Bond" version, linked to a scene in the 1981 Bond movie *For Your Eyes Only* in which Roger Moore makes a get-away in a 2CV.

The car historian, LJK Setright, author of *Drive On! A Social*

History of the Motor Car, described the 2CV as "the most intelligent application of minimalism ever to succeed as a car". A British motoring journalist, less flatteringly, once described a 2CV as the "result of an illicit liaison between a deckchair and a Nissen Hut".

In Britain, and elsewhere, the strange little vehicle failed to compete properly with the original VW Beetle or even the Morris Minor and Morris Mini. French car industry historians blame Citroën for failing to realise that it had a potential winner abroad until it was too late. Much less money was invested in foreign factories and promotion than was invested by VW in its Beetle.

The Beetle often cost twice as much as the 2CV but it went on to sell 20,000,000 vehicles worldwide, compared to just over 5,000,000 for all the variants of the 2CV.

By the late 1970s, nonetheless, the 2CV became a lifestyle statement, popular with hippies and early ecologists. There was once a joke that part of the factory finish of a 2CV was a back-window sticker saying "Nuclear? No thanks."

A dashing young French prime minister, Laurent Fabius (38 when he took office in 1984) established the 2CV as an urban runabout for the chattering classes. He self-consciously drove to the prime ministerial offices each morning in one of the later, trendy versions of the former rural egg and sheep carrier.

Nonetheless, 2CV production in France ceased in 1989 and in Portugal in 1990. It is alleged by car industry historians and 2CV fans that Citroën was, by then, embarrassed by its "umbrella on wheels". The car failed to meet modern expectations of safety or speed, the company said at the time. Much the same arguments were given for killing off the original British Mini and the VW Beetle.

In all three cases, the popularity and longevity of the surviving cars suggest that they were abandoned too soon: victims of corporate strategy and image-consciousness rather than true market research or customer-friendliness. The 2CV was also, it is whispered by some car industry experts, too tough for its own good. What use to a manufacturer is a little car which can easily last for 200,000 miles without needing significant new parts?

Surviving 2CVs, often painted in dazzling colours which jar

with the car's utilitarian origins, are much sought after. In Britain, they go for up to £4,000 in the second hand market—and for somewhat less in France. There is also a thriving market, in both France and Britain, in 2CV "re-builds": cars which are all but new, reconstructed according to the original specifications but with extras unheard of by the car's designers (and my Belgian godmother). Is a 2CV with a multiple choice stereo CD player still a 2CV? In 2004 the American pop musician, Billy Joel, gave the street-credibility of the 2CV an enormous boost when he had an accident while driving one on Long Island.

In an eco-conscious age, car manufacturers all over the world are beginning to re-examine the concept of a cheap, economical, basic, reliable, easily maintained car. Peugeot-Citroën is promising a "new Deux CV" for next year but, judging by the advance images, the Citroën Cactus is a snappy little economy run-about. It is not the kind of car that you would carry sheep or eggs in.

Ironically, perhaps, it was not Peugeot-Citroën but the other French car giant, Renault, which led the way in Europe in exploring the possibilities of a retro car, stripped back to the basics. The Logan is, however, a stretched limousine compared to the odd little car with Noddy wheels and a soft roof which appeared sixty years ago.

■ Train Spotting in France
OCTOBER 2008

Everyone knows the strange feeling of déjà vu. Here is an example of its even stranger sister, "jamais vu": a moment when you are forced, finally, to confront the evidence that the world of your youth has changed forever.

I had an hour to kill at Chambéry railway station in the French Alps. An hour at a railway station is never completely wasted for a partially-reformed train spotter. I was watching the familiar French trains coming and going: TGVs, local trains, freight trains. Abruptly, out of the Alpine mist, there loomed the unmistakeable shape of a British freight locomotive. I walked to the end of the platform to stare.

It was a vast American-designed locomotive, as long as two buses, based according to the lettering on its side at Toton depot, between Derby and Nottingham.

Under European Union competition rules, the French state railways, the SNCF, were bludgeoned two years ago into allowing access to other freight operators. My enormous locomotive belonged to a British-based, German-owned company called Euro Cargo Rail. In other words it was an American-designed, Canadian-built, British locomotive operating in France for a German company.

That, however, was not my moment of "jamais vu".

The immense locomotive was changing drivers. The departing driver removed a bright yellow safety jacket and revealed a fleecy, gold cardigan and elegant, brown trousers. She—French, early forties, frizzy hair, rather beautiful—strode down the platform, as if bound for a night on the town.

■ Fame, With Strings Attached
MARCH 2009

France's long-running satirical TV puppets celebrated twenty years on the air this week with a marathon tribute to themselves and a new puppet: me.

Les Guignols de l'Info, the most insolent and creative programme on French television, startled its viewers on Monday night by persuading real-life personalities—including Nicolas Sarkozy and Karl Lagerfeld—to stand in for their own puppet characters.

A retrospective of twenty years of the show, stretching over more than five hours, demonstrated that there has only been one true hero in French politics in recent times: Jacques Chirac. The rascally, lovable, irascible, gravel-voiced Chirac puppet—creepily close to the real thing—emerged as the most compelling character in what the programme's creators call the "sit-com of modern French politics".

But who was the enigmatic, soft-spoken puppet who made a brief appearance early in the Guignols' tribute to themselves on the cable channel, Canal Plus? The puppet was introduced as

"John, the correspondent of a British newspaper in France". He was tall with curly grey hair and glasses.

Could it be...? Surely not. Was this the first puppet in the history of the Guignols to be less grotesque than the original? My wife and work-colleagues insist that the "John" puppet is either an uncanny coincidence or a better-looking, and better-dressed, version of me. Immortality beckons.

The British correspondent was shown teaching an allegedly biased French radio interviewer how to write a newspaper story at the height of the 2007 presidential elections. The interviewer wrote: "Ségolène Royal is a tart." "My" character said primly, in poor French: "No, you will have to change that. It's a personal opinion and not generally accepted." The interviewer changed his words to: "Everyone knows that Ségolène Royal is a tart." The British correspondent looked exasperated. End of my thirty seconds of fame.

Les Guignols de l'Info began as a French homage to *Spitting Image*, the British satirical puppet show which ran on ITV from 1984 to 1996. The French show, which appears for about eight minutes each weekday at around 8 p.m., has far outlived the British original.

Over 300 people work on the show. To remain topical, it is mostly scripted, rehearsed and acted out on the day of broadcast. Up to 3,000,000 viewers tune in each night. Although sometimes cruel, and not always uproariously funny, it has become a French institution. In a television landscape notorious for its blandness and often obsequious approach to politicians, *Les Guignols de l'Info* (literally, the "news puppets") is an island of inventiveness and insolence.

Perhaps surprisingly, it is adored by most of the politicians that it mocks. (There are some spoil-sport exceptions.) Part of Monday night's marathon tribute was therefore a spoof of a spoof in which real celebrities stood in for their puppet characters on screen.

After a long sequence of puppets answering e-mailed questions from viewers, an unmistakable Nicolas Sarkozy "puppet" was shown, from behind, responding to the question: "Do the Guignols influence voters?" The "puppet" turned out to be the president in person, who replied: "Unfortunately, yes."

There was also a much longer sequence, imitating a typical show, which is always presented by a puppet version of Patrick Poivre d'Arvor, the veteran news presenter who was sacked last year after the intervention of President Sarkozy. The spoof sequence was presented by the real Poivre d'Arvor, successfully imitating the puppet which imitates him. He introduced a string of personalities who had agreed to replace their own puppets, including the former Socialist Party leader, François Hollande, the mayor of Paris, Bertrand Delanoë, the fashion designer, Karl Lagerfeld and the former France football manager, Aimé Jacquet.

Maybe, they will allow me to appear in person next time. Or would that be too grotesque?

■ The End of *Le Monde*? Never
MAY 2009

Many of the great French institutions—those things which once made France indelibly French—have vanished or nearly so. Where are the yellow cigarettes of yesteryear? What became of the Paris Metro smell of burned rubber and cheap perfume? What happened to yellow headlights?

Frenchmen wearing berets and striped jerseys with baguettes under their arms still exist—but only in British cartoons.

There is, however, one great landmark of French life which remains, through all passing changes, largely itself. The daily newspaper, *Le Monde*, which has just published its 20,000th edition, is accused by some diehard readers, and ex-readers, of betraying its ideals in recent years.

Le Monde was once uncompromisingly intellectual. It now covers football. And pop music. It publishes photographs, even on its front page. Long gone are the days when the front-page headline might be longer and more complex than three opening paragraphs in rival newspapers. Here is the "splash" headline from the edition of 12 May, 1981, the day after an epoch-making French presidential election. "The very clear victory of M. François Mitterrand goes beyond a unification of the whole

of the left and widens the divisions of the outgoing majority."
Very snappy.

The example comes from a wonderful collection of *Le Monde*
front pages from 1945 to 2008, published by the newspaper to
commemorate its 20,000th edition. Only from the early 1980s was
the jumble of grey on the front relieved by a cartoon and, finally,
in the last few years, photographs.

Purists mourn the old *Le Monde* but I find the new version
more penetrating, wittier, less infuriatingly po-faced. Some things
never change. *Le Monde* is still broadly centre-left in its attitudes
(although not entirely immune to the charms of President Nicolas
Sarkozy). The newspaper still insists on being published in the early
afternoon rather than the morning. It still carries, confusingly, the
next day's date.

It remains a beautifully written, usually reliable, intelligent
and dryly funny newspaper: a perfect argument for why print
newspapers deserve to survive in the internet age. How is *Le
Monde* doing? It is suffering badly like all the rest.

■ Bottom Gear
OCTOBER 2009

By their cars shall you know them. Not any more, it appears.

Parisian motorists, disliked all over France for being over-
aggressive, under-friendly and simply for being Parisian, have
found a way to camouflage their origins. Since last April, France
has switched to a new system of car registration. The number no
longer finishes with the two-digit code of the *département* (75
for Paris, 13 for the Bouches-du-Rhône and so on). Instead, the
number-plate carries a separate sticker indicating its département
and region.

The choice of these stickers is voluntary. Cars can legally display
any département number code that their owner desires. You can,
if you wish, live in Paris and drive around in a car displaying the
code number of a faraway, backwoods département.

The number of new cars carrying the dreaded Paris code, "75", has fallen by more than half. The départements of choice are 2a and 2b (upper and lower Corsica), 87 (Haute-Vienne in Limousin) and 56 (Morbihan in Brittany). Parisians, it seems, are choosing to identify with the département of their grand-parents; or their holiday homes.

It so happens that my leased car came due for renewal this autumn. I faced an existential choice. Should I remain, in automobile terms, a Parisian? Or should I migrate to Calvados (14), where we own a small cottage? I ordered a "14" sticker.

My fiercely Parisian children were dismayed. They call the new car the "ploucmobile". *Plouc* is the rude French word for yokel.

In lower Normandy, however, I am finally accepted as a local and possibly also a yokel. As I trundle along the lanes in my number 14 car, the incidence of rude gestures has diminished dramatically.

———

Armani Man is back. A couple of years ago, I wrote about a man with an Italian accent who was touring Paris in a battered car offering people free Giorgio Armani suits. The article provoked a lengthy correspondence about similar Armani Men operating all over the western world. There was clearly some kind of scam. But what?

I was strolling to work the other day when a man with an Italian accent beckoned me towards his battered car. After pretending to be lost, he offered me a free Armani suit. "I have XL," he said. Blasted cheek. I greeted him like a long-lost friend and asked him to explain the scam. People all over the world were anxious to know what was going on, I said. He wound up his window and drove away. The mystery continues.